THE PLAYBOY

A Comic Book By
CHESTER BROWN

DRAWN & QUARTERLY

The Playboy. ISBN 0-9696701-1-7
Written and drawn by Chester Brown.
Entire contents ©copyright 1992 Chester Brown.
All rights reserved. Published by Drawn &
Quarterly Publications.
Chris Oliveros and Marina Lesenko:
Publishers. No part of this book may
be reproduced in any manner whatsoever
(except small portions for review purposes)
without written permission from the
publishers and author.
The Playboy was originally serialized, in
somewhat different form, in Chester Brown's
comic book, Yummy Fur, in issues 21 - 23,
which were published by Vortex Comics.
First Printing: December, 1992
PRINTED IN CANADA.

For a complete list of other fine comic
books published by D&Q, write for our
free mail order catalogue:
Drawn & Quarterly Publications,
5550 Jeanne Mance Street, No. 16
Montreal, Quebec,
Canada H2V 4K6.

Dedicated to Seth
for his example
as an artist

THE
PLAYBOY

PART ONE

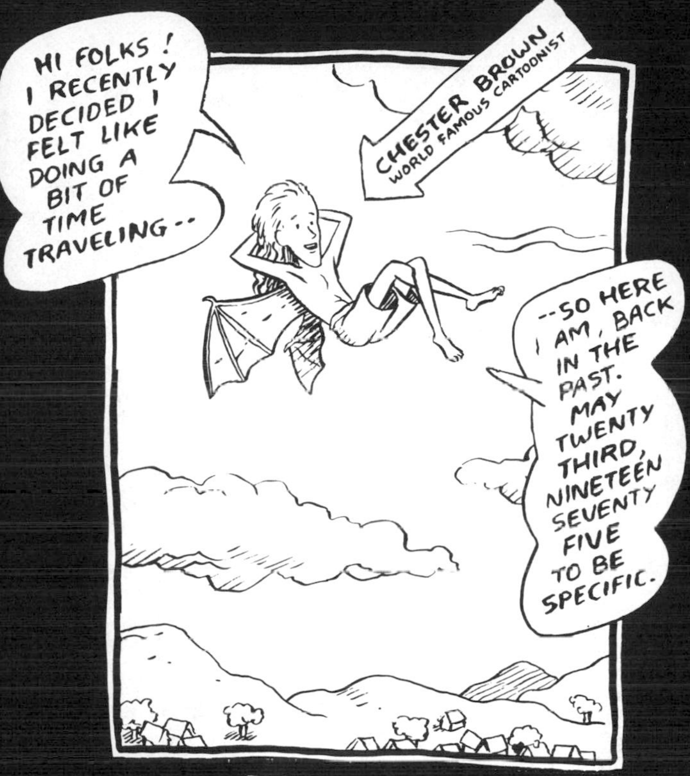
HI FOLKS! I RECENTLY DECIDED I FELT LIKE DOING A BIT OF TIME TRAVELING--
CHESTER BROWN
WORLD FAMOUS CARTOONIST
--SO HERE I AM, BACK IN THE PAST. MAY TWENTY THIRD, NINETEEN SEVENTY FIVE TO BE SPECIFIC.

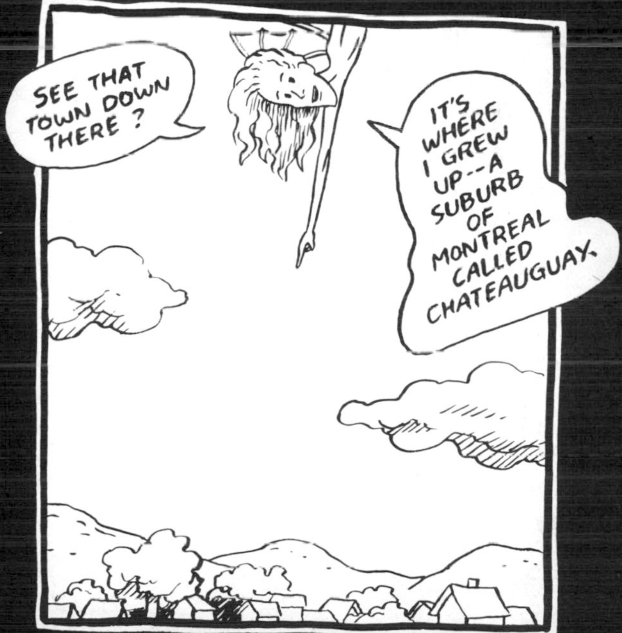
SEE THAT TOWN DOWN THERE?
IT'S WHERE I GREW UP--A SUBURB OF MONTREAL CALLED CHATEAUGUAY.

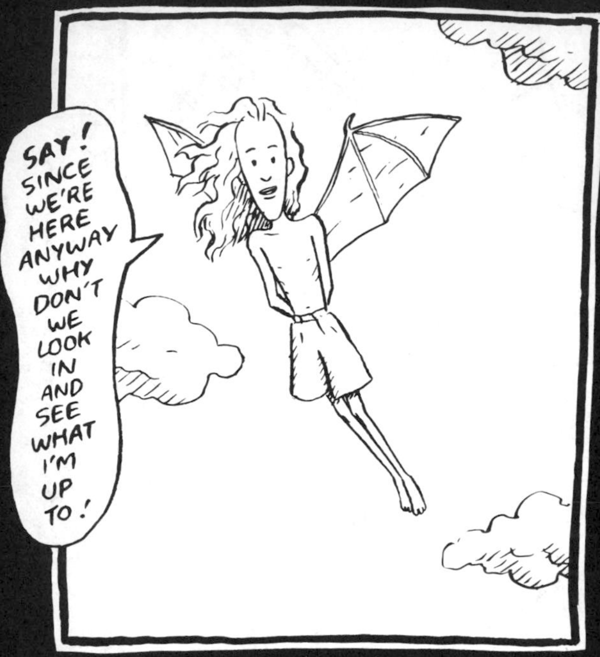
SAY! SINCE WE'RE HERE ANYWAY WHY DON'T WE LOOK IN AND SEE WHAT I'M UP TO!

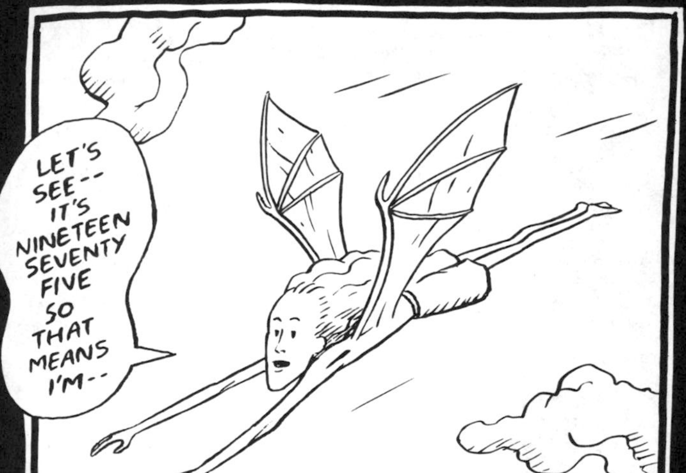
LET'S SEE-- IT'S NINETEEN SEVENTY FIVE SO THAT MEANS I'M--

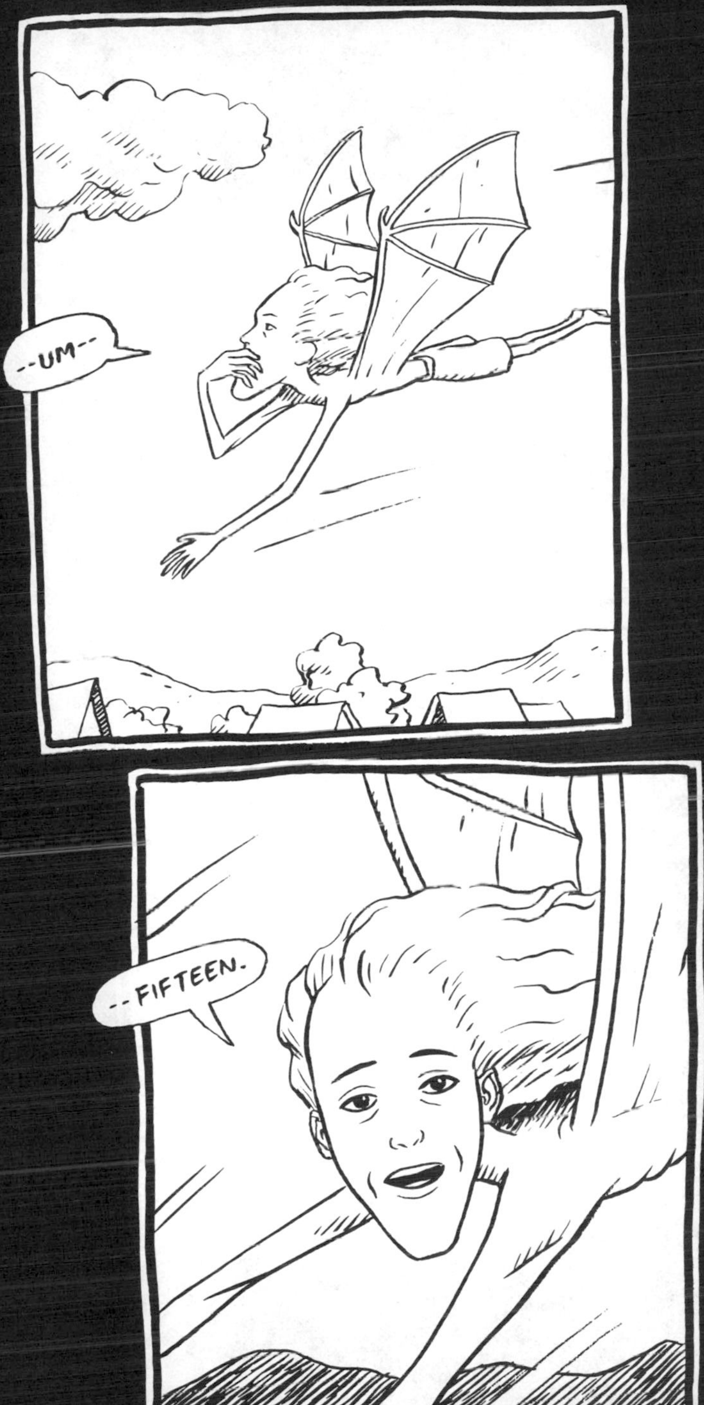
--UM--
--FIFTEEN.

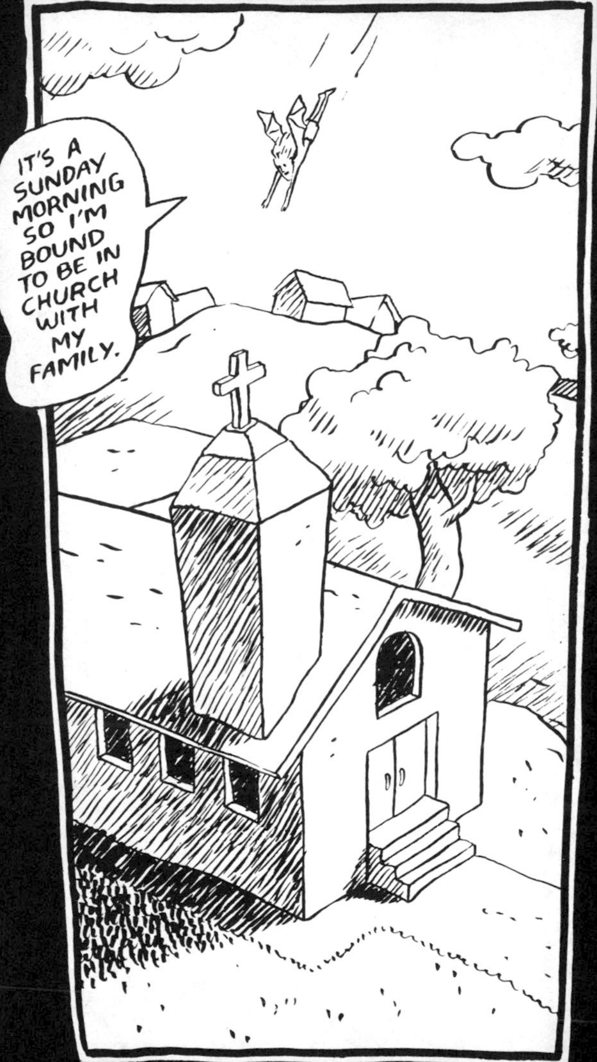
IT'S A SUNDAY MORNING SO I'M BOUND TO BE IN CHURCH WITH MY FAMILY.

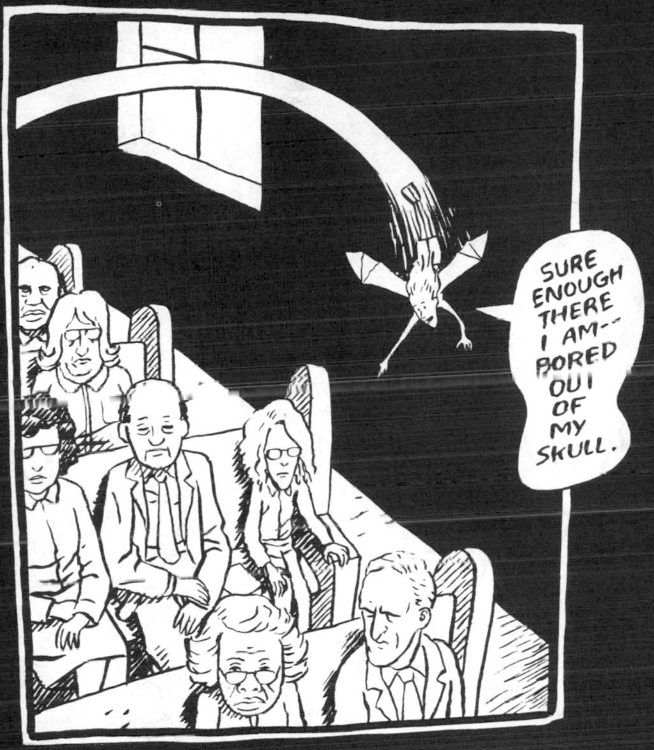
SURE ENOUGH THERE I AM-- BORED OUT OF MY SKULL.

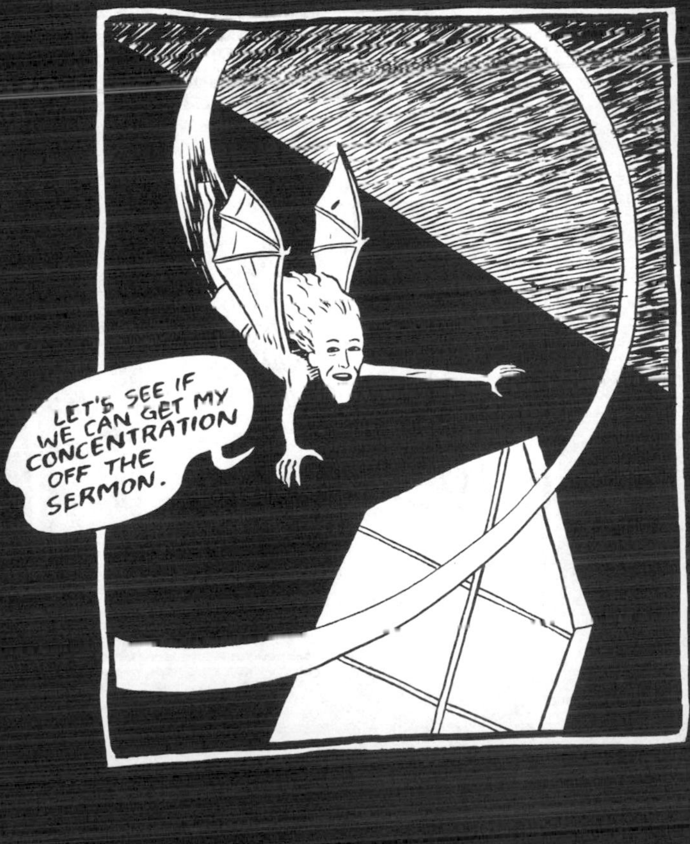
LET'S SEE IF WE CAN GET MY CONCENTRATION OFF THE SERMON.

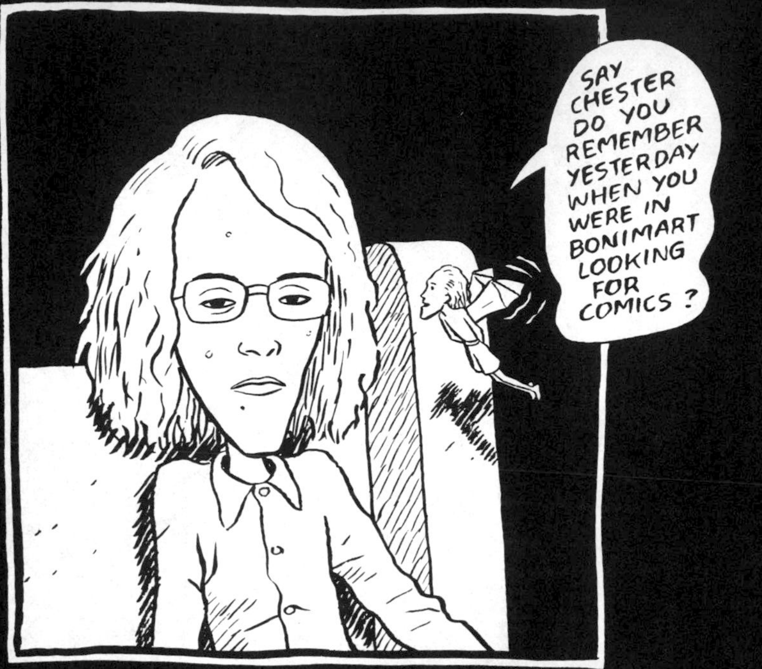
SAY CHESTER DO YOU REMEMBER YESTERDAY WHEN YOU WERE IN BONIMART LOOKING FOR COMICS ?

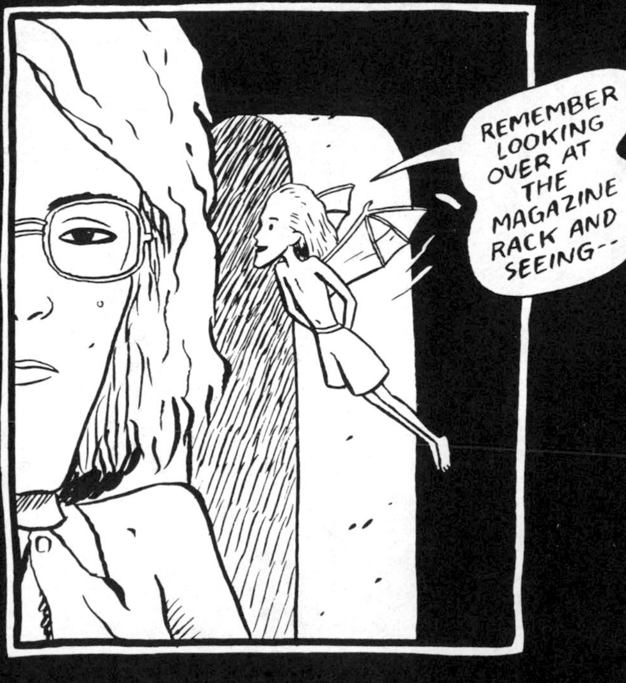
REMEMBER LOOKING OVER AT THE MAGAZINE RACK AND SEEING--

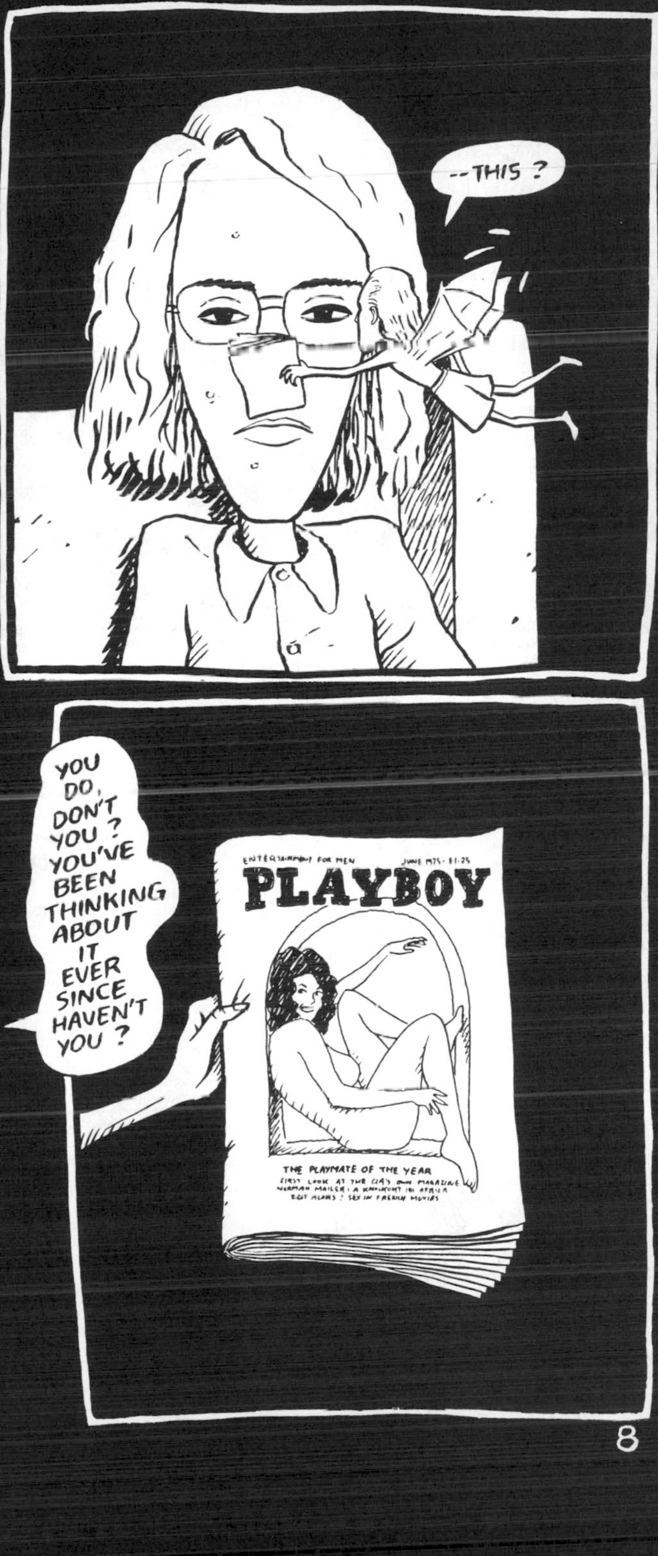
--THIS ?
YOU DO, DON'T YOU ? YOU'VE BEEN THINKING ABOUT IT EVER SINCE HAVEN'T YOU ?
ENTERTAINMENT FOR MEN
JUNE 1975 · $1.25
PLAYBOY
THE PLAYMATE OF THE YEAR
NORMAN MAILER: A KNOCKOUT IN AFRICA
SEX IN FRENCH MOVIES

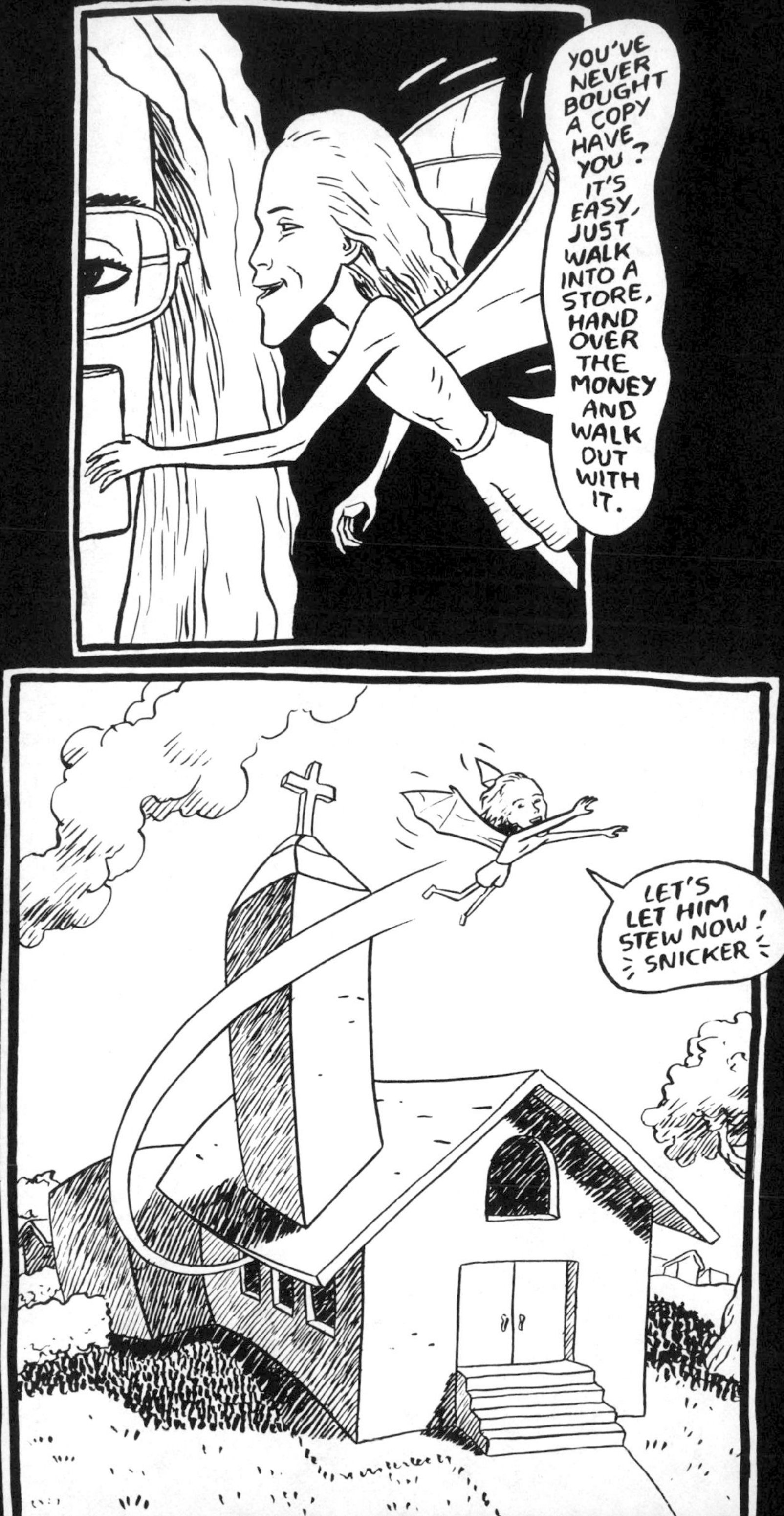
YOU'VE NEVER BOUGHT A COPY HAVE YOU? IT'S EASY, JUST WALK INTO A STORE, HAND OVER THE MONEY AND WALK OUT WITH IT.
LET'S LET HIM STEW NOW! SNICKER

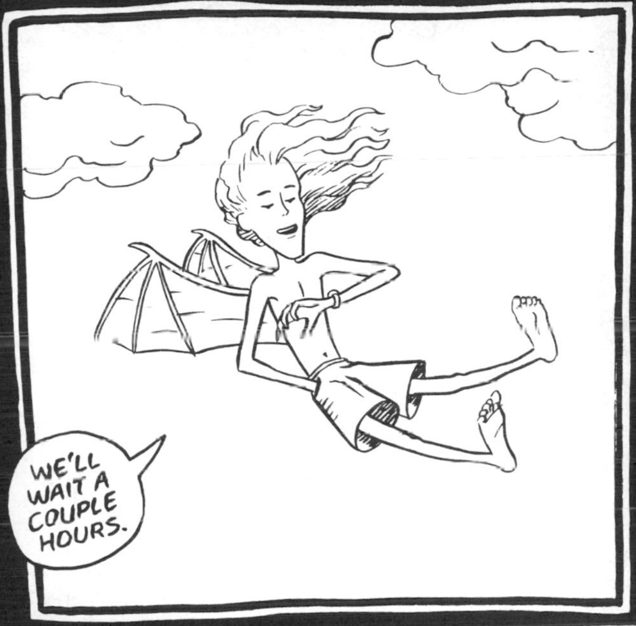
WE'LL WAIT A COUPLE HOURS.

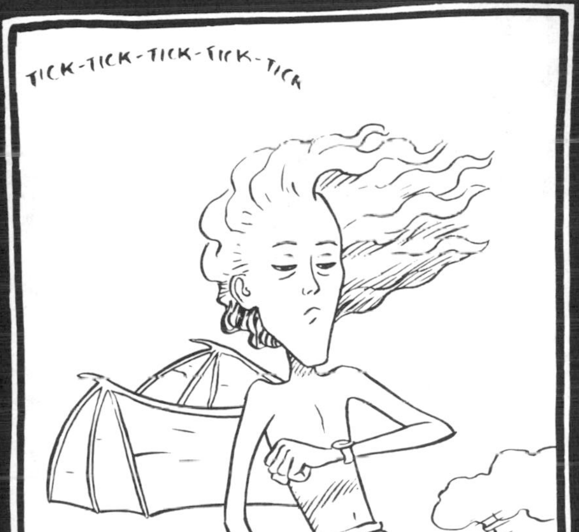
TICK-TICK-TICK-TICK-TICK

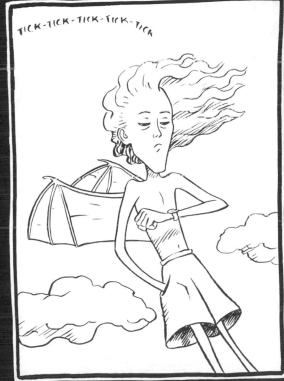

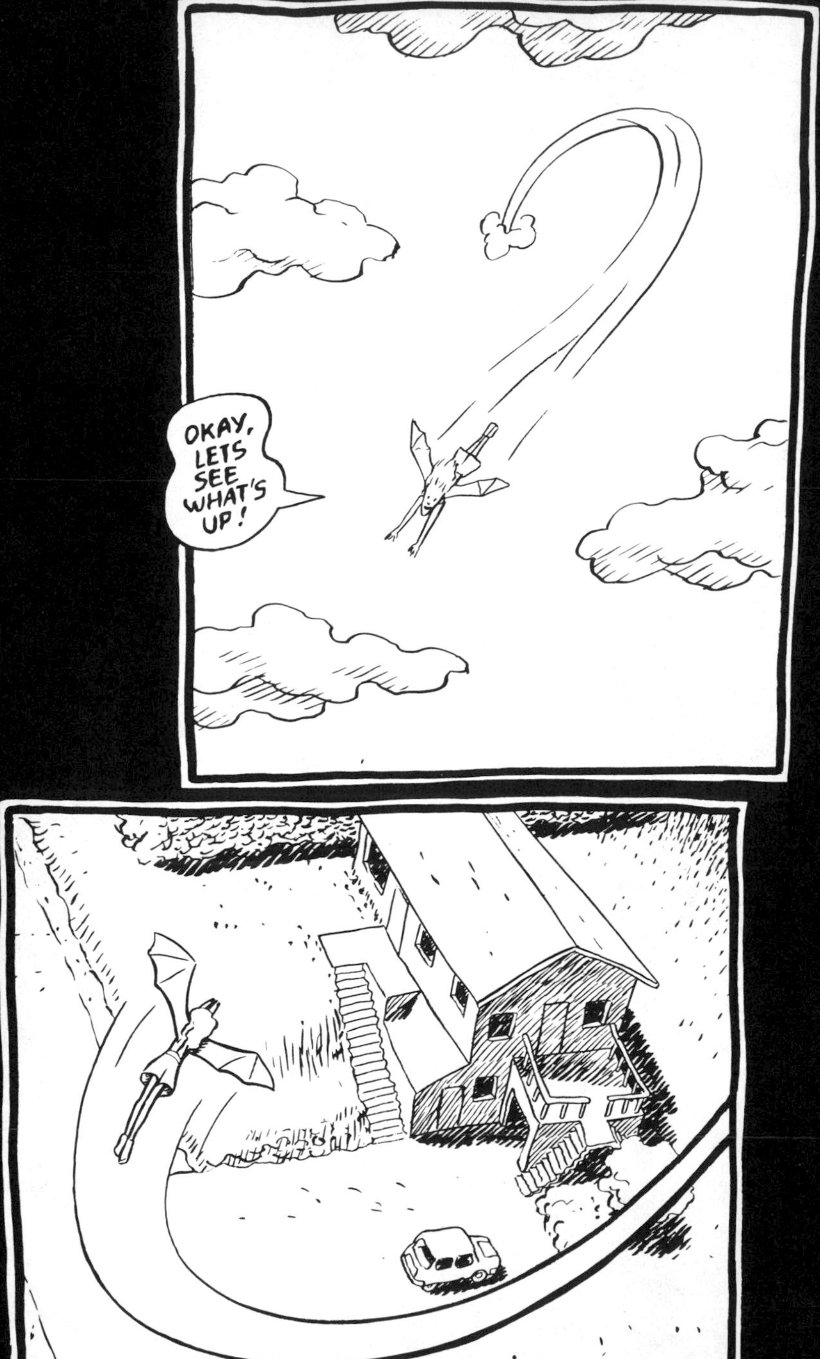
OKAY, LETS SEE WHAT'S UP!

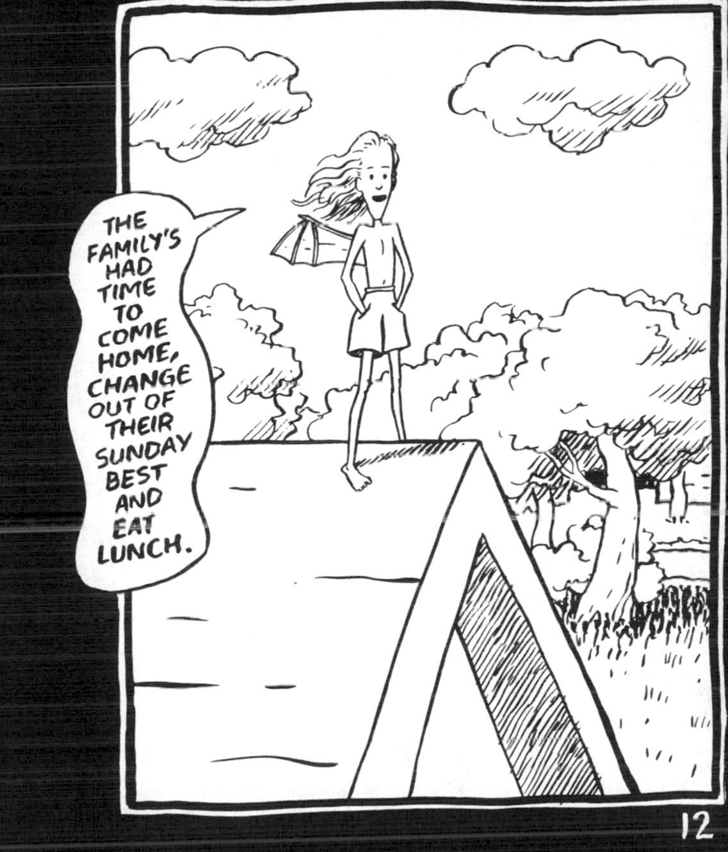
THE FAMILY'S HAD TIME TO COME HOME, CHANGE OUT OF THEIR SUNDAY BEST AND EAT LUNCH.

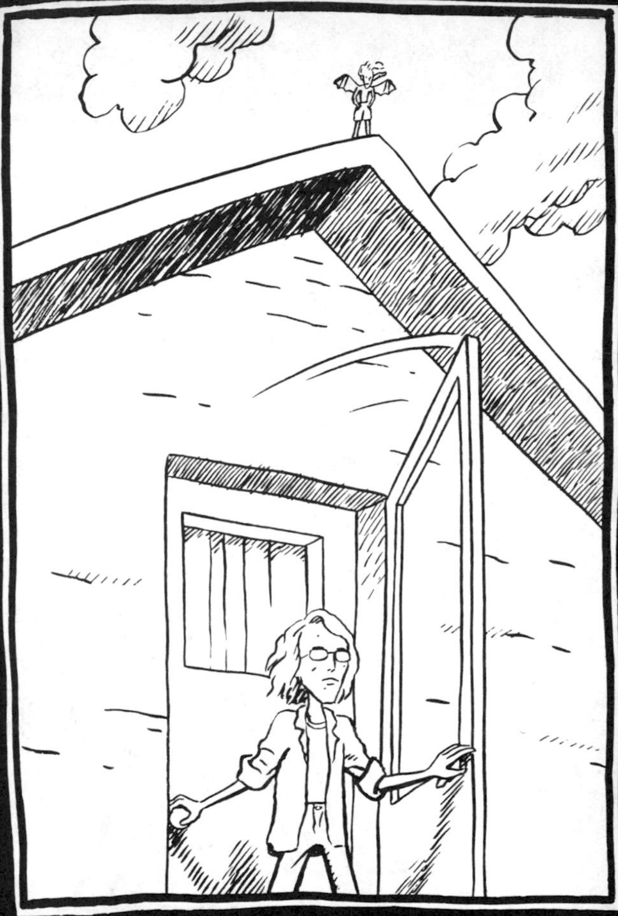

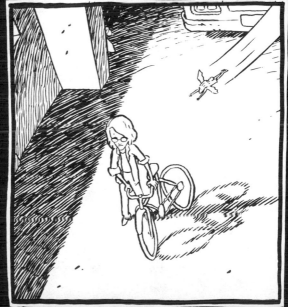

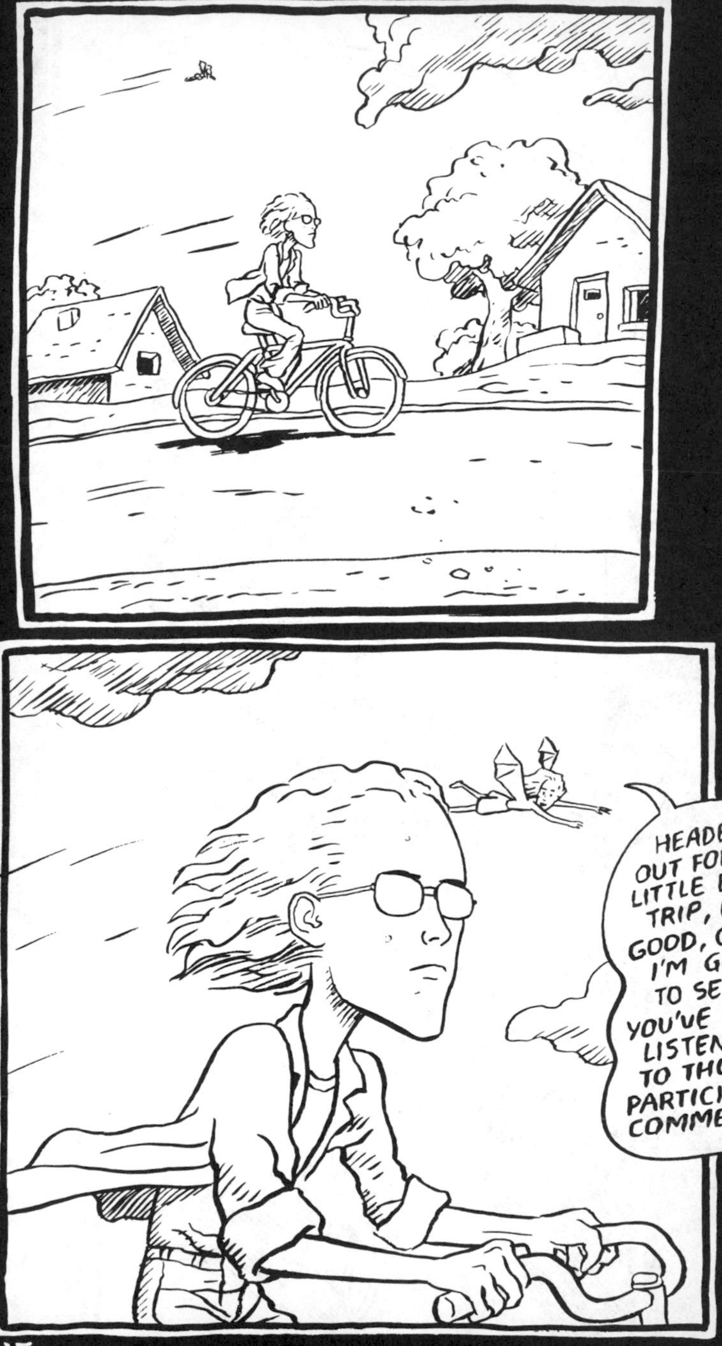
HEADED OUT FOR A LITTLE BIKE TRIP, EH? GOOD, GOOD. I'M GLAD TO SEE YOU'VE BEEN LISTENING TO THOSE PARTICIPACTION COMMERCIALS.

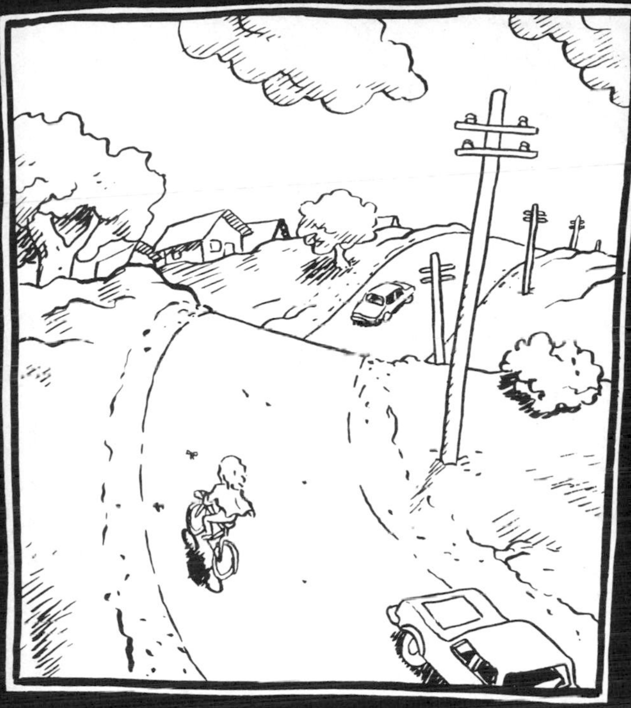

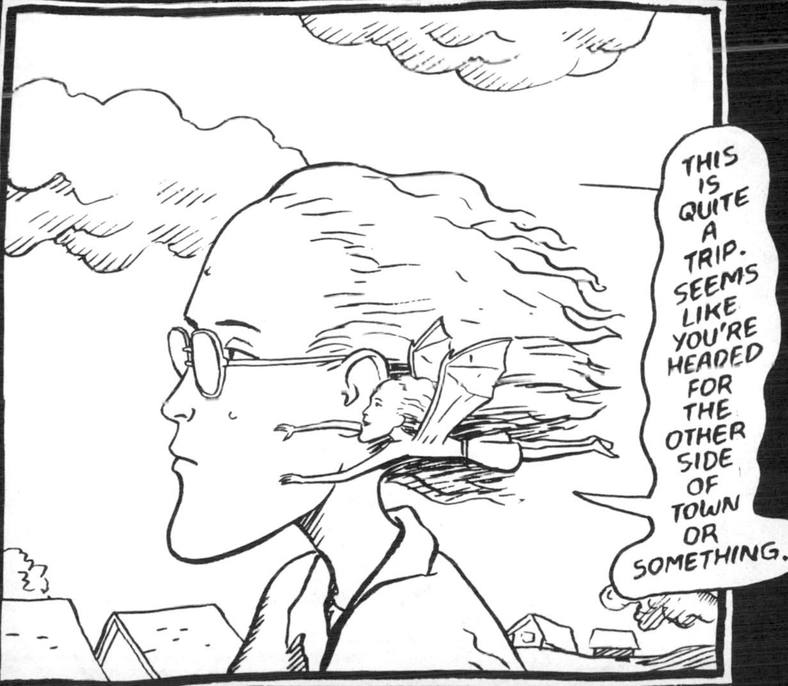
THIS IS QUITE A TRIP. SEEMS LIKE YOU'RE HEADED FOR THE OTHER SIDE OF TOWN OR SOMETHING.

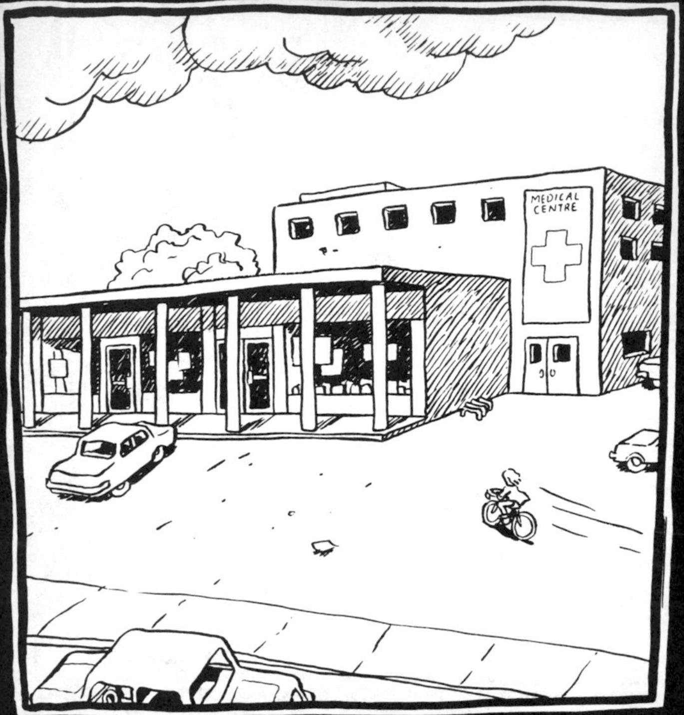
MEDICAL CENTRE

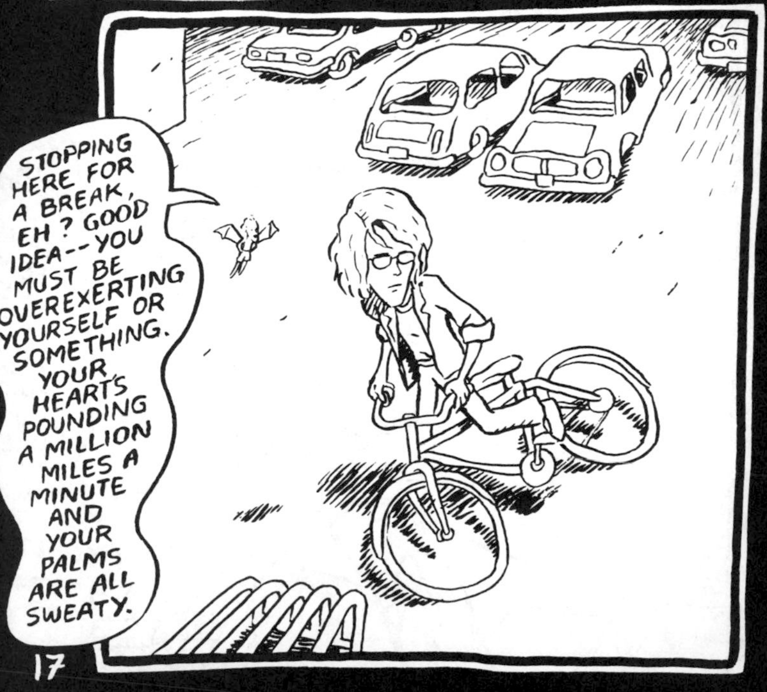
STOPPING HERE FOR A BREAK, EH ? GOOD IDEA-- YOU MUST BE OVEREXERTING YOURSELF OR SOMETHING. YOUR HEART'S POUNDING A MILLION MILES A MINUTE AND YOUR PALMS ARE ALL SWEATY.

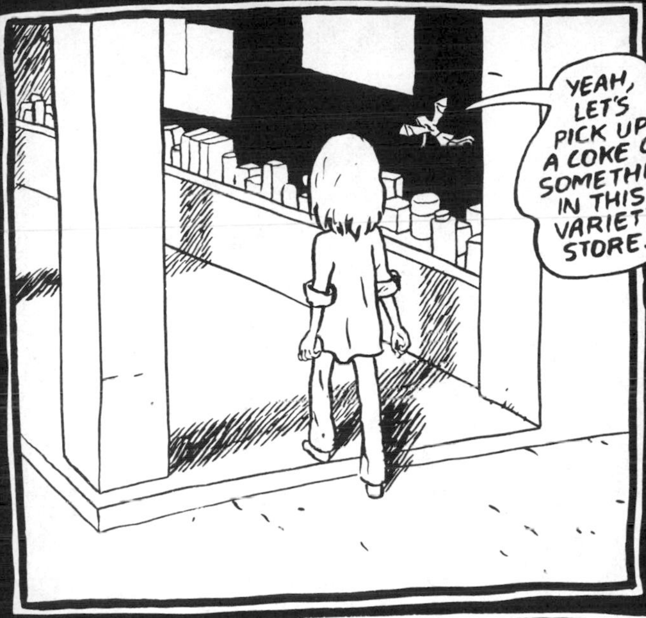
YEAH, LET'S PICK UP A COKE OR SOMETHING IN THIS VARIETY STORE.

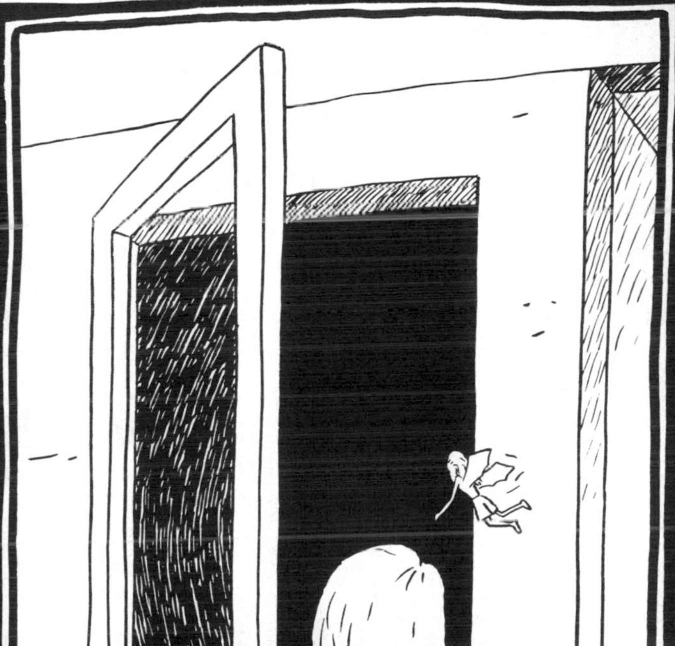

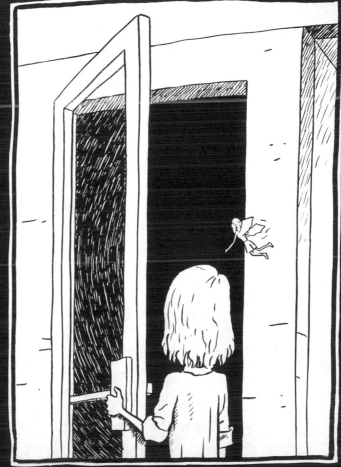

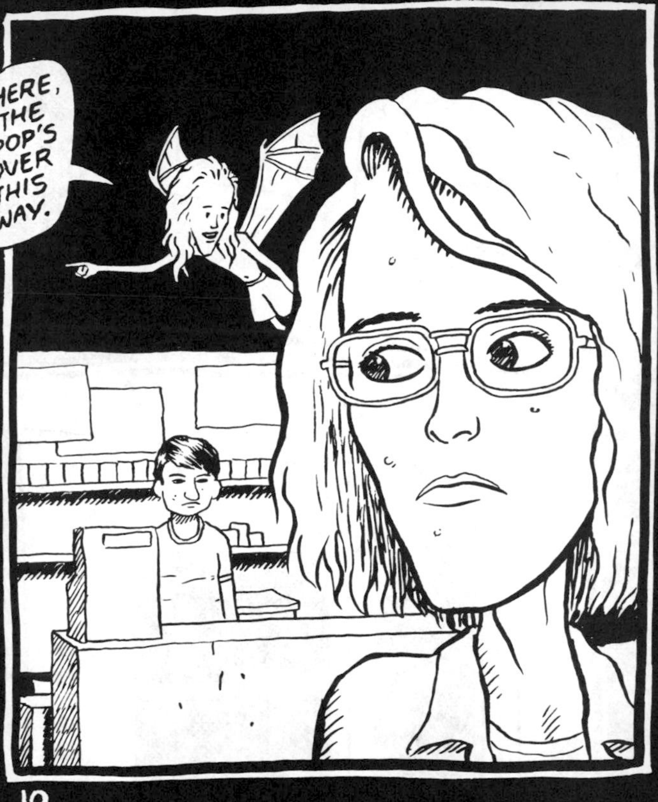
HERE, THE POP'S OVER THIS WAY.

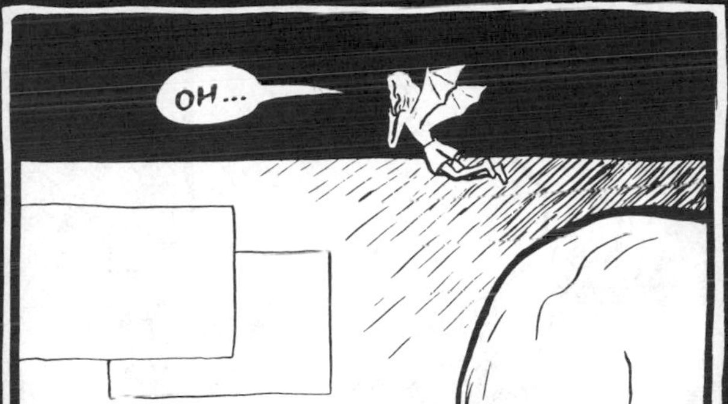
OH...

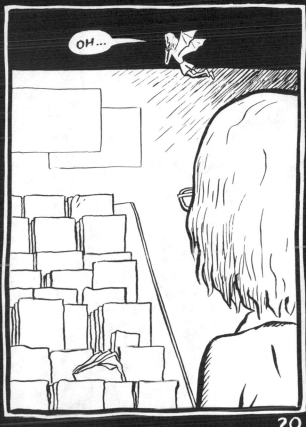

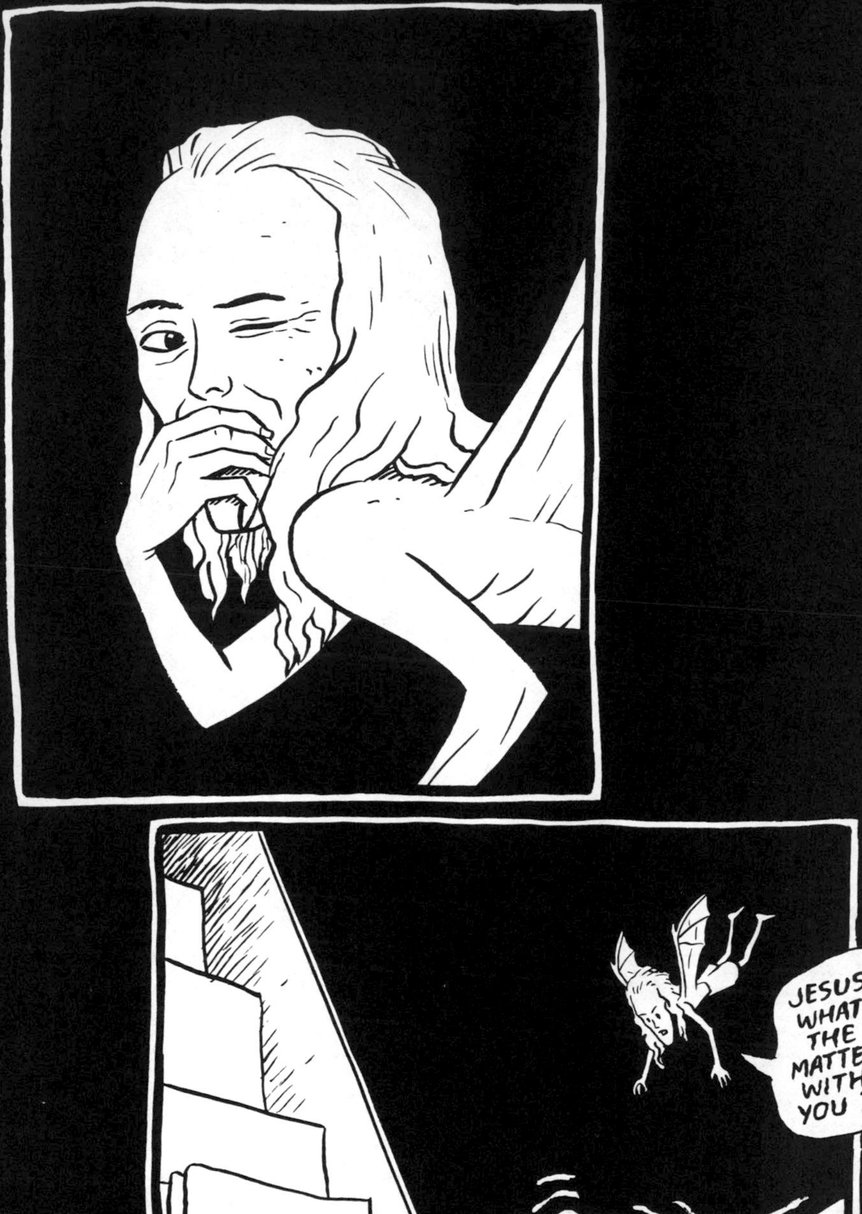
PLAYBOY
JESUS! WHAT'S THE MATTER WITH YOU?

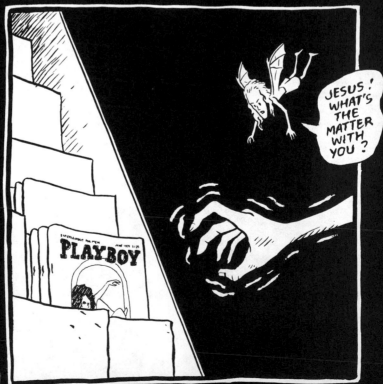

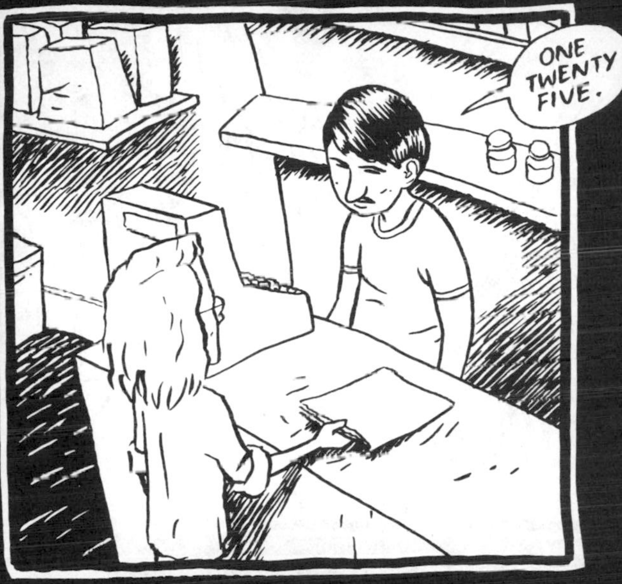
ONE TWENTY FIVE.

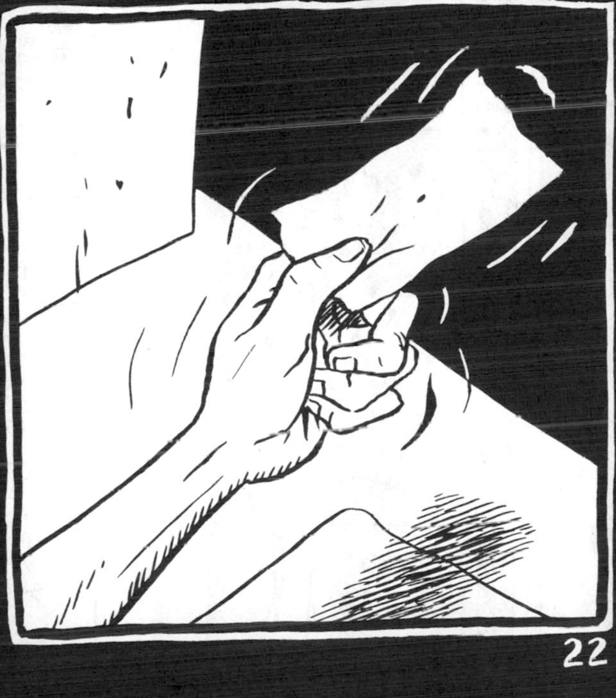

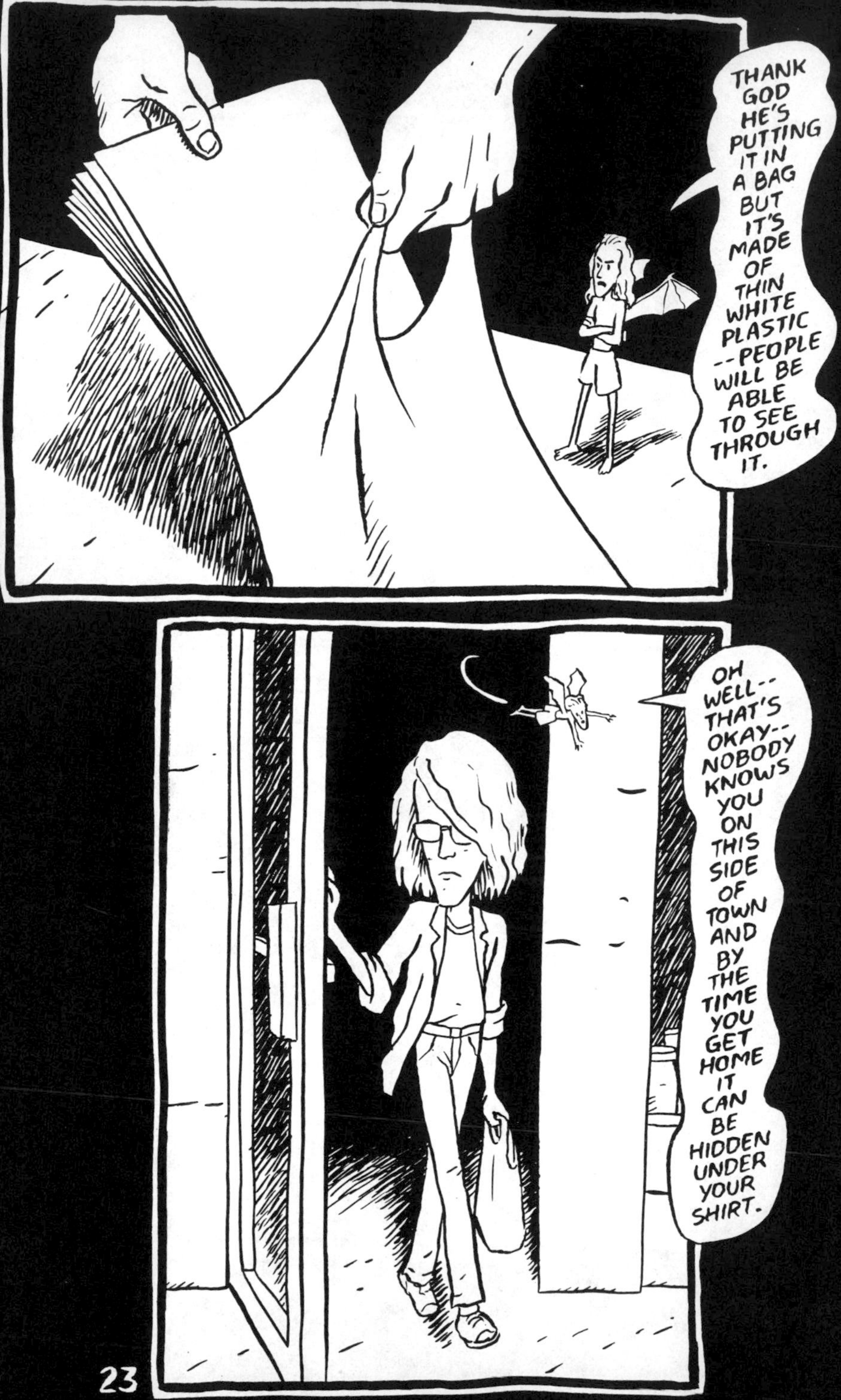
THANK GOD HE'S PUTTING IT IN A BAG BUT IT'S MADE OF THIN WHITE PLASTIC --PEOPLE WILL BE ABLE TO SEE THROUGH IT.
OH WELL-- THAT'S OKAY-- NOBODY KNOWS YOU ON THIS SIDE OF TOWN AND BY THE TIME YOU GET HOME IT CAN BE HIDDEN UNDER YOUR SHIRT.

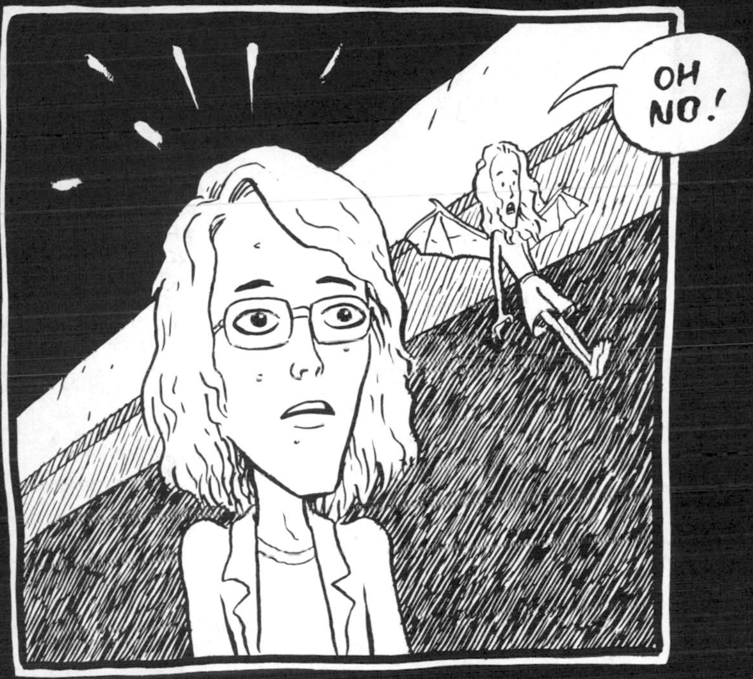
OH NO!

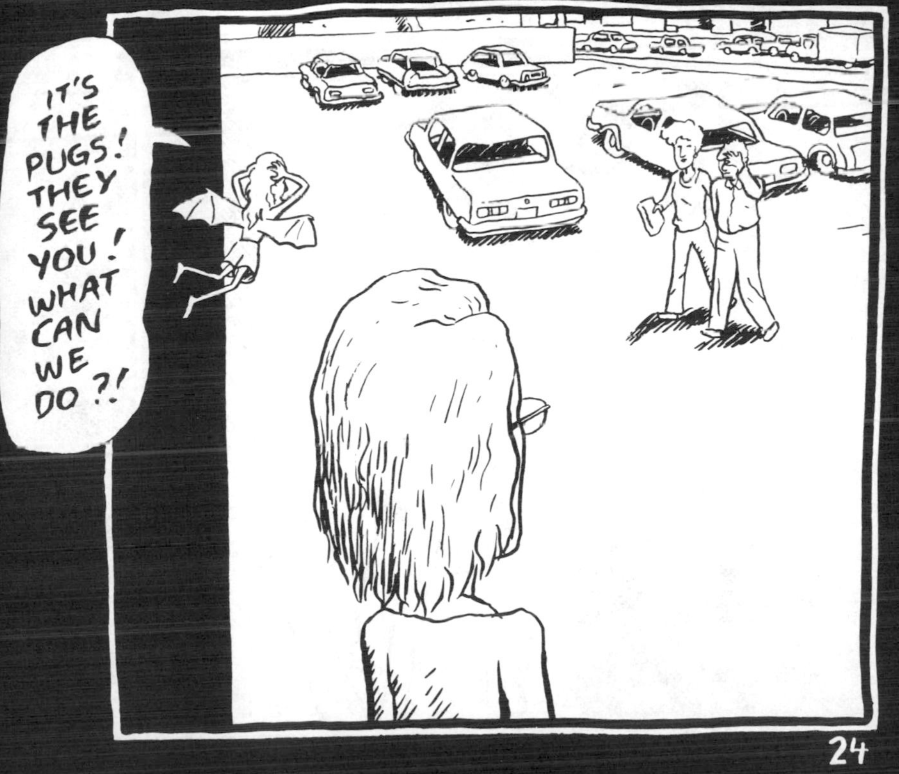
IT'S THE PUGS! THEY SEE YOU! WHAT CAN WE DO?!

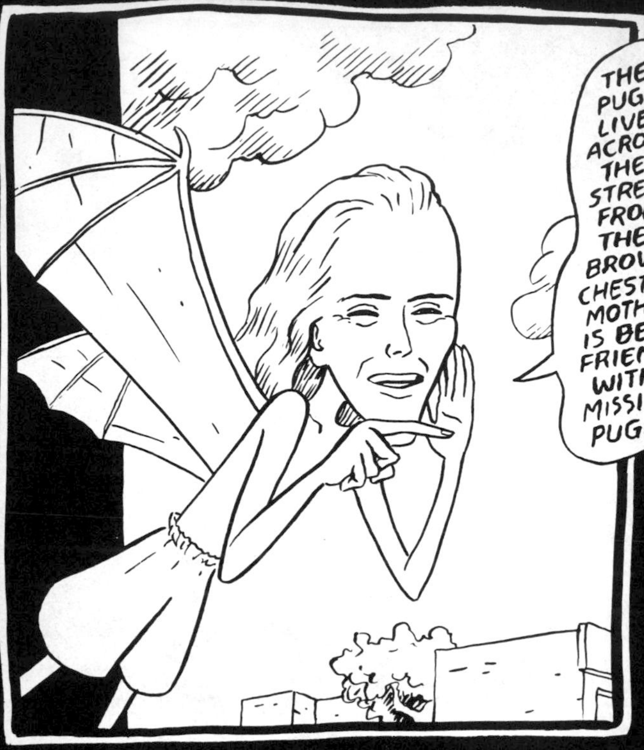
THE PUGS LIVE ACROSS THE STREET FROM THE BROWNS. CHESTER'S MOTHER IS BEST FRIENDS WITH MISSIZ PUG.

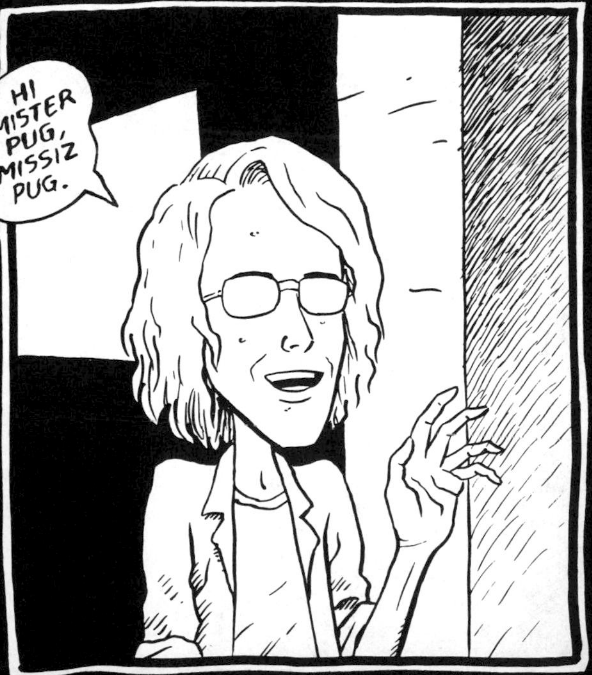
HI MISTER PUG, MISSIZ PUG.

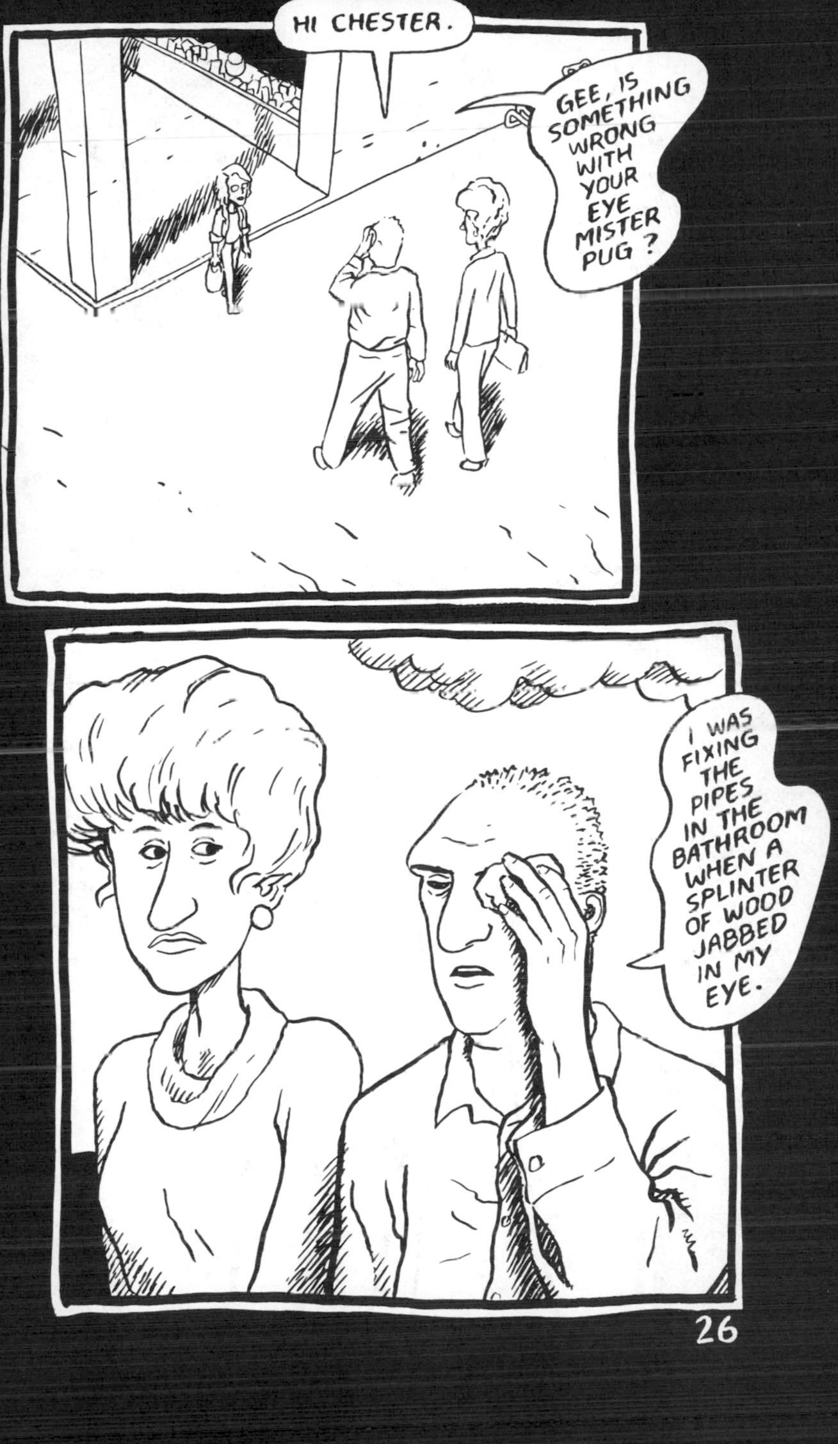
HI CHESTER.
GEE, IS SOMETHING WRONG WITH YOUR EYE MISTER PUG?
I WAS FIXING THE PIPES IN THE BATHROOM WHEN A SPLINTER OF WOOD JABBED IN MY EYE.

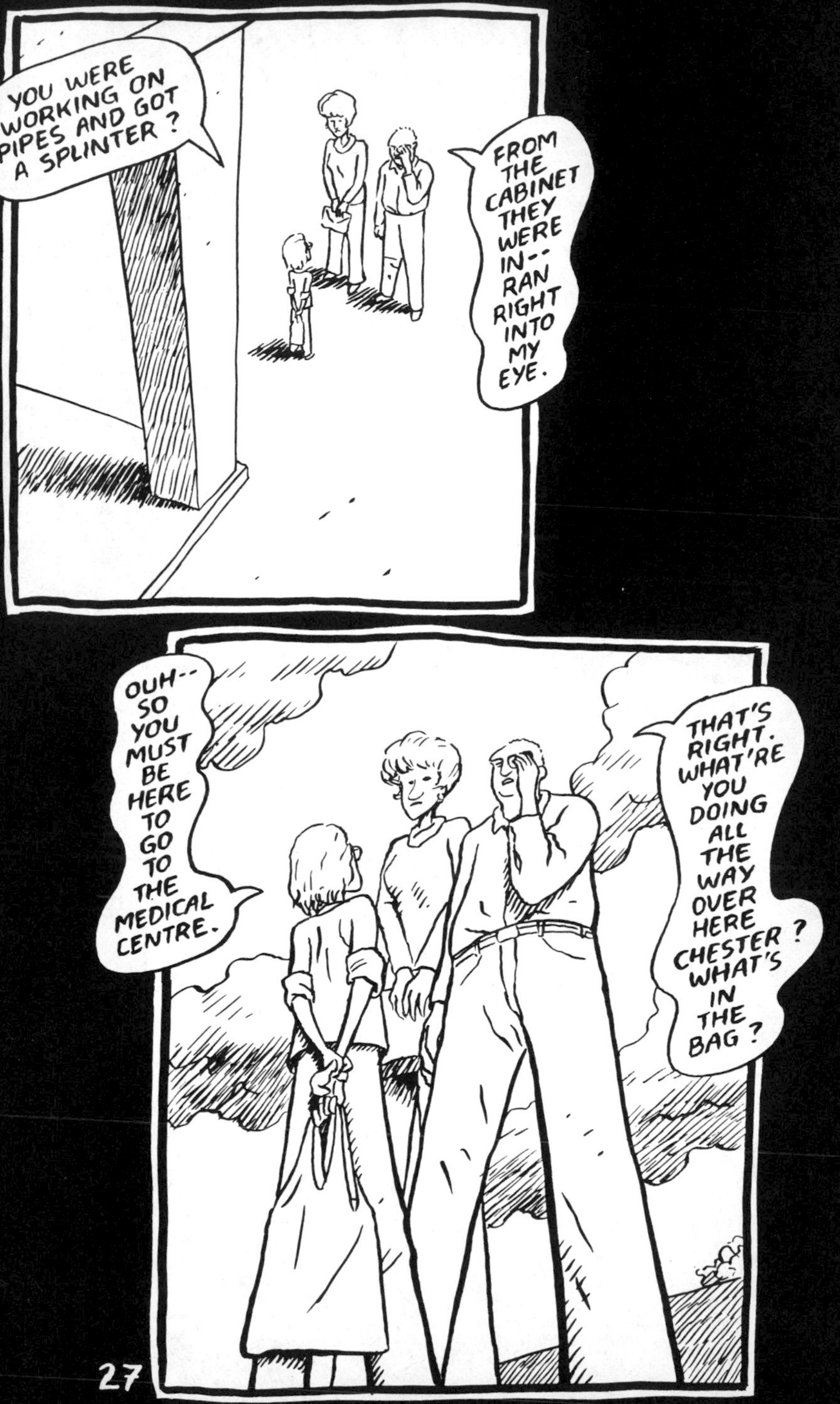
YOU WERE WORKING ON PIPES AND GOT A SPLINTER ?
FROM THE CABINET THEY WERE IN-- RAN RIGHT INTO MY EYE.
OUH-- SO YOU MUST BE HERE TO GO TO THE MEDICAL CENTRE.
THAT'S RIGHT. WHAT'RE YOU DOING ALL THE WAY OVER HERE CHESTER ? WHAT'S IN THE BAG ?

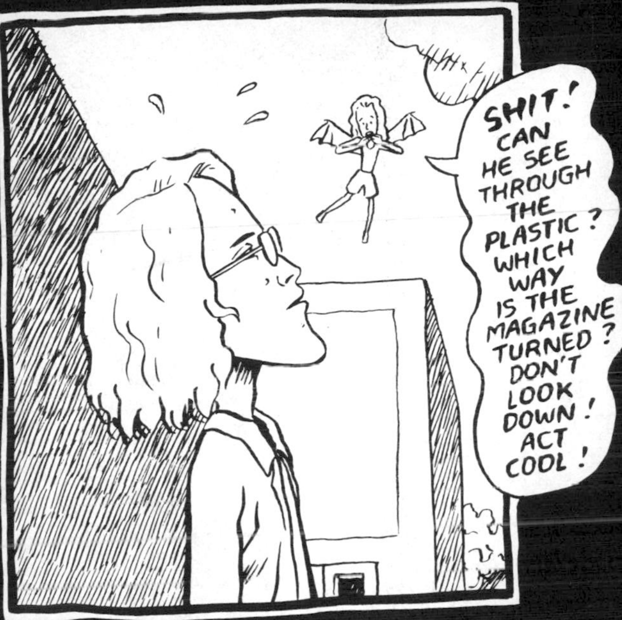
SHIT! CAN HE SEE THROUGH THE PLASTIC? WHICH WAY IS THE MAGAZINE TURNED? DON'T LOOK DOWN! ACT COOL!

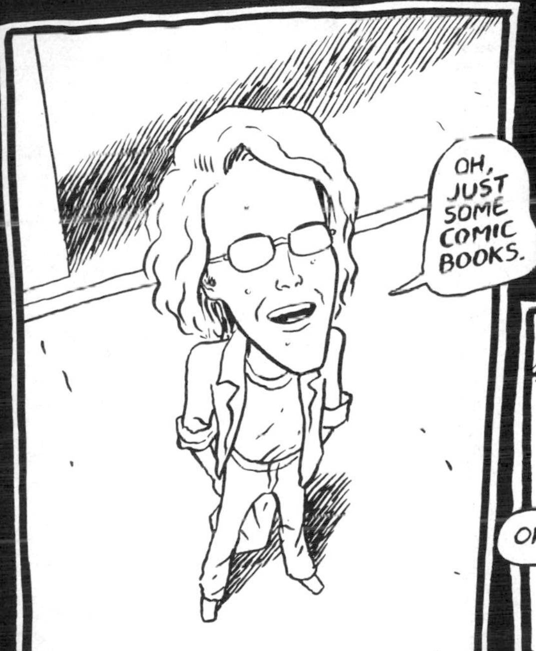
OH, JUST SOME COMIC BOOKS.

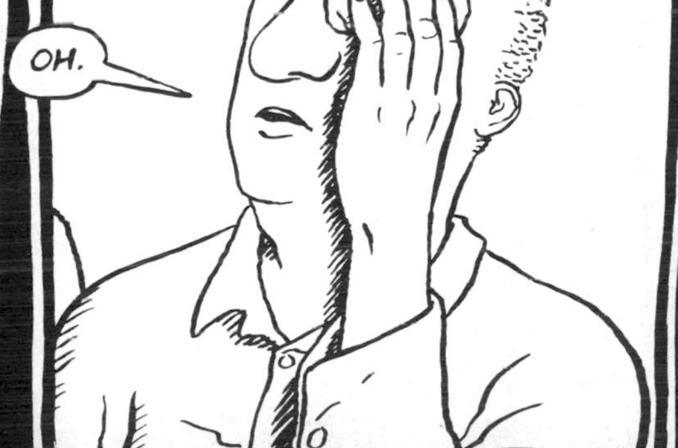
OH.

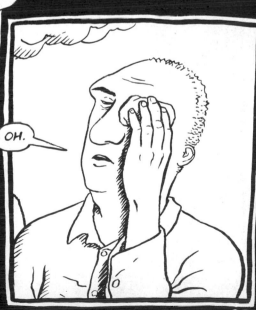

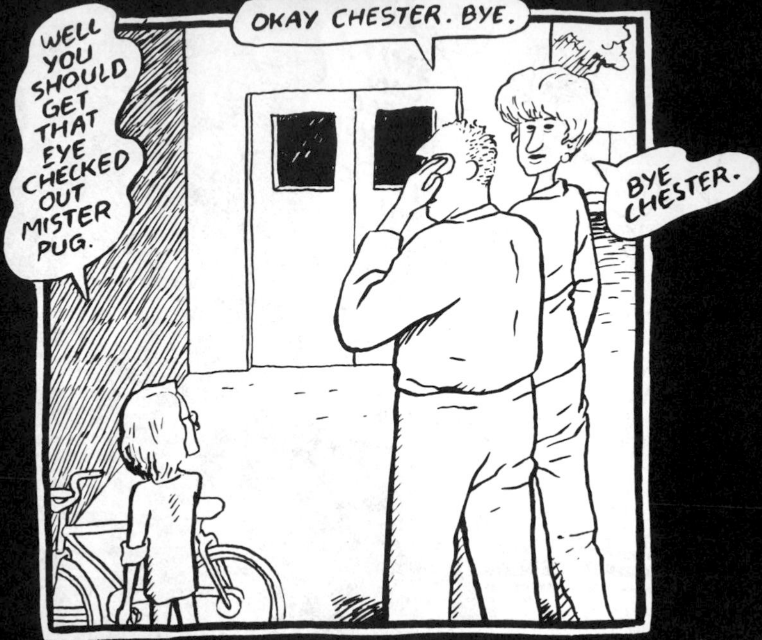
WELL YOU SHOULD GET THAT EYE CHECKED OUT MISTER PUG.
OKAY CHESTER. BYE.
BYE CHESTER.

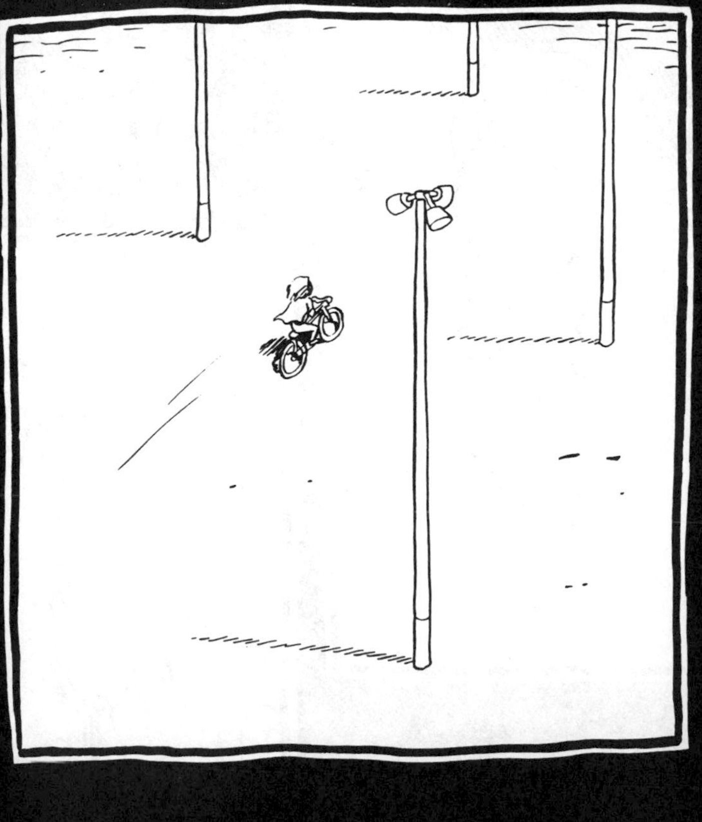

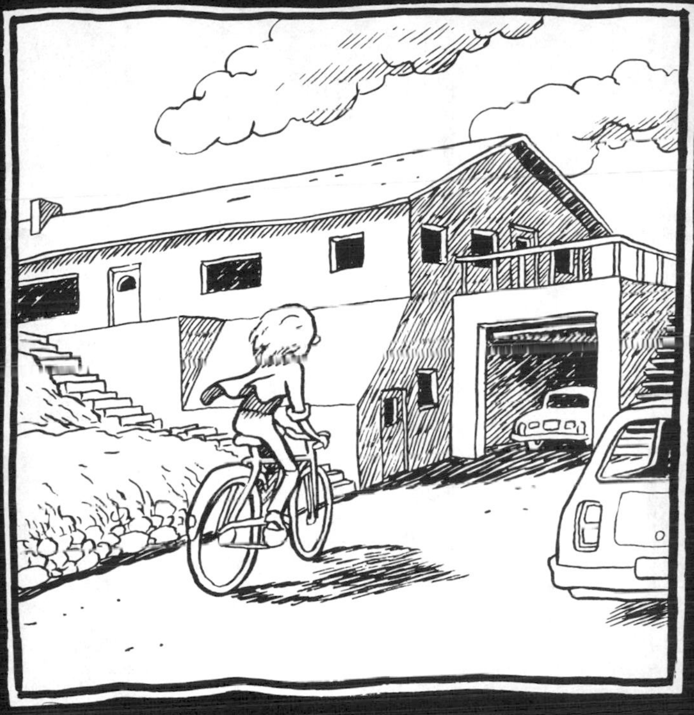

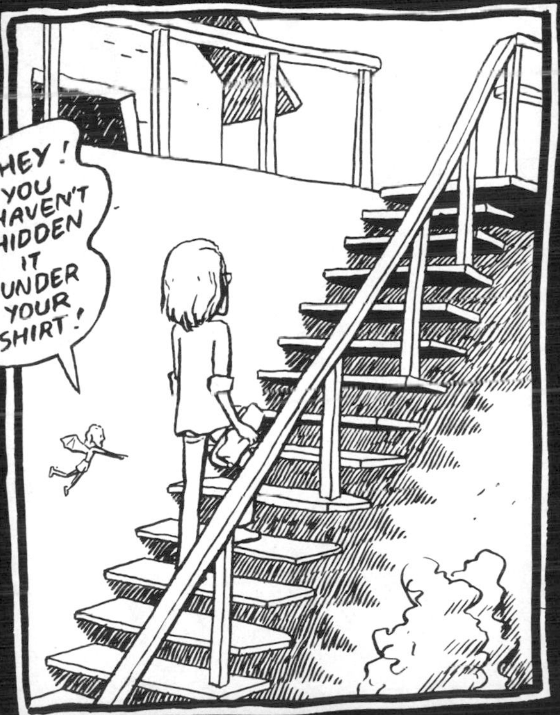
HEY! YOU HAVEN'T HIDDEN IT UNDER YOUR SHIRT!

I SEE- THE BEST WAY TO HIDE SOMETHING IS TO HAVE IT OUT IN THE OPEN, EH ?
NO ONE AROUND THE SIDE DOOR.

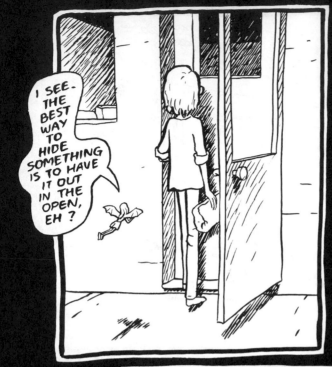

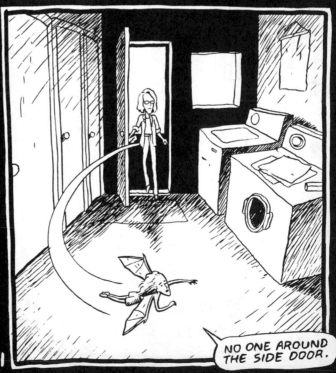

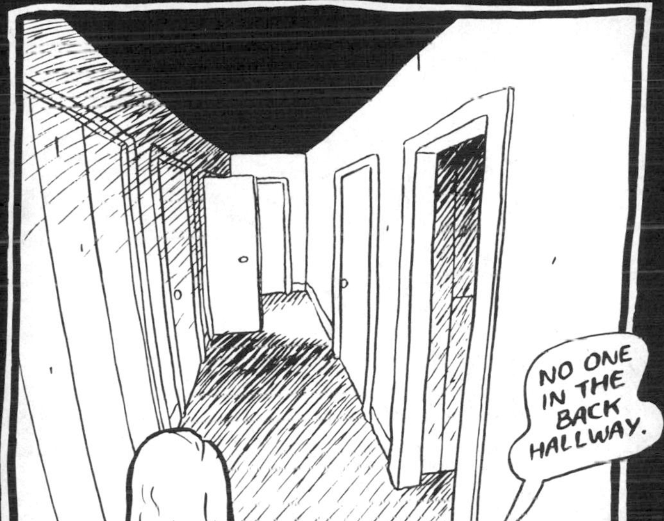
NO ONE IN THE BACK HALLWAY.

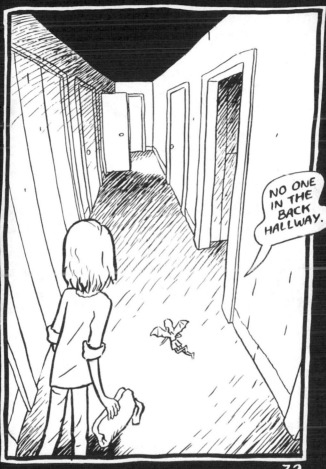

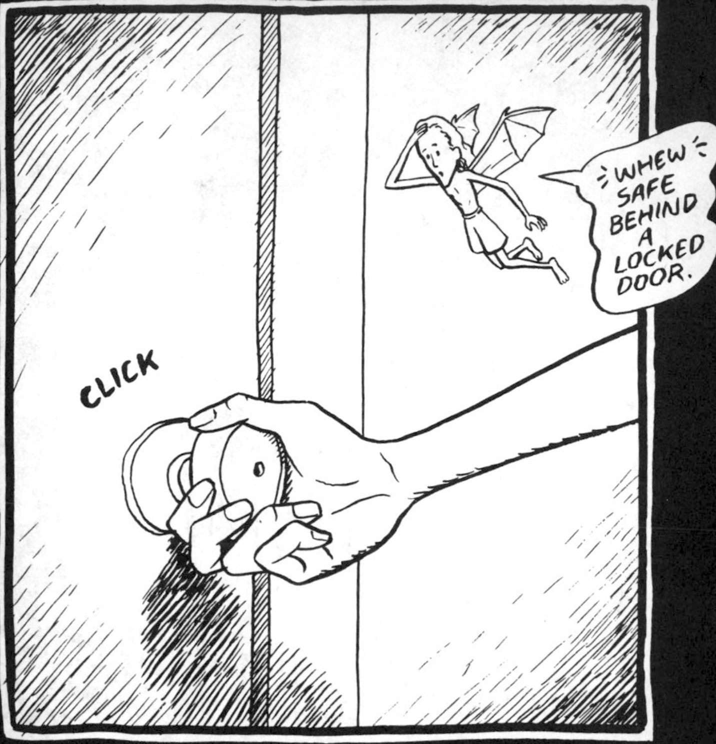
WHEW
SAFE BEHIND A LOCKED DOOR.
CLICK

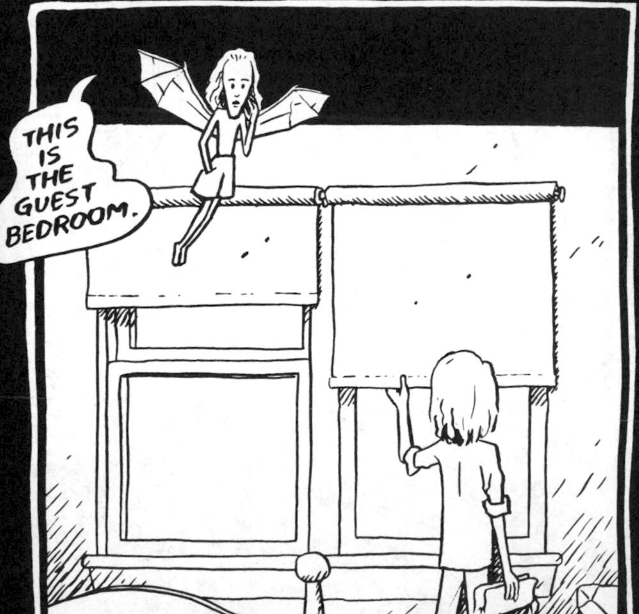
THIS IS THE GUEST BEDROOM.

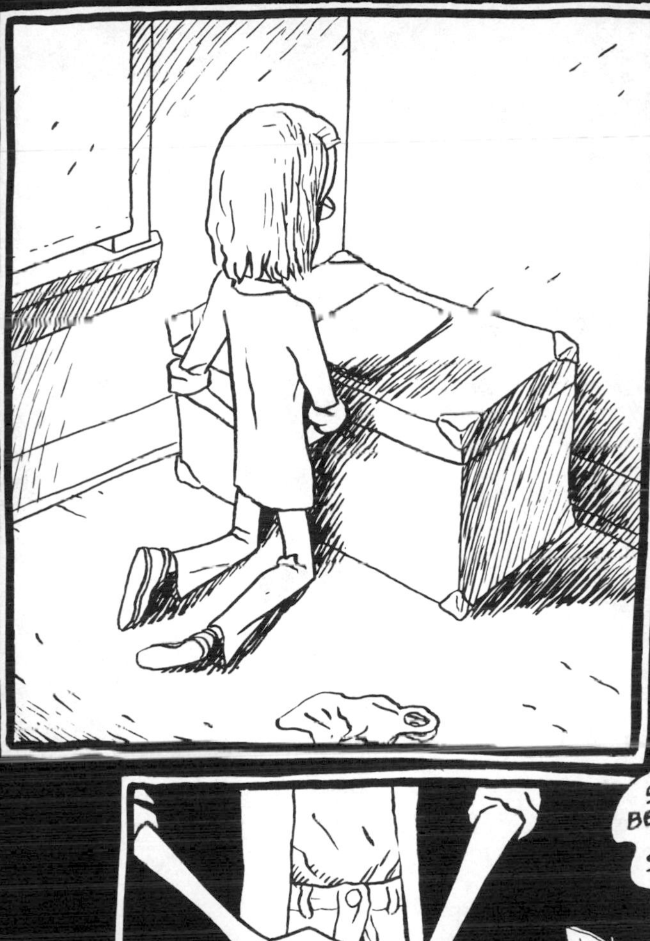

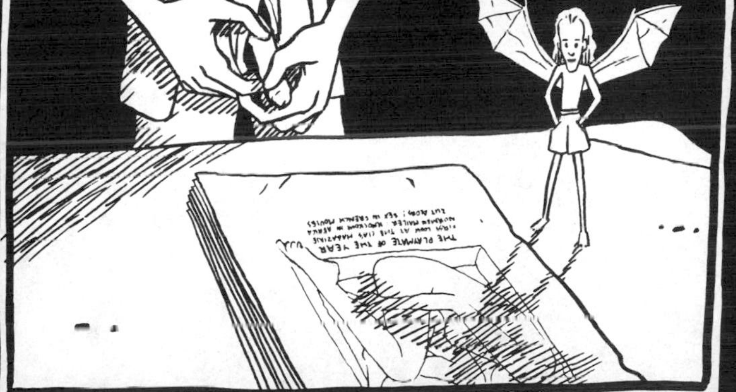
SHE IS BEAUTIFUL ISN'T SHE ?

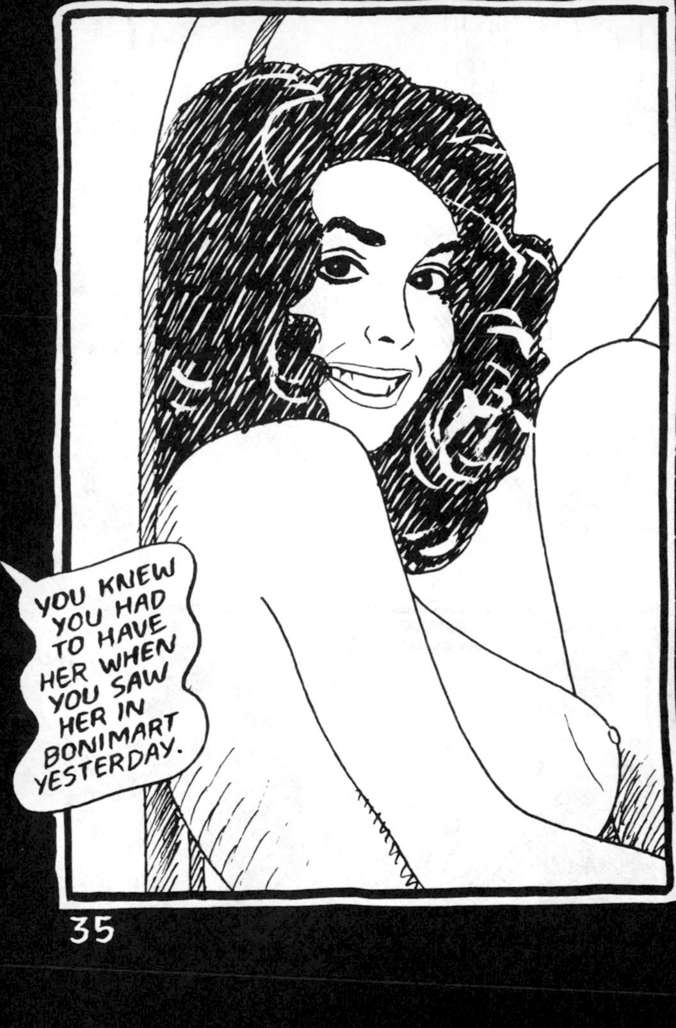
YOU KNEW YOU HAD TO HAVE HER WHEN YOU SAW HER IN BONIMART YESTERDAY.

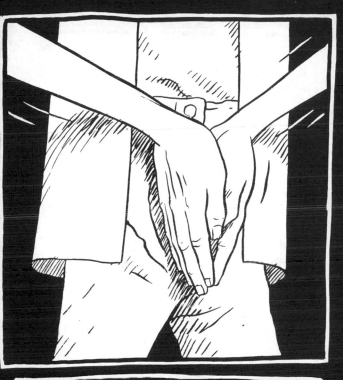

36

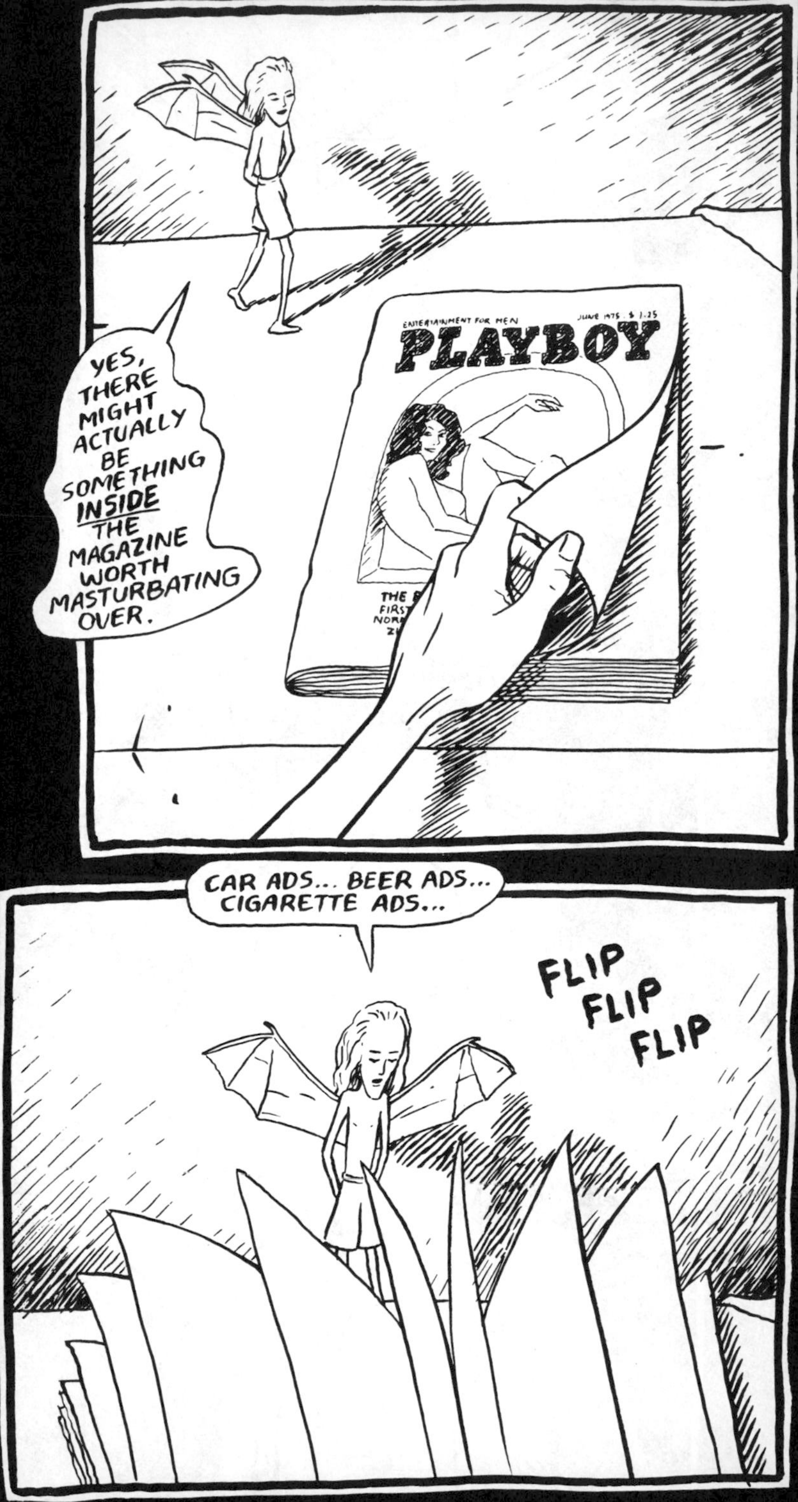
ENTERTAINMENT FOR MEN
JUNE 1975 $1.25
PLAYBOY
YES, THERE MIGHT ACTUALLY BE SOMETHING INSIDE THE MAGAZINE WORTH MASTURBATING OVER.
CAR ADS... BEER ADS... CIGARETTE ADS...
FLIP FLIP FLIP

FLIP
SMACK
OH NO!

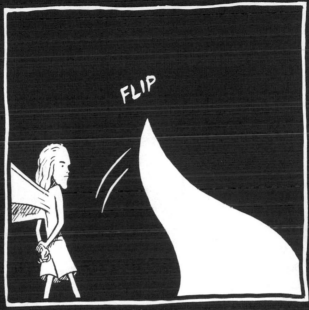

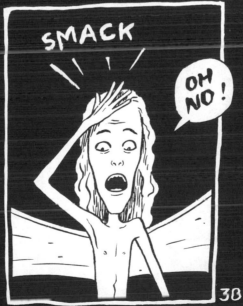

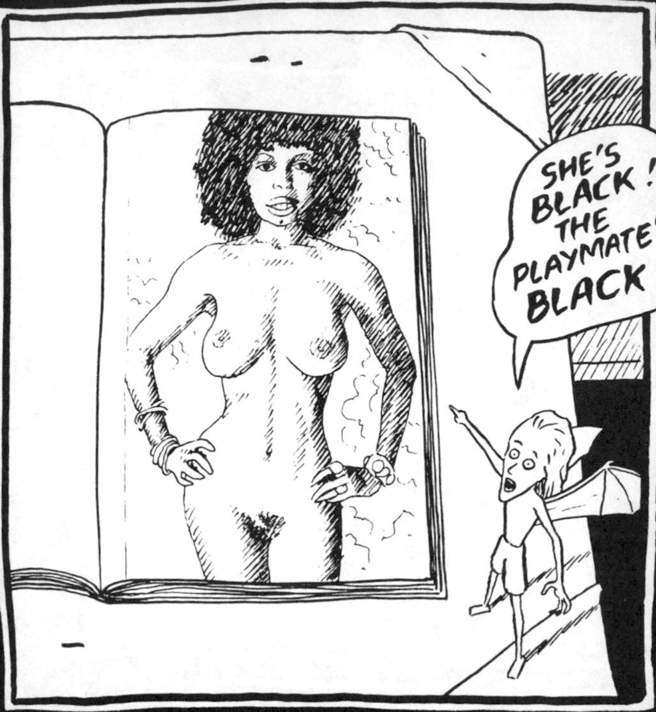
SHE'S BLACK! THE PLAYMATE'S BLACK!

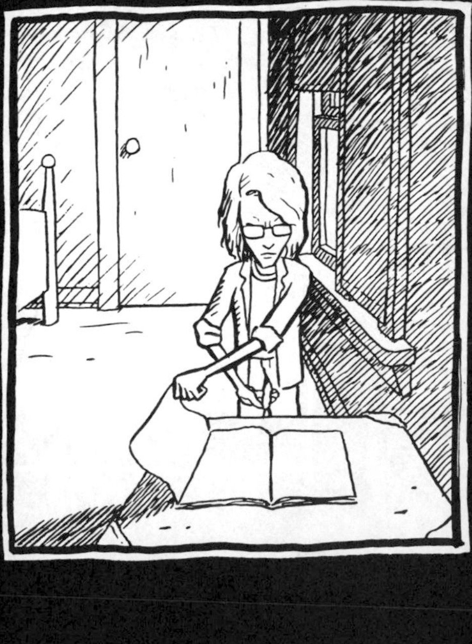

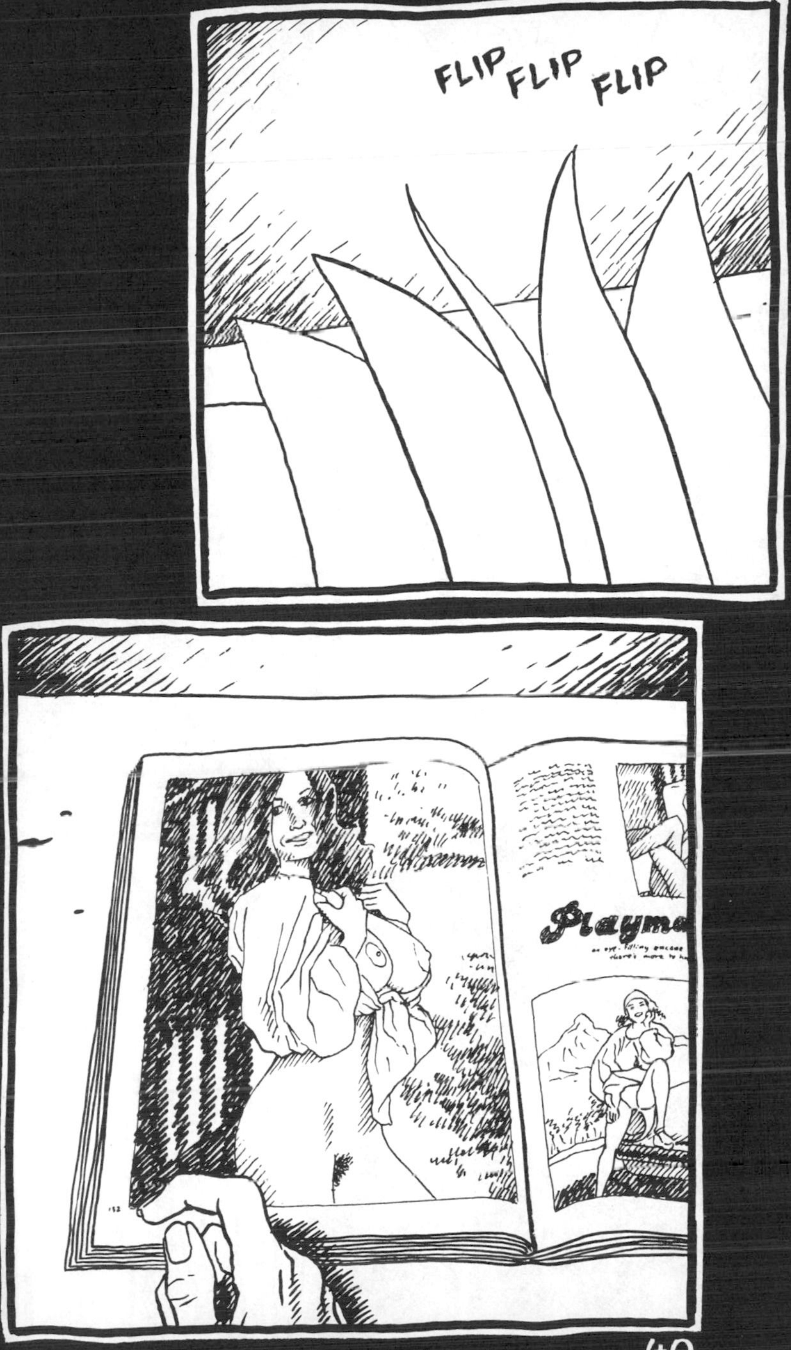
FLIP FLIP FLIP

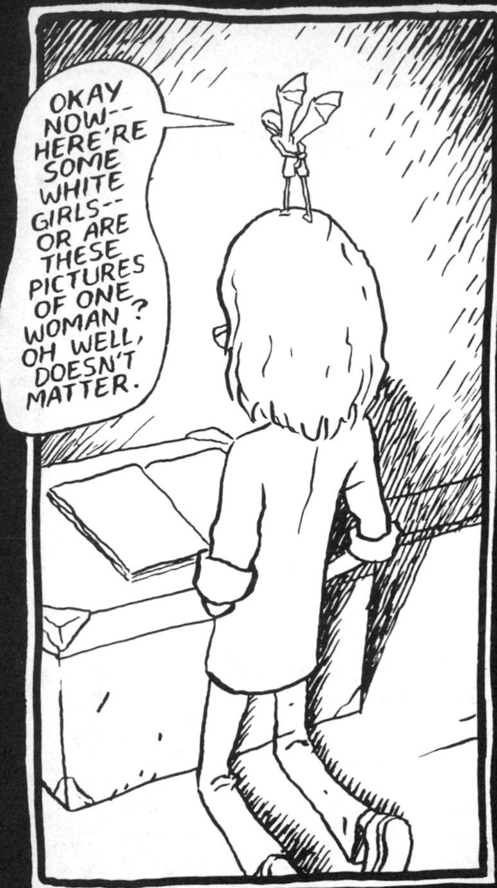
OKAY NOW-- HERE'RE SOME WHITE GIRLS-- OR ARE THESE PICTURES OF ONE WOMAN? OH WELL, DOESN'T MATTER.

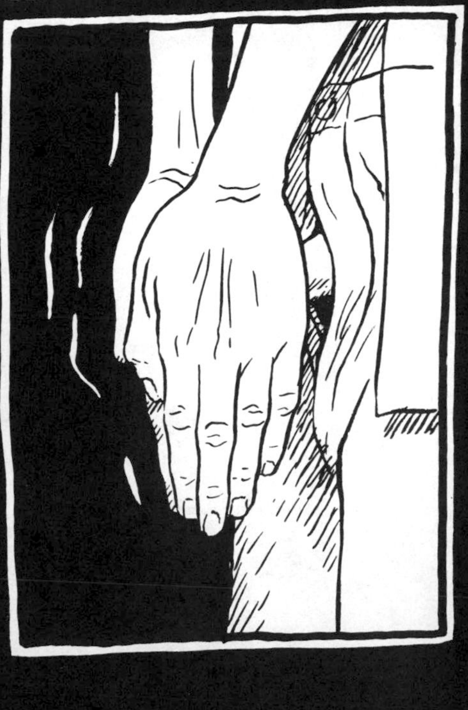

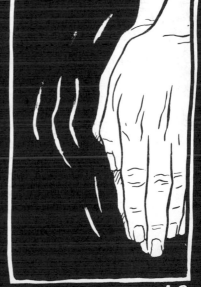

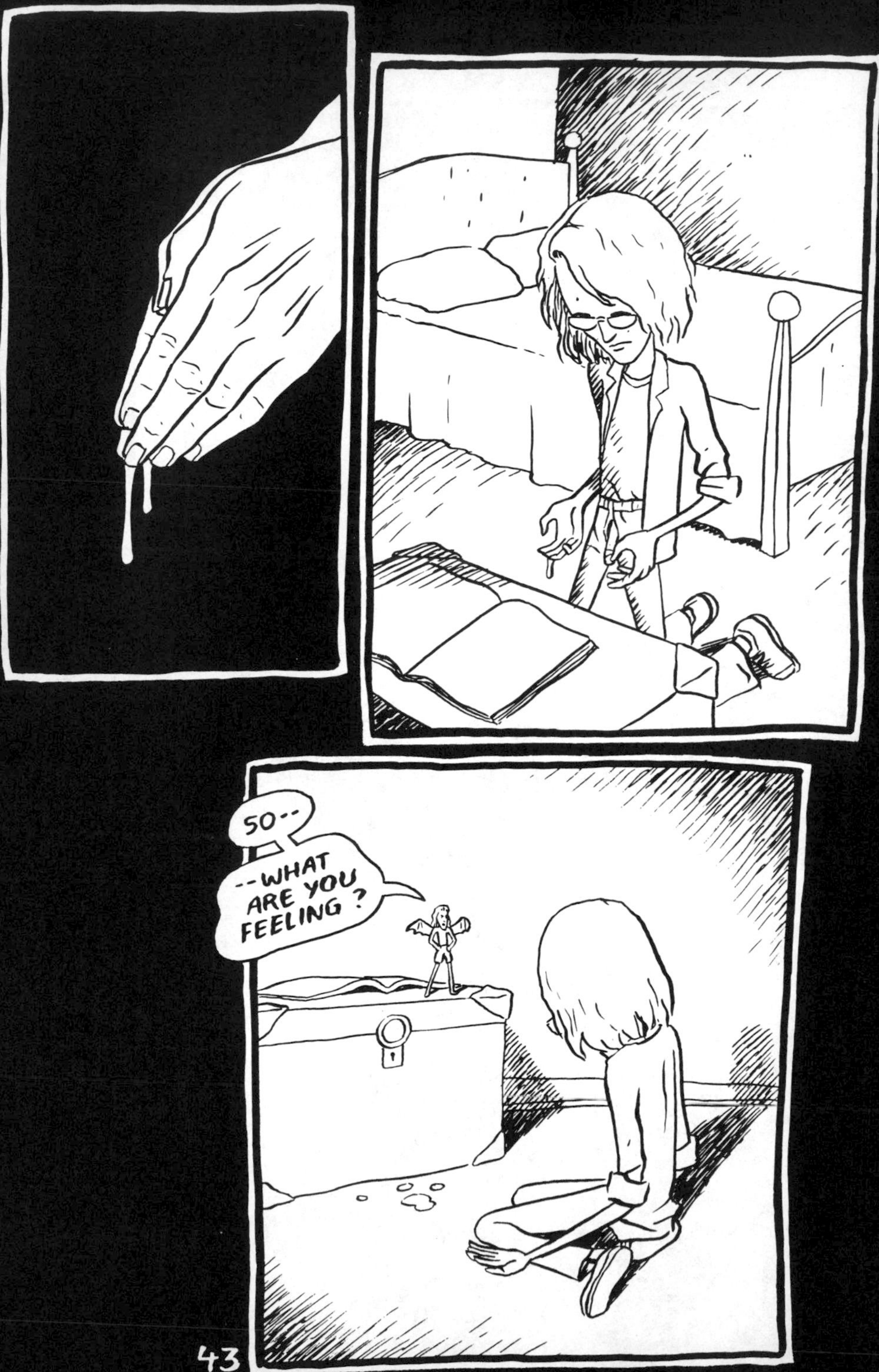
SO--
--WHAT ARE YOU FEELING ?

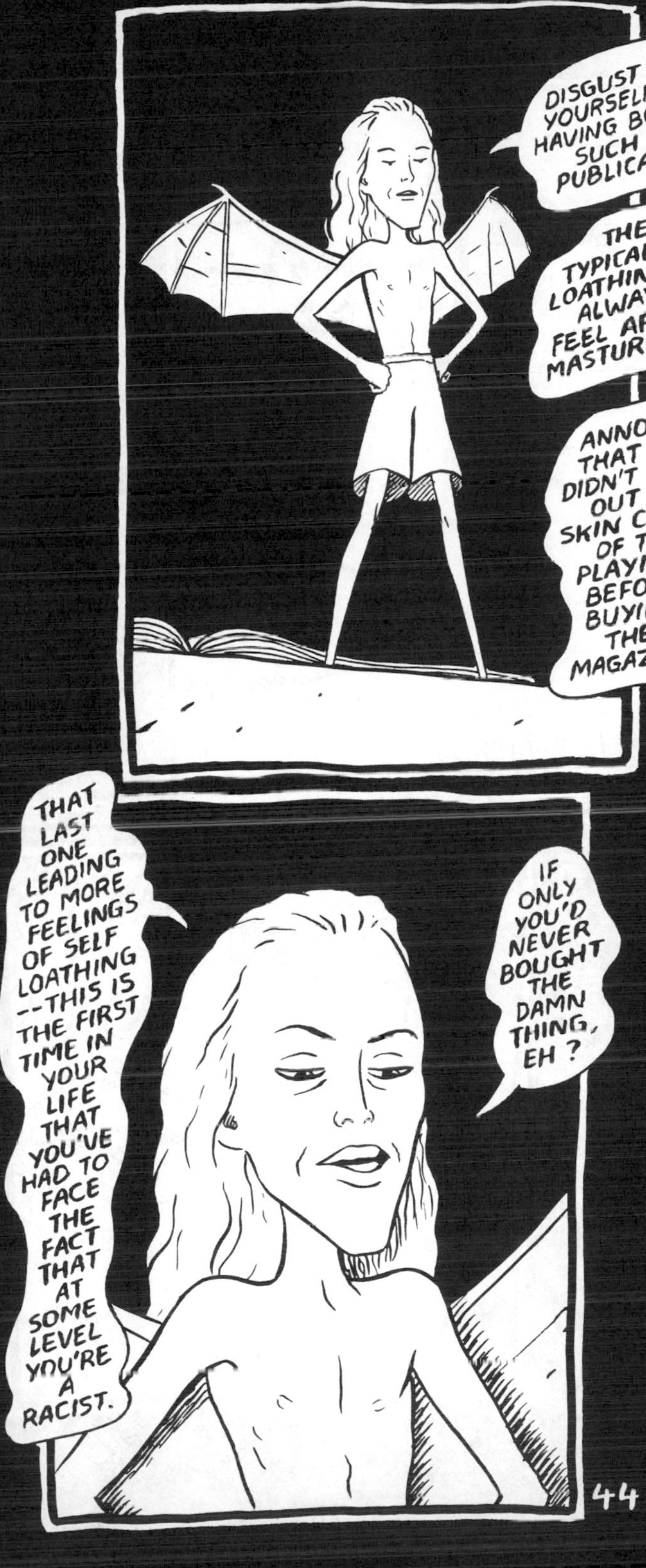
DISGUST WITH YOURSELF FOR HAVING BOUGHT SUCH A PUBLICATION.
THE TYPICAL SELF LOATHING YOU ALWAYS FEEL AFTER MASTURBATING.
ANNOYANCE THAT YOU DIDN'T CHECK OUT THE SKIN COLOUR OF THE PLAYMATE BEFORE BUYING THE MAGAZINE.
THAT LAST ONE LEADING TO MORE FEELINGS OF SELF LOATHING --THIS IS THE FIRST TIME IN YOUR LIFE THAT YOU'VE HAD TO FACE THE FACT THAT AT SOME LEVEL YOU'RE A RACIST.
IF ONLY YOU'D NEVER BOUGHT THE DAMN THING, EH ?

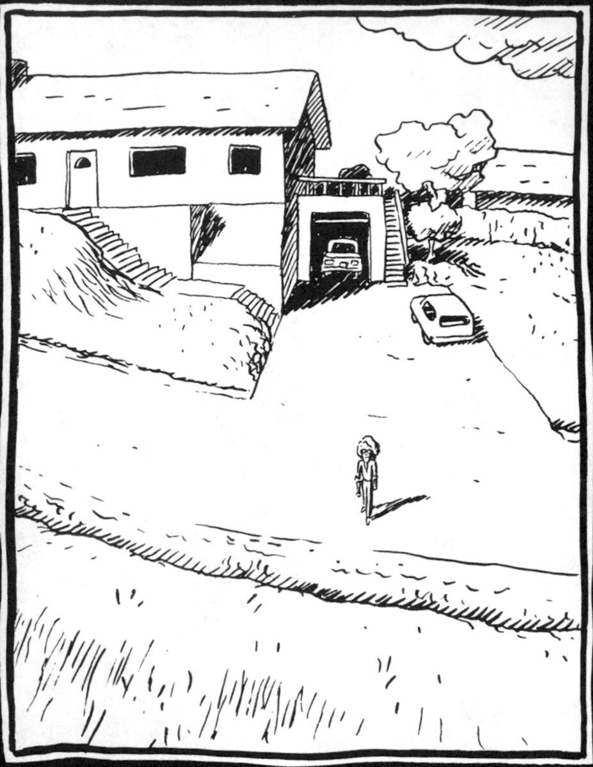

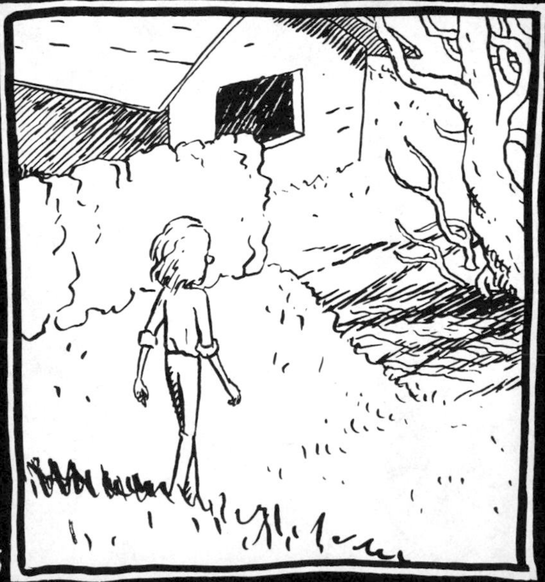

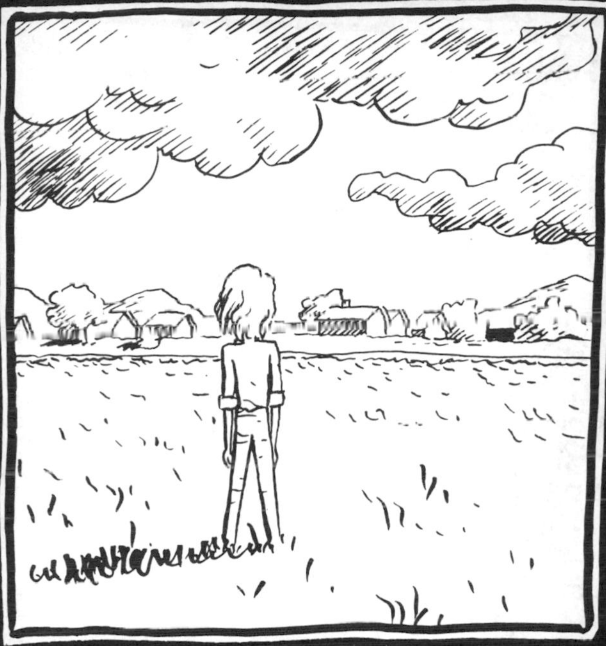

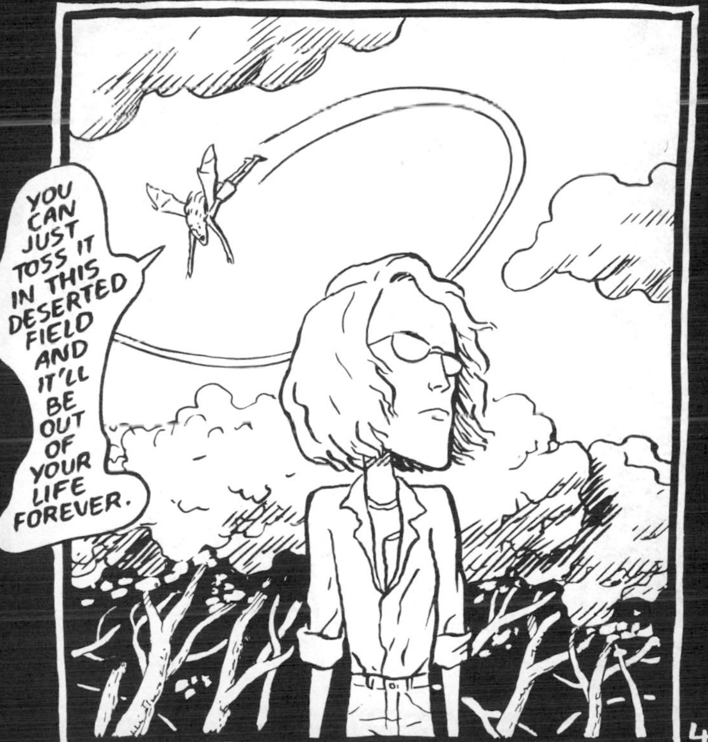
YOU CAN JUST TOSS IT IN THIS DESERTED FIELD AND IT'LL BE OUT OF YOUR LIFE FOREVER.

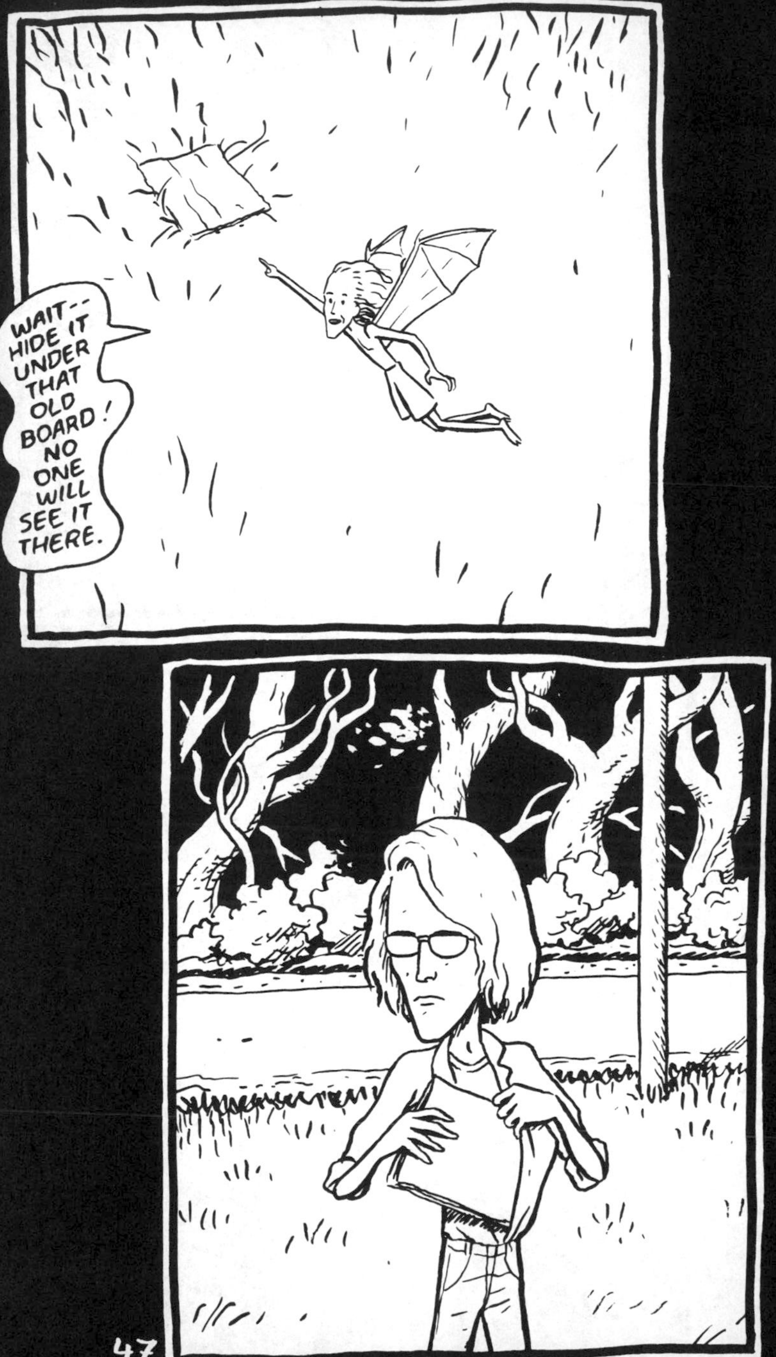
WAIT-- HIDE IT UNDER THAT OLD BOARD! NO ONE WILL SEE IT THERE.

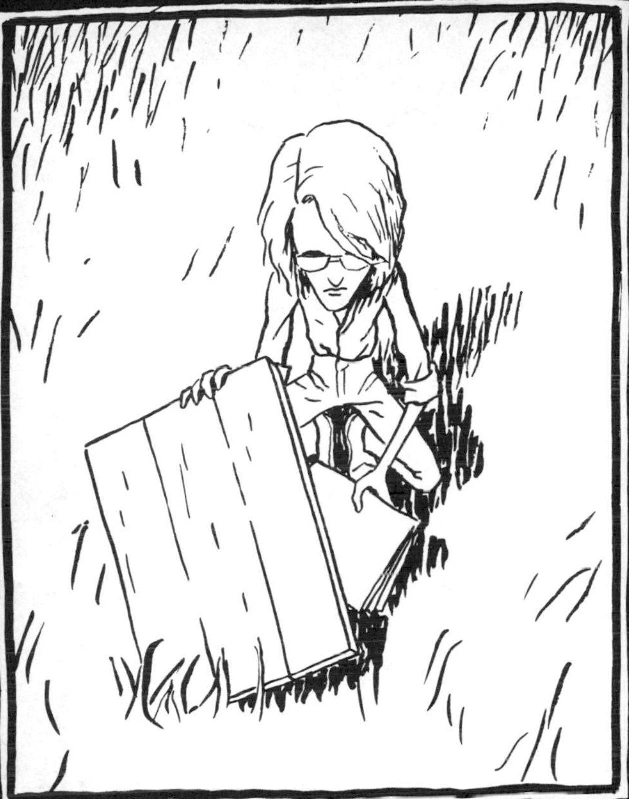

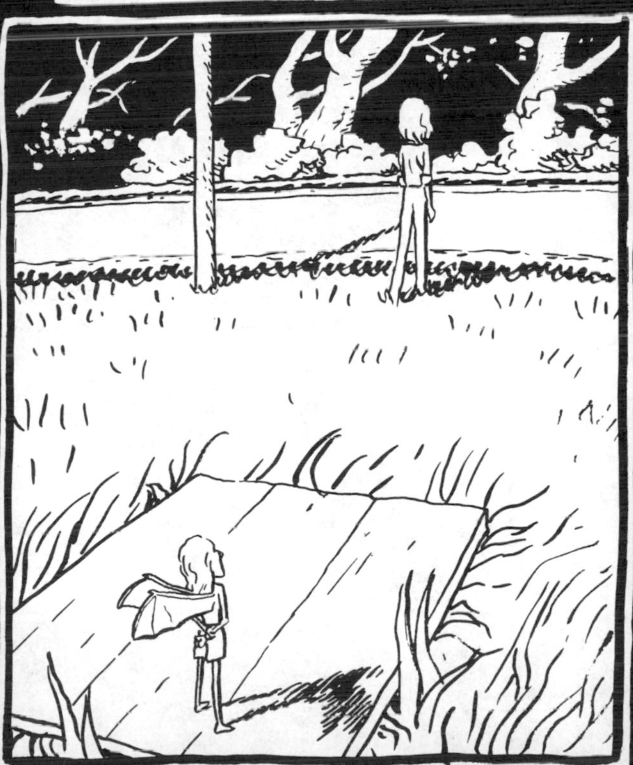

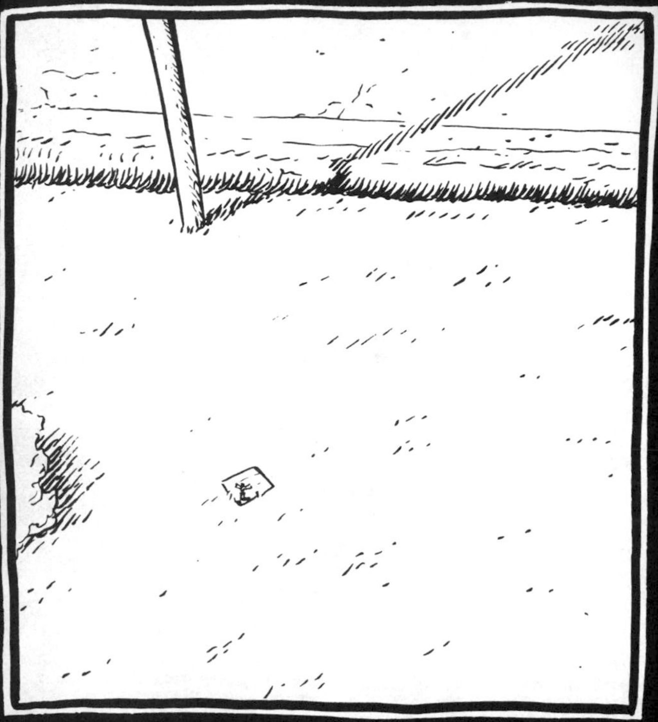

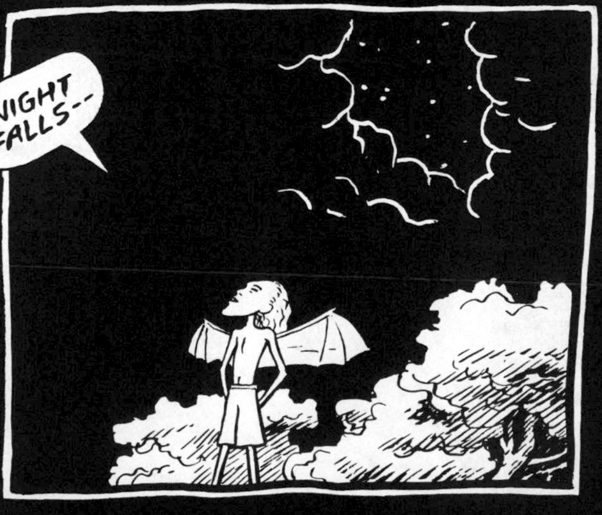
NIGHT FALLS--

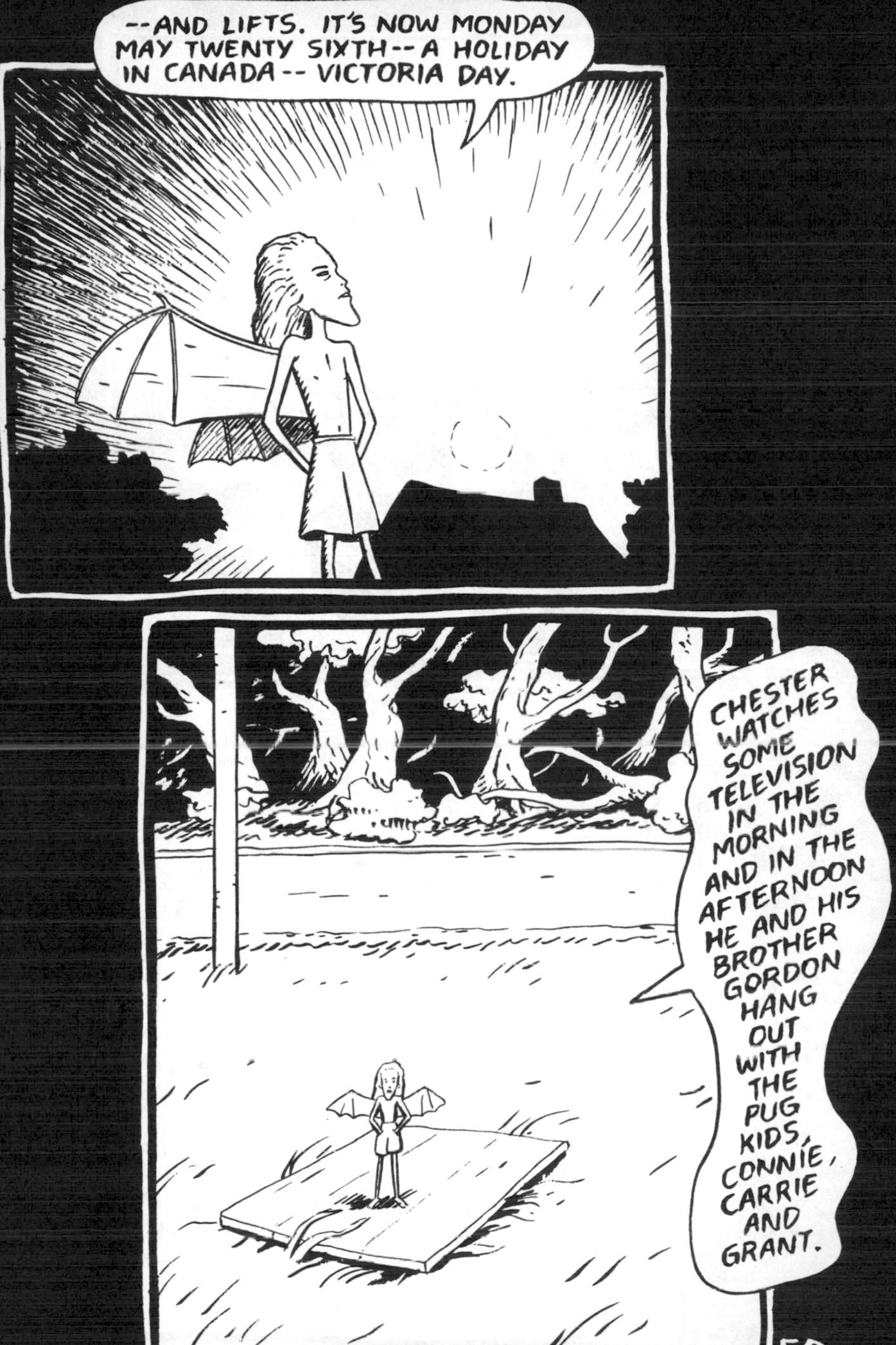
--AND LIFTS. IT'S NOW MONDAY MAY TWENTY SIXTH--A HOLIDAY IN CANADA--VICTORIA DAY.
CHESTER WATCHES SOME TELEVISION IN THE MORNING AND IN THE AFTERNOON HE AND HIS BROTHER GORDON HANG OUT WITH THE PUG KIDS, CONNIE, CARRIE AND GRANT.

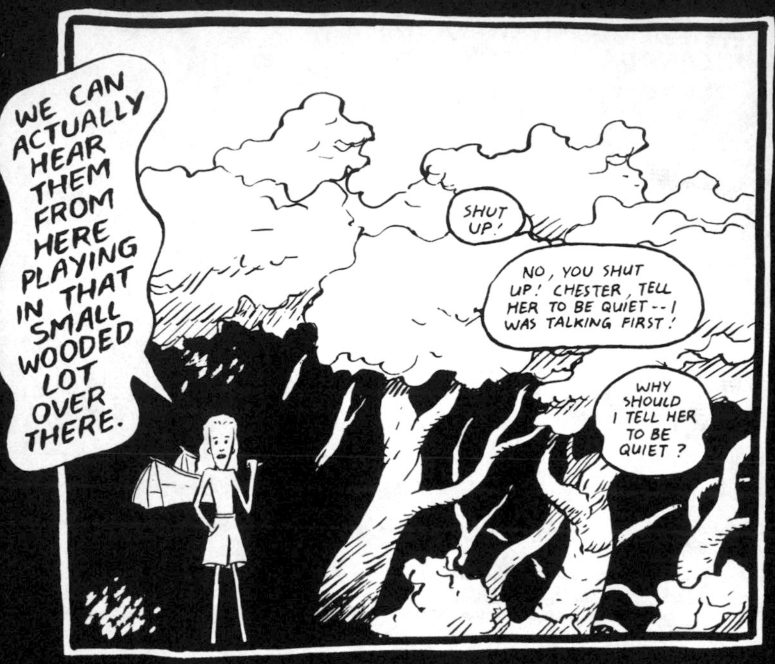
WE CAN ACTUALLY HEAR THEM FROM HERE PLAYING IN THAT SMALL WOODED LOT OVER THERE.
SHUT UP!
NO, YOU SHUT UP! CHESTER, TELL HER TO BE QUIET -- I WAS TALKING FIRST!
WHY SHOULD I TELL HER TO BE QUIET?

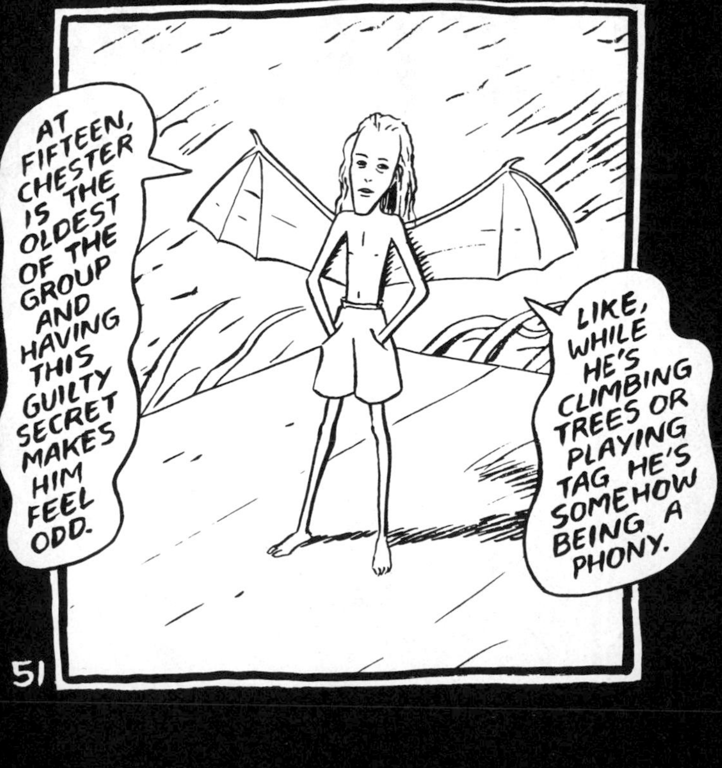
AT FIFTEEN, CHESTER IS THE OLDEST OF THE GROUP AND HAVING THIS GUILTY SECRET MAKES HIM FEEL ODD.
LIKE, WHILE HE'S CLIMBING TREES OR PLAYING TAG HE'S SOMEHOW BEING A PHONY.

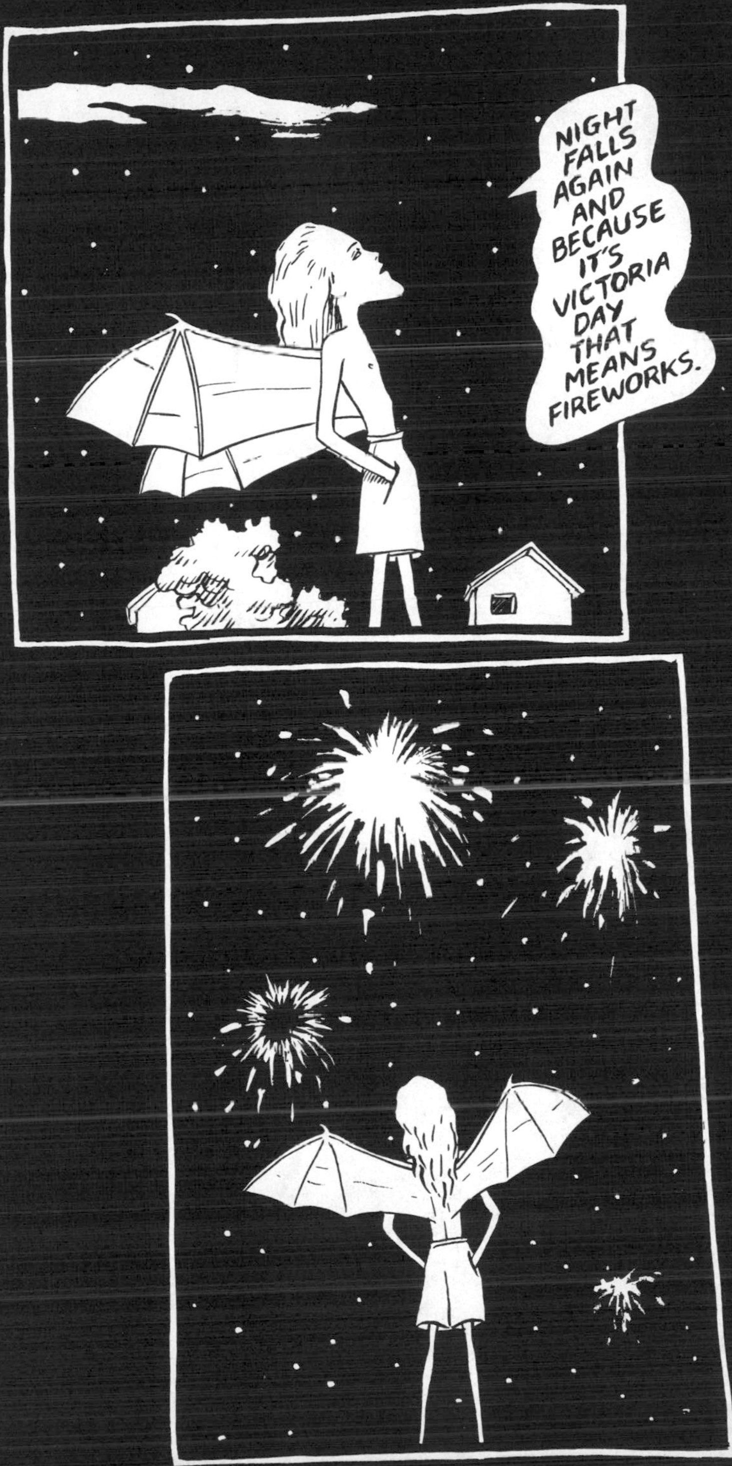
NIGHT FALLS AGAIN AND BECAUSE IT'S VICTORIA DAY THAT MEANS FIREWORKS.

THE NEXT DAY IS TUESDAY, MAY TWENTY SEVENTH AND IT'S BACK TO SCHOOL. THE DREARY DULL DAY GIVES CHESTER PLENTY OF TIME TO THINK ABOUT WHAT'S UNDER THIS BOARD. WHEN SCHOOL LETS OUT AT THREE O'CLOCK HE DOESN'T HEAD STRAIGHT HOME.

53

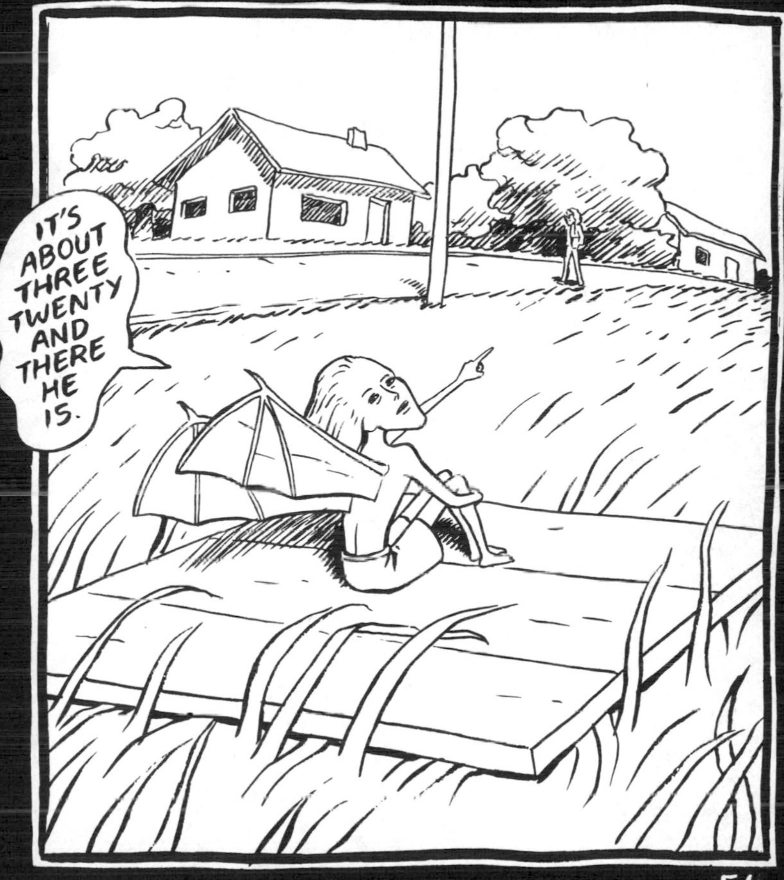
IT'S ABOUT THREE TWENTY AND THERE HE IS.

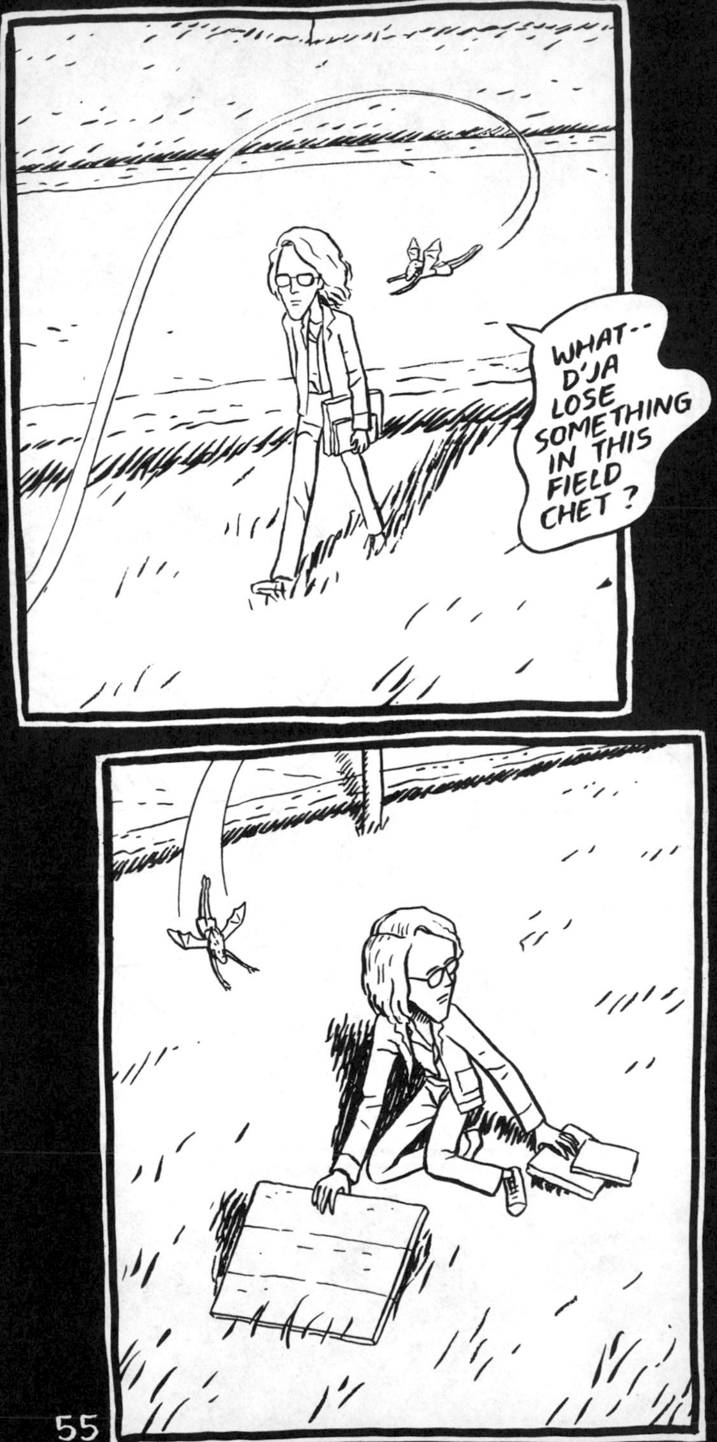
WHAT-- D'JA LOSE SOMETHING IN THIS FIELD CHET?

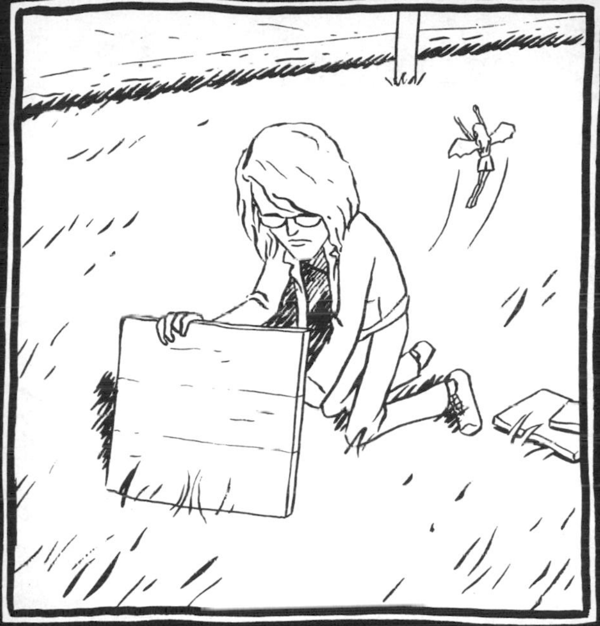

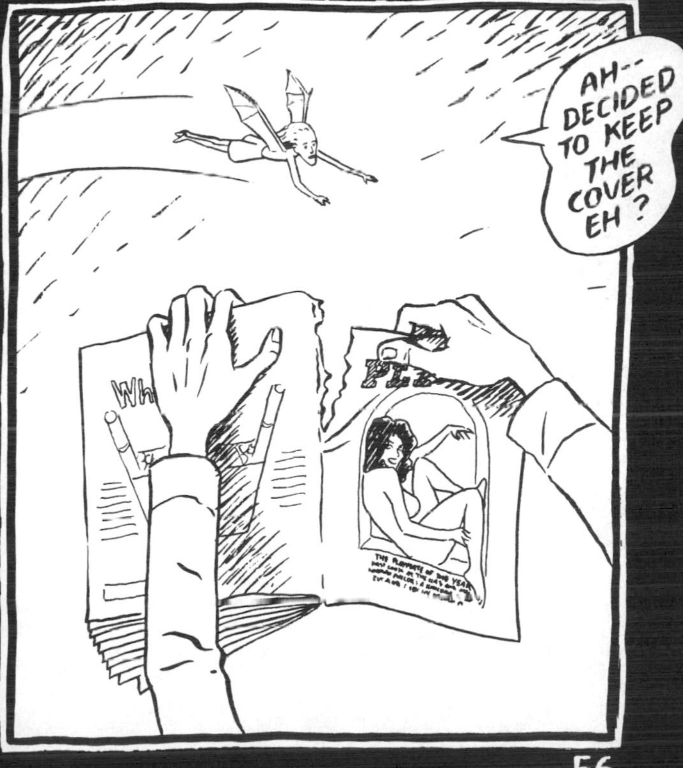
AH-- DECIDED TO KEEP THE COVER EH ?

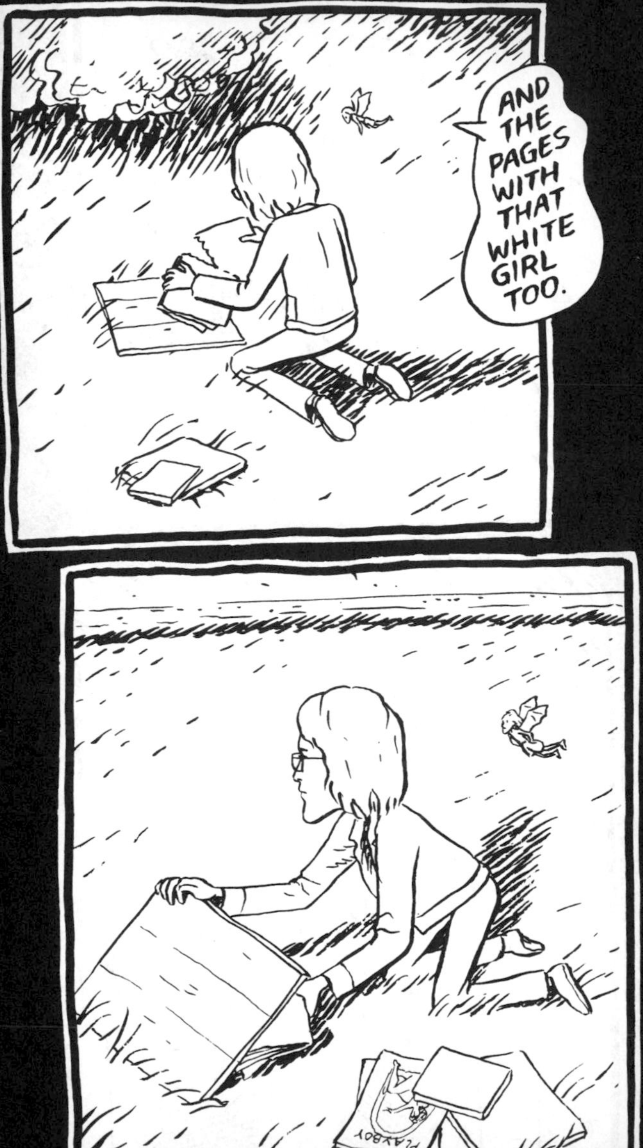
AND THE PAGES WITH THAT WHITE GIRL TOO.
PLAYBOY

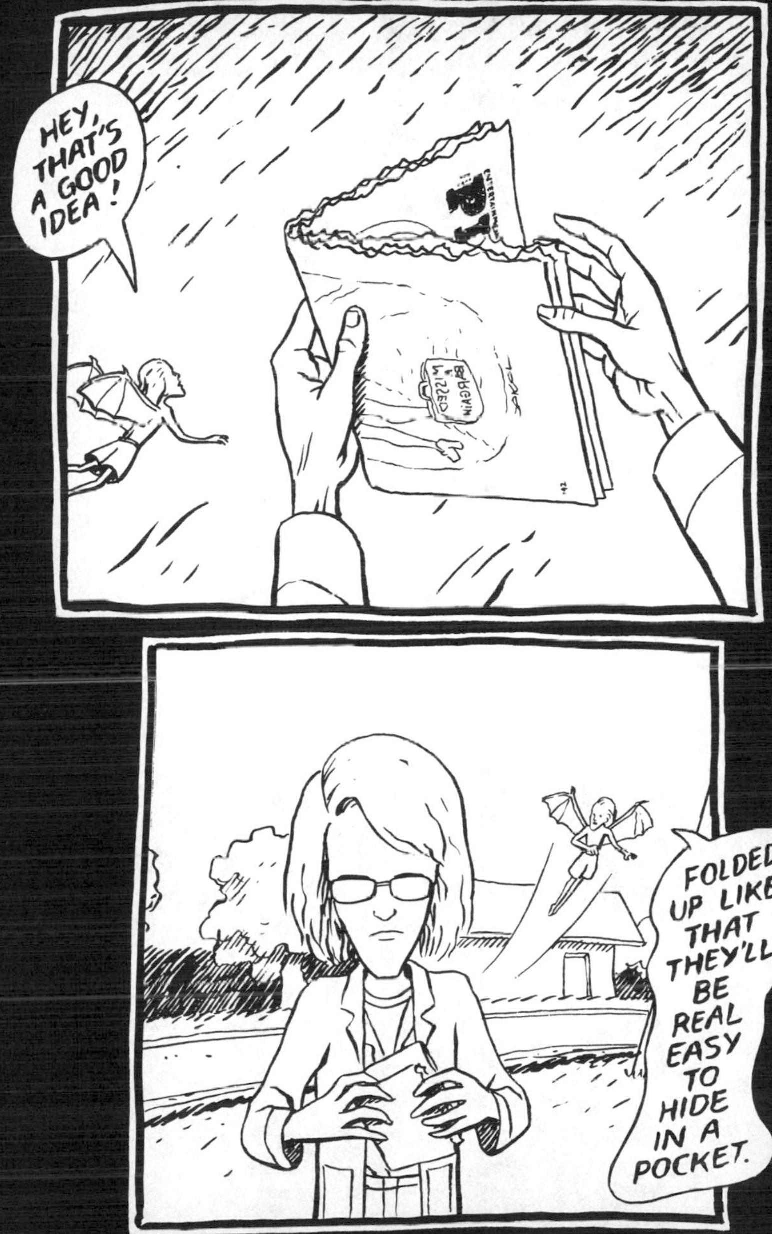
HEY, THAT'S A GOOD IDEA!
FOLDED UP LIKE THAT THEY'LL BE REAL EASY TO HIDE IN A POCKET.

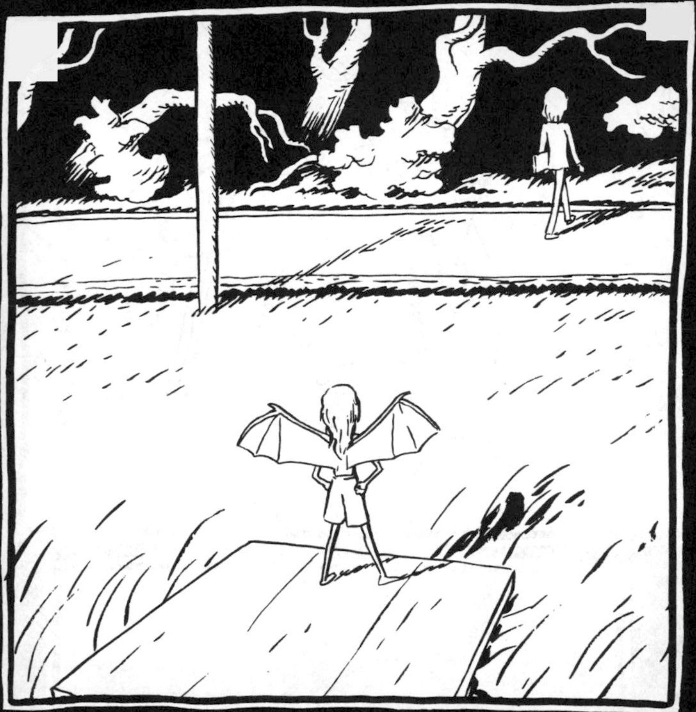

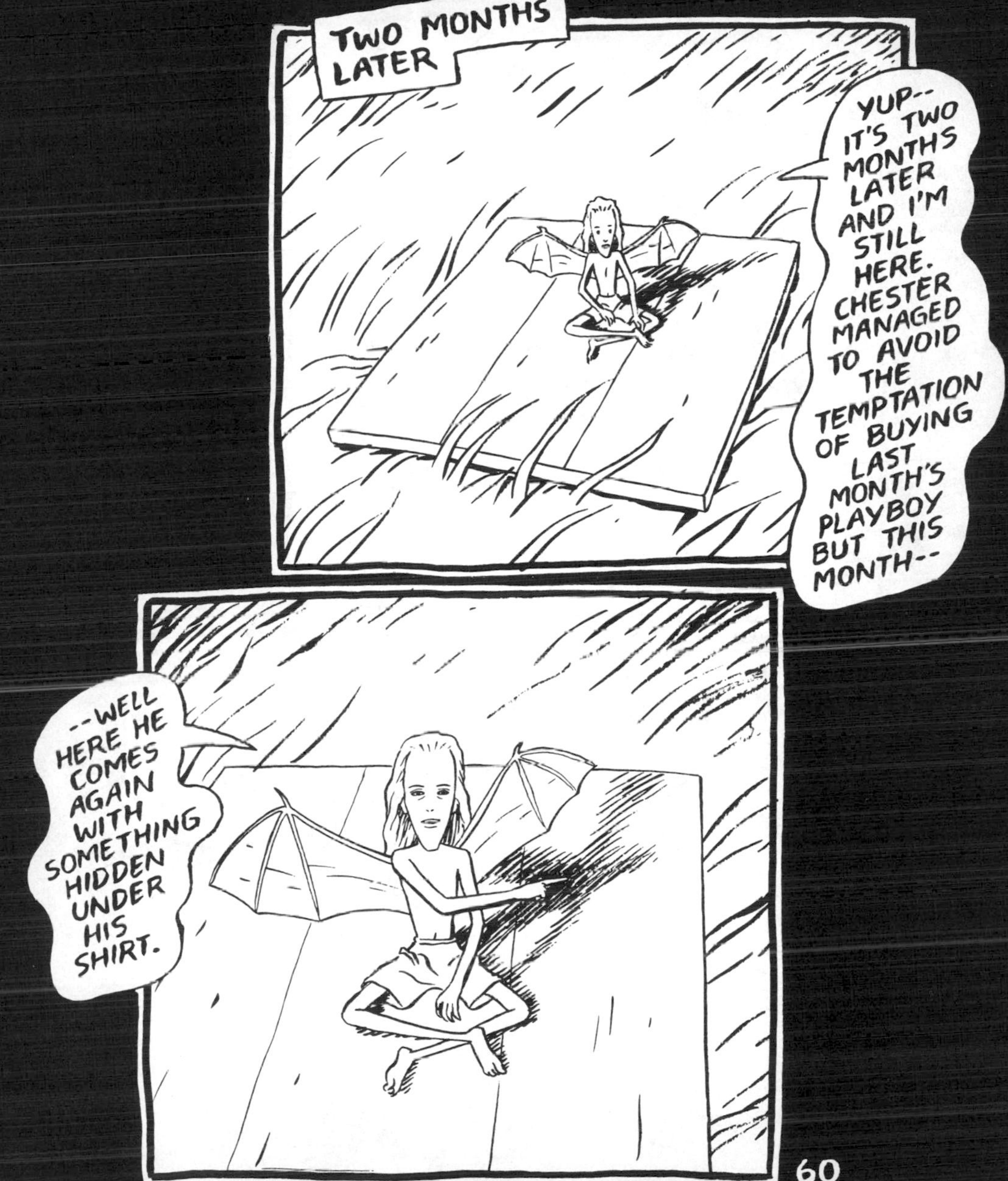
TWO MONTHS LATER
YUP-- IT'S TWO MONTHS LATER AND I'M STILL HERE. CHESTER MANAGED TO AVOID THE TEMPTATION OF BUYING LAST MONTH'S PLAYBOY BUT THIS MONTH--
--WELL HERE HE COMES AGAIN WITH SOMETHING HIDDEN UNDER HIS SHIRT.

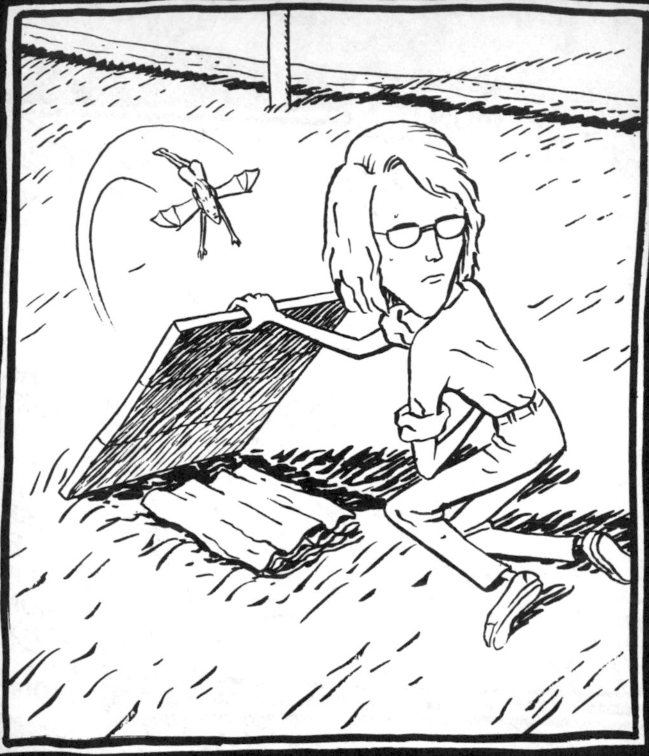

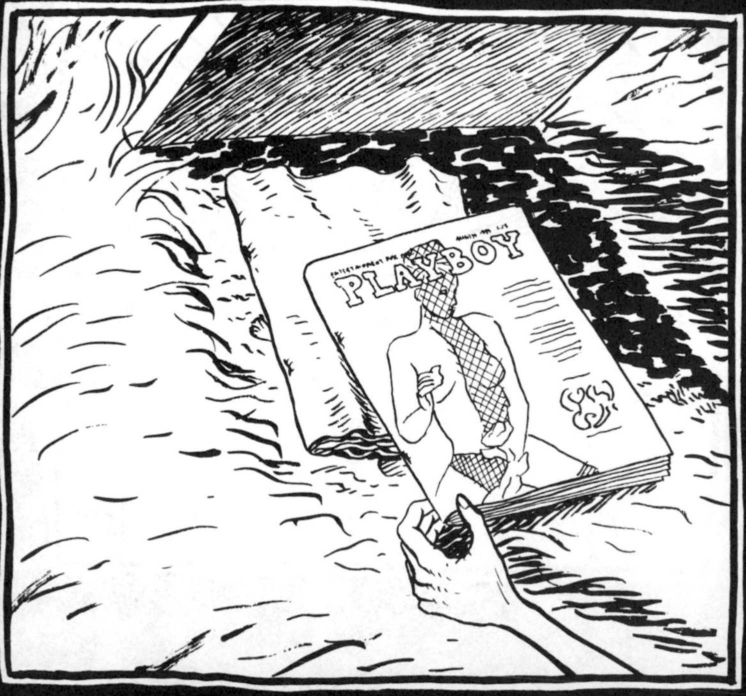
PLAYBOY

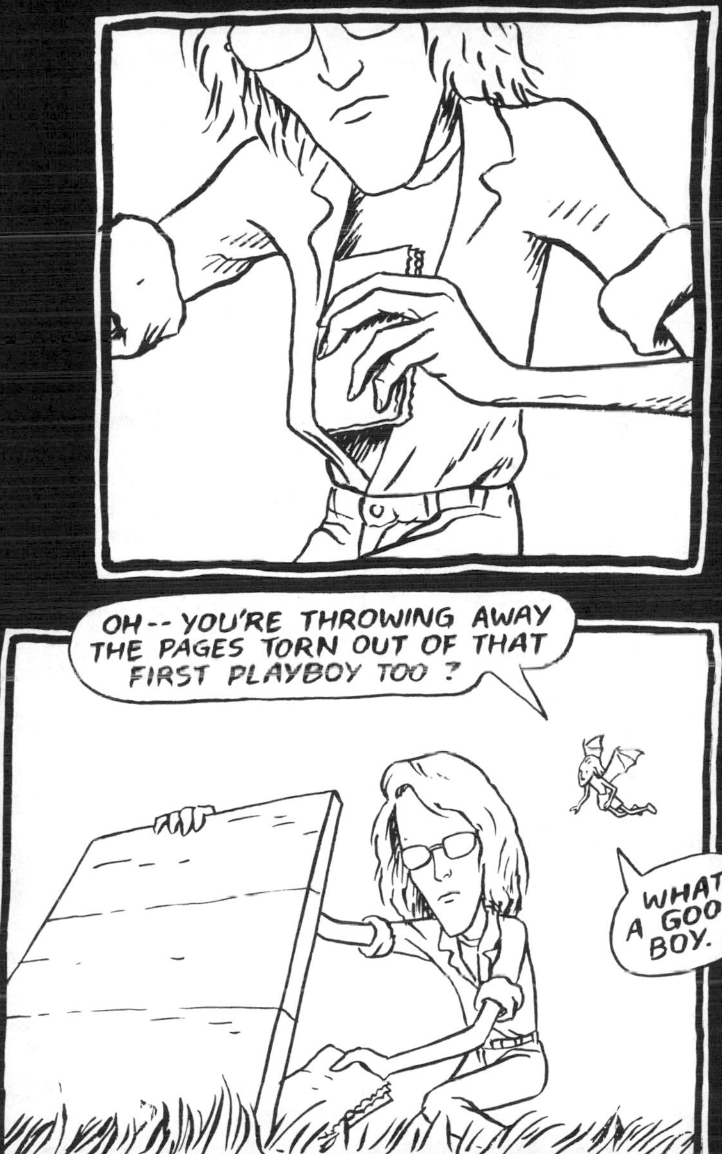
OH -- YOU'RE THROWING AWAY THE PAGES TORN OUT OF THAT FIRST PLAYBOY TOO ?
WHAT A GOOD BOY.

THAT NIGHT

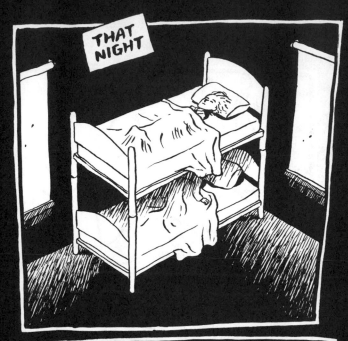

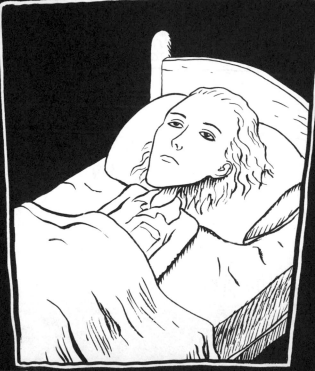

ON SECOND THOUGHT MAYBE IT WASN'T SUCH A GOOD IDEA THROWING ALL THAT PLAYBOY STUFF OUT.
REMEMBER ?
PLAYBOY
THE PLAYMATE OF THE YEAR

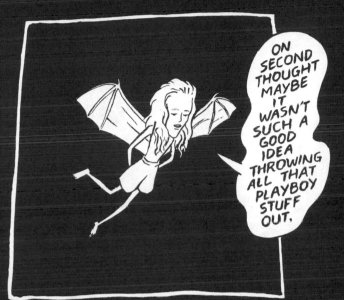

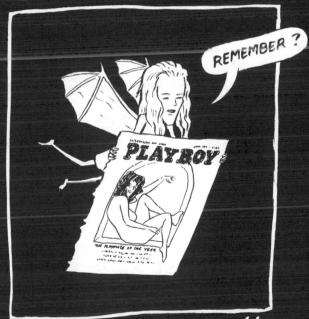

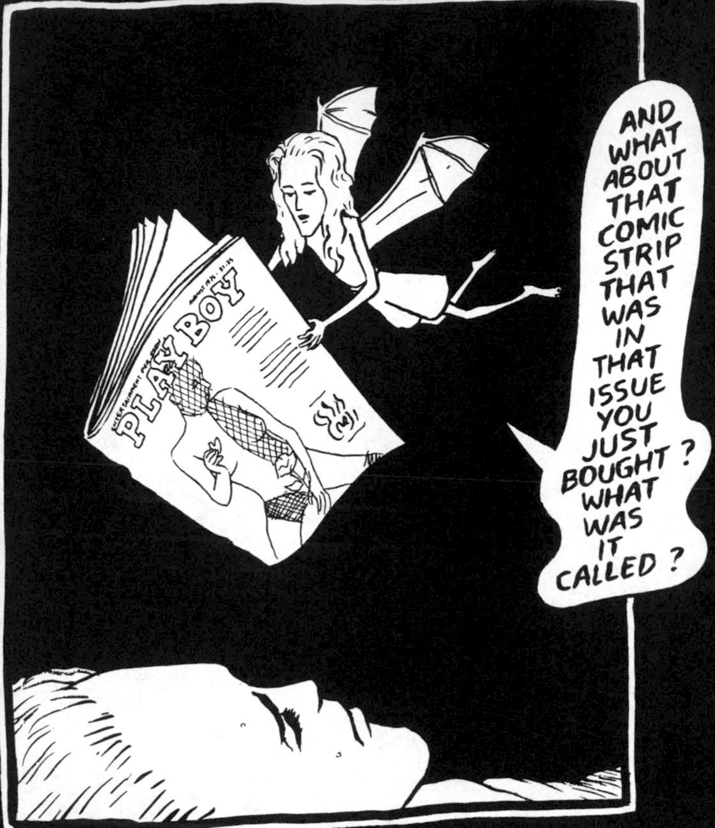
AND WHAT ABOUT THAT COMIC STRIP THAT WAS IN THAT ISSUE YOU JUST BOUGHT? WHAT WAS IT CALLED?
PLAYBOY

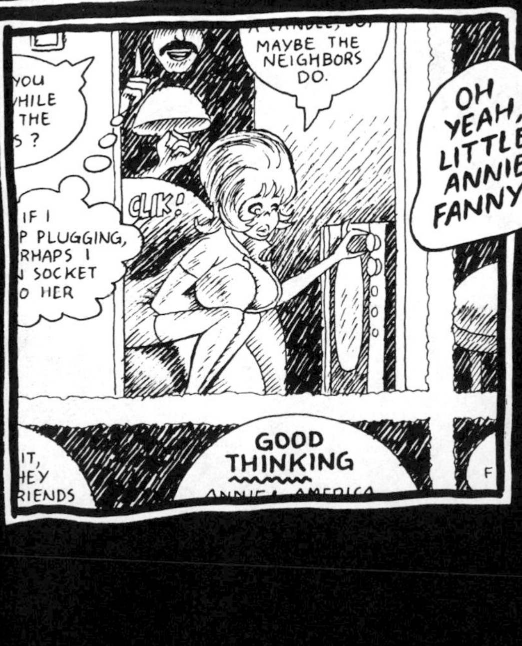
MAYBE THE NEIGHBORS DO.
CLIK!
GOOD THINKING
OH YEAH, LITTLE ANNIE FANNY.

THE
NEXT
DAY

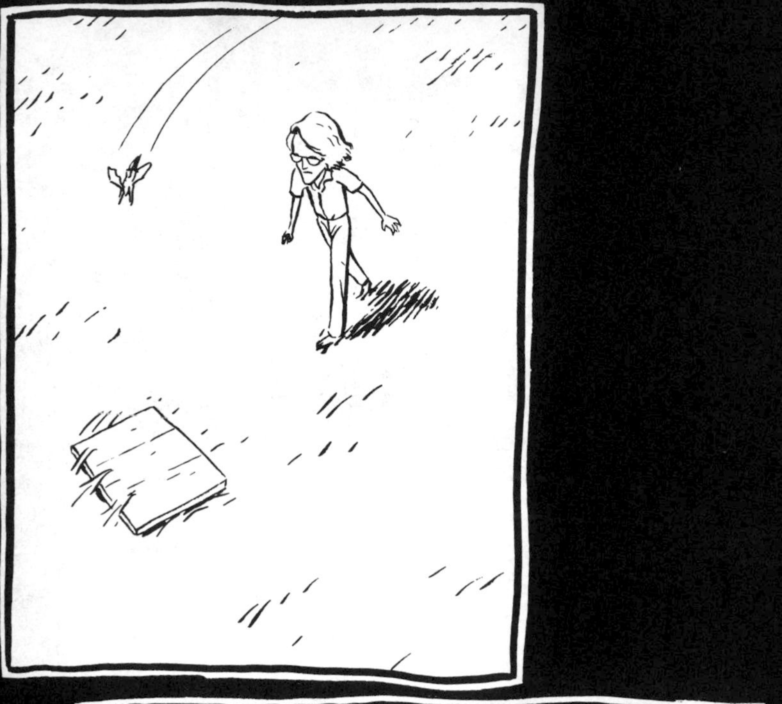

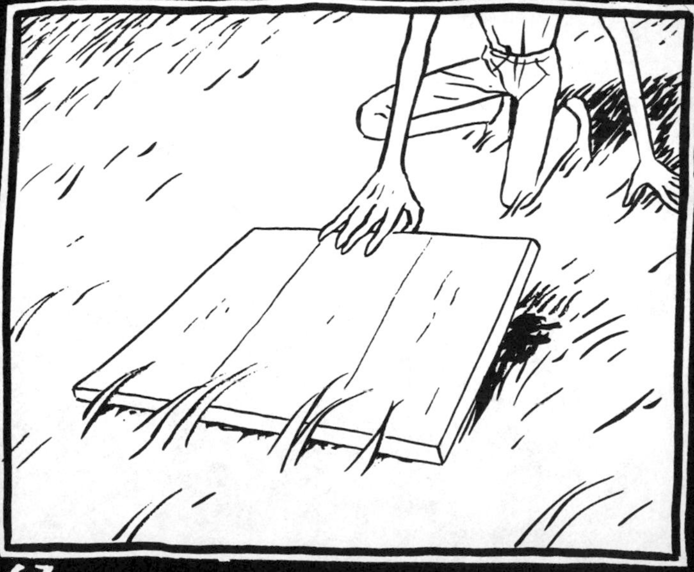

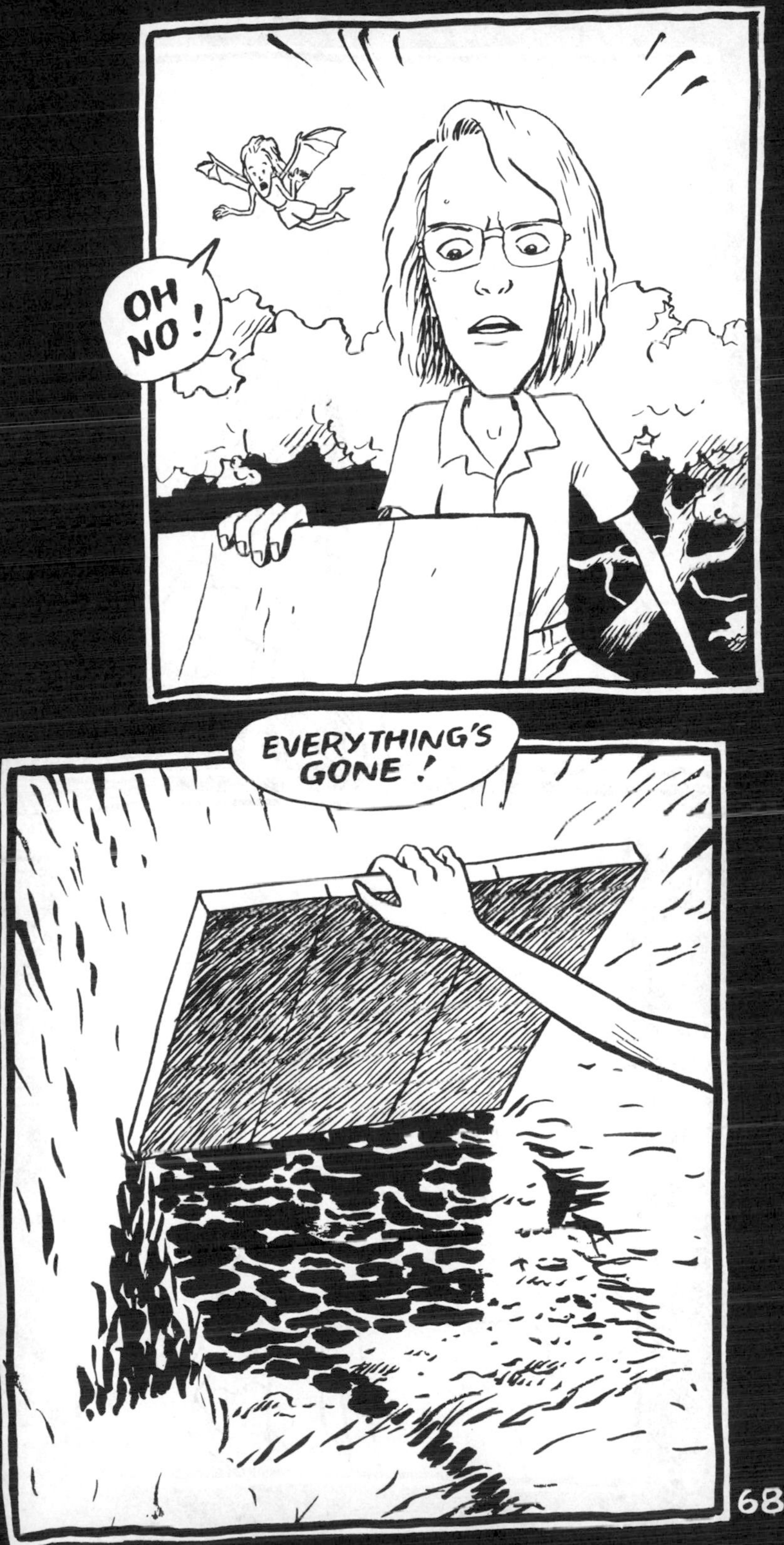
OH NO!
EVERYTHING'S GONE!

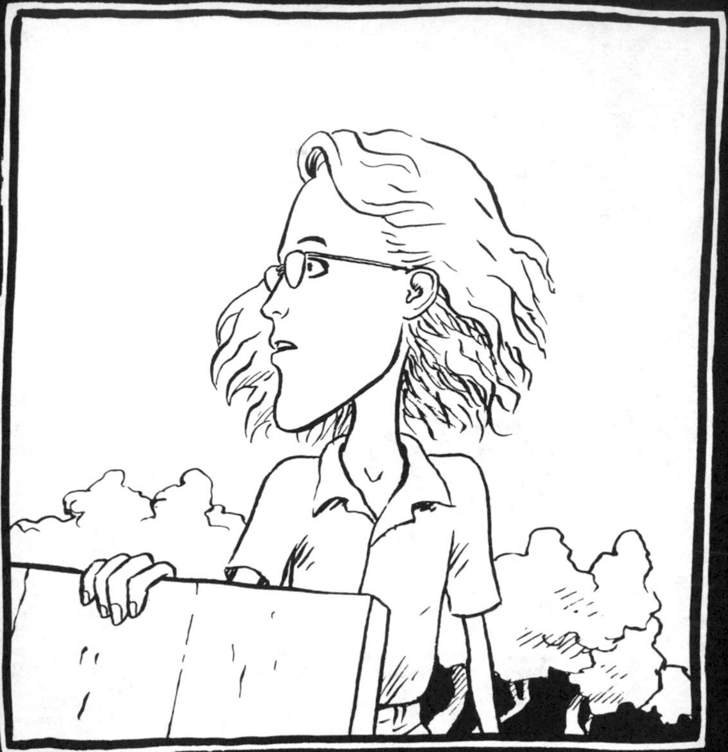

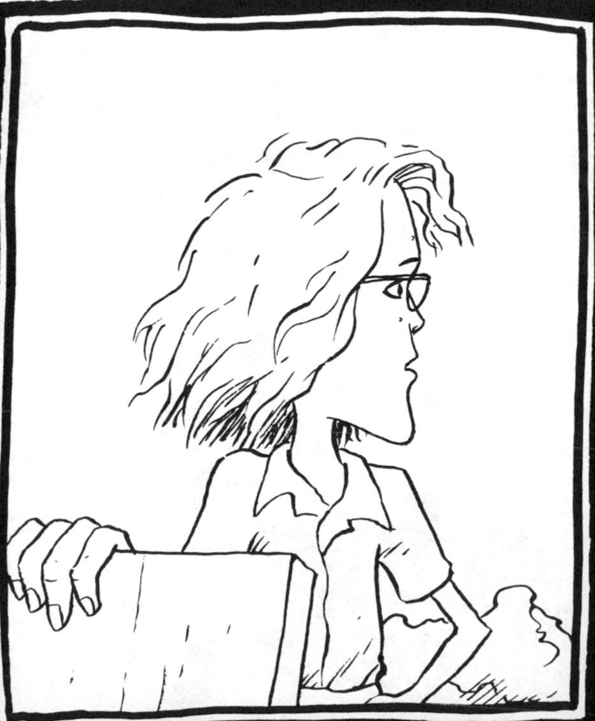

70

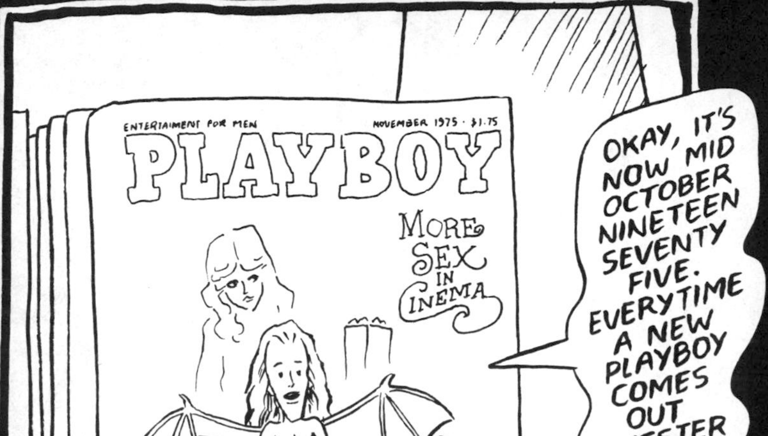
ENTERTAINMENT FOR MEN
NOVEMBER 1975 · $1.75
PLAYBOY
MORE SEX IN CINEMA
OKAY, IT'S NOW MID OCTOBER NINETEEN SEVENTY FIVE. EVERYTIME A NEW PLAYBOY COMES OUT CHESTER HAS TO CHECK OUT THE GIRLS IN IT BUT HE HASN'T PICKED UP THE LAST TWO ISSUES.

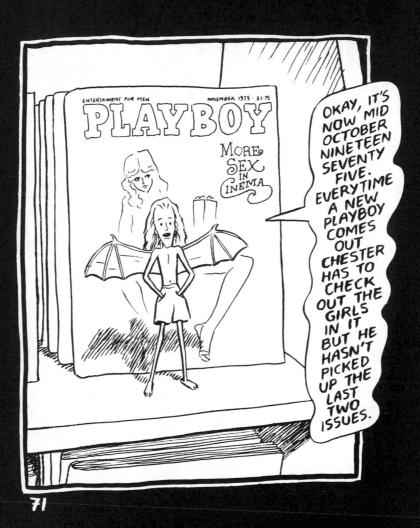

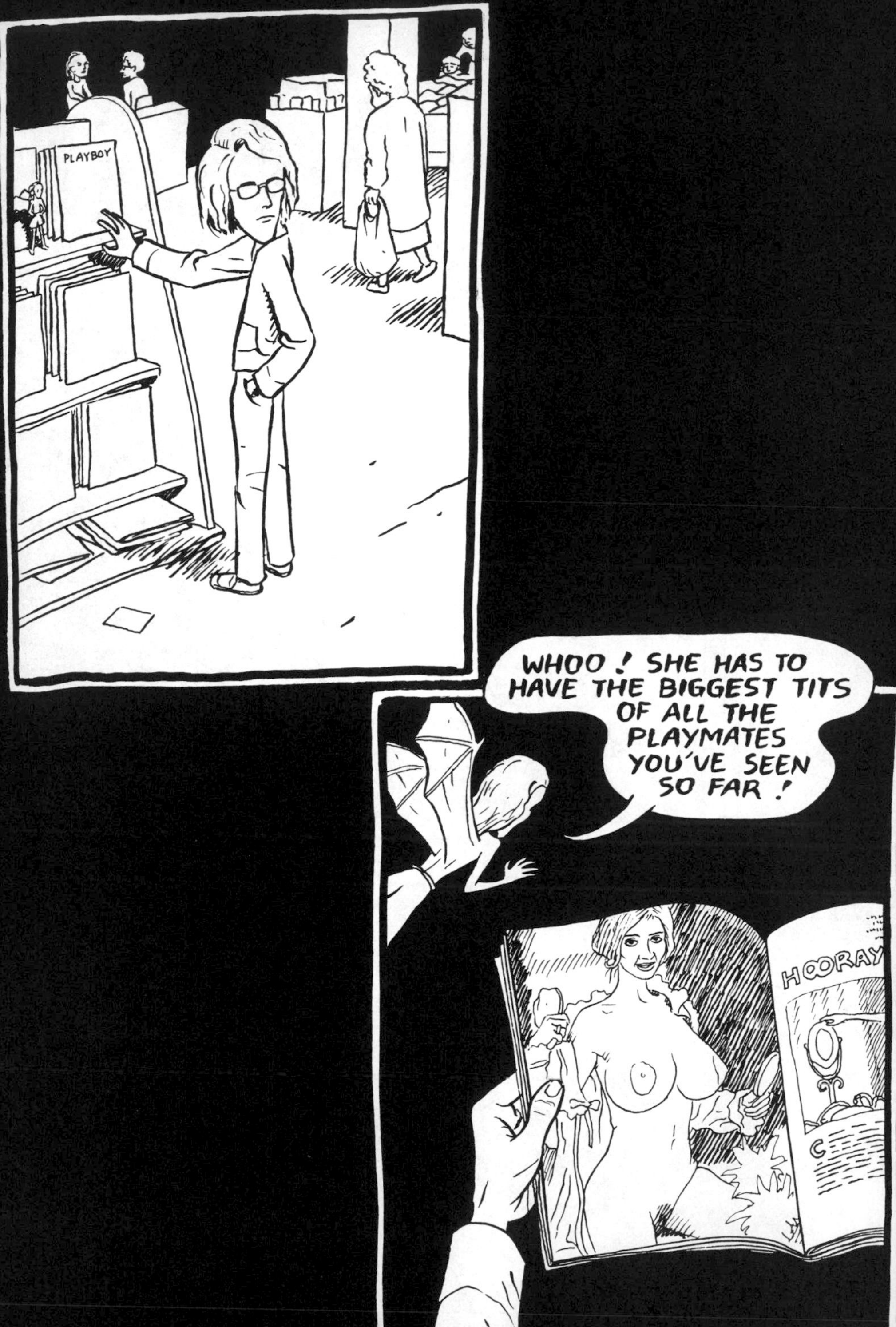
PLAYBOY
WHOO! SHE HAS TO HAVE THE BIGGEST TITS OF ALL THE PLAYMATES YOU'VE SEEN SO FAR!
HOORAY

"Why Viceroy? Because I'd never smoke a boring cigarette".
PLAYBOY
MORE SEX IN CINEMA
YOU HAVE TO BUY THIS ISSUE!
PLAYBOY
MORE SEX IN CINEMA

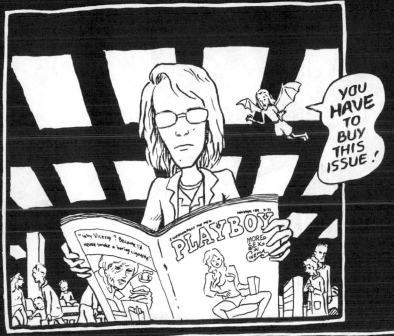

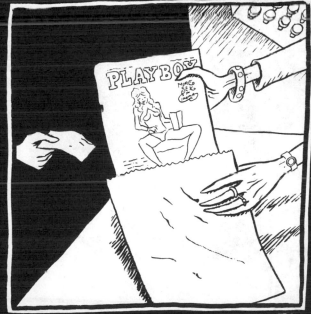

CHNG

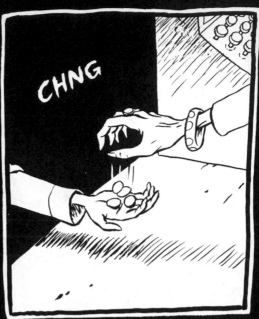

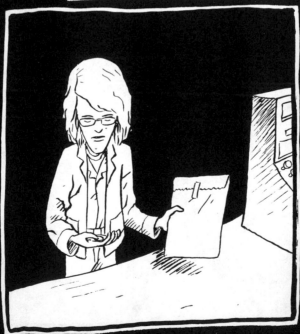

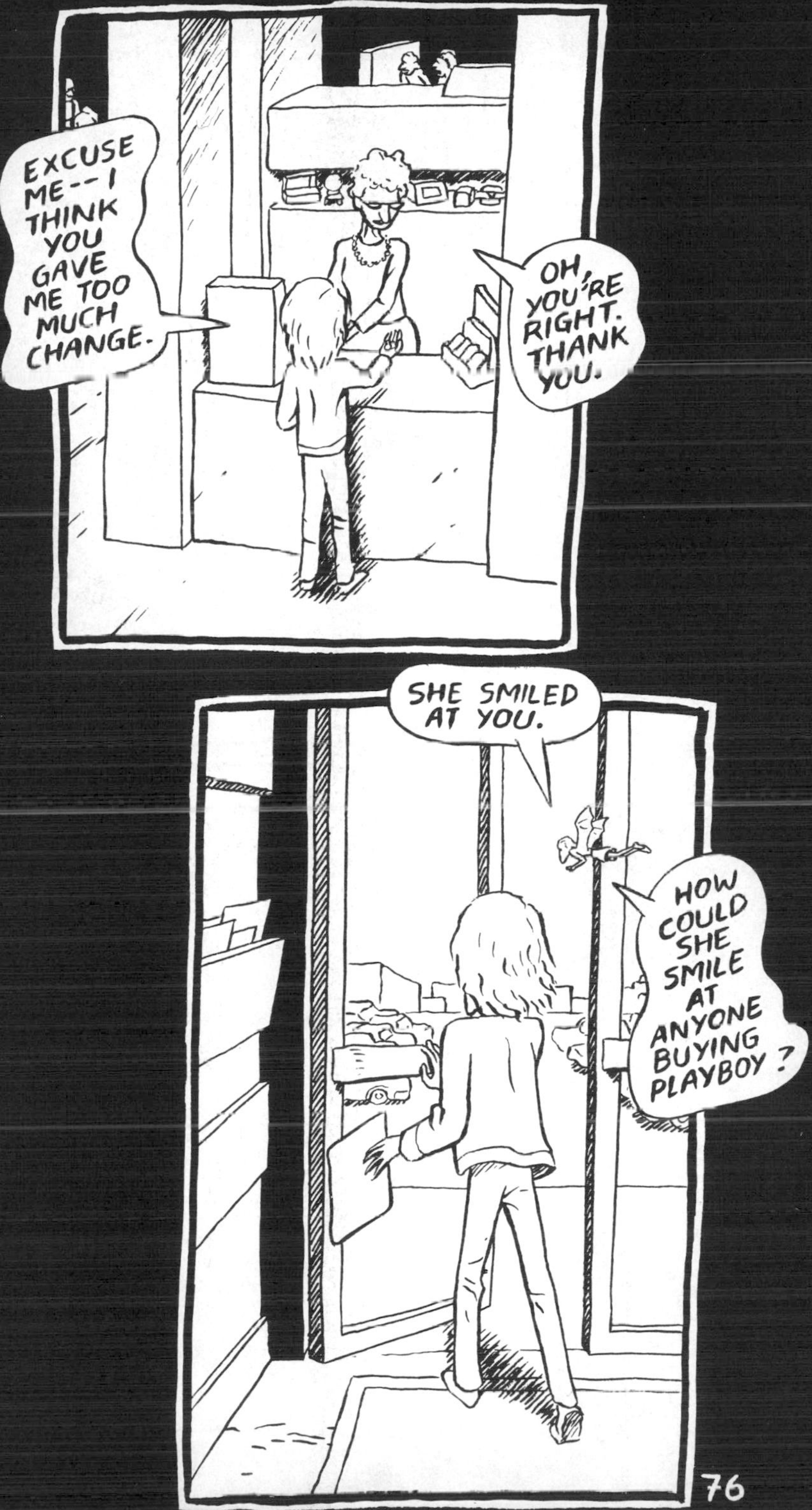
EXCUSE ME--I THINK YOU GAVE ME TOO MUCH CHANGE.
OH, YOU'RE RIGHT. THANK YOU.
SHE SMILED AT YOU.
HOW COULD SHE SMILE AT ANYONE BUYING PLAYBOY?

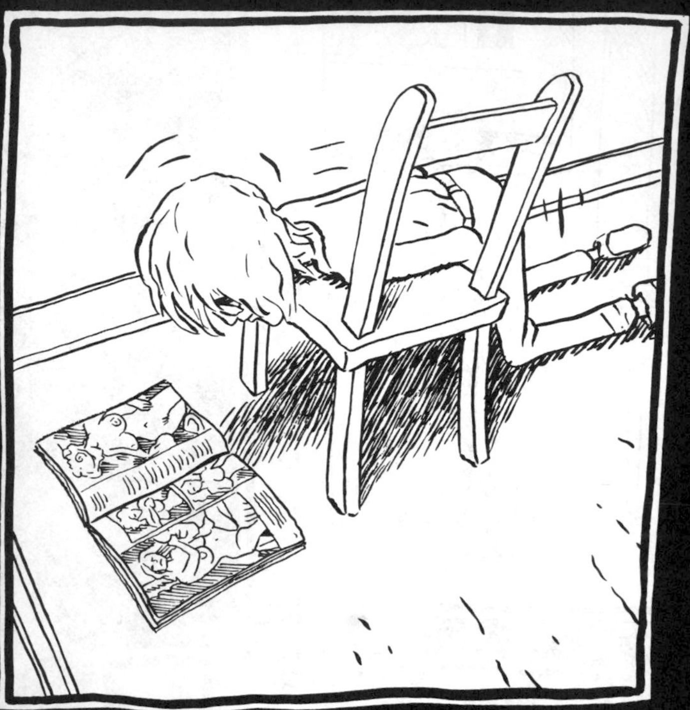

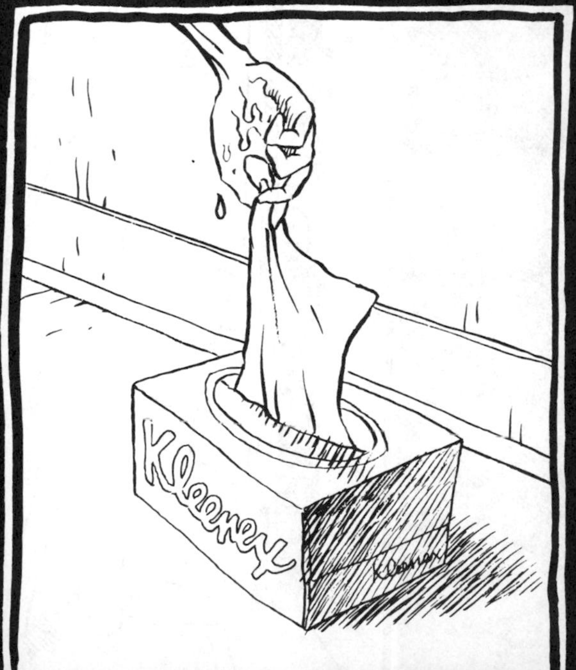
Kleenex

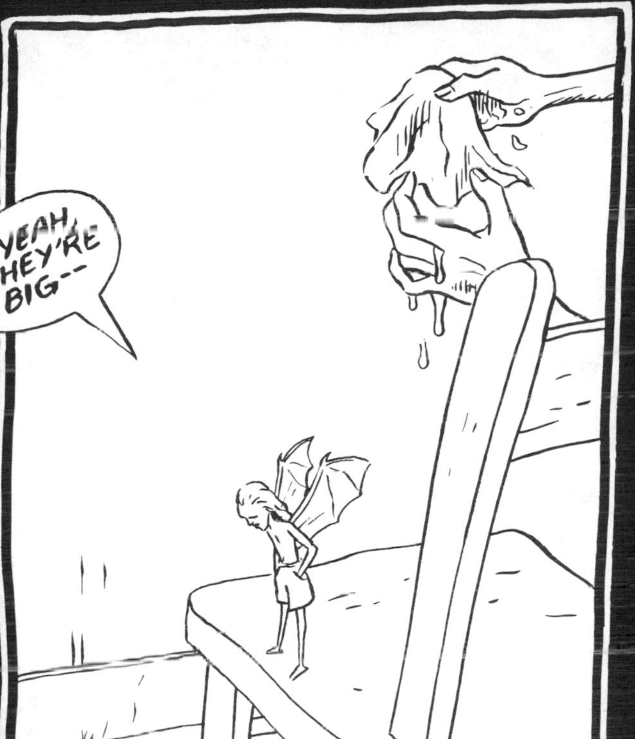
YEAH, THEY'RE BIG--

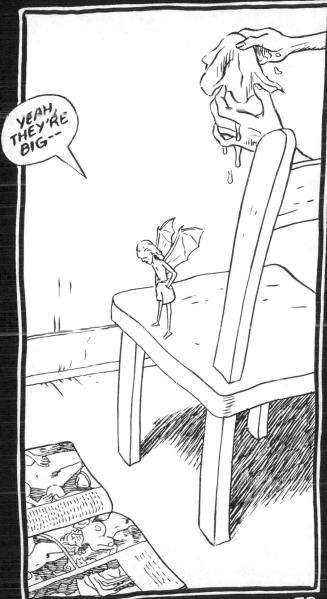

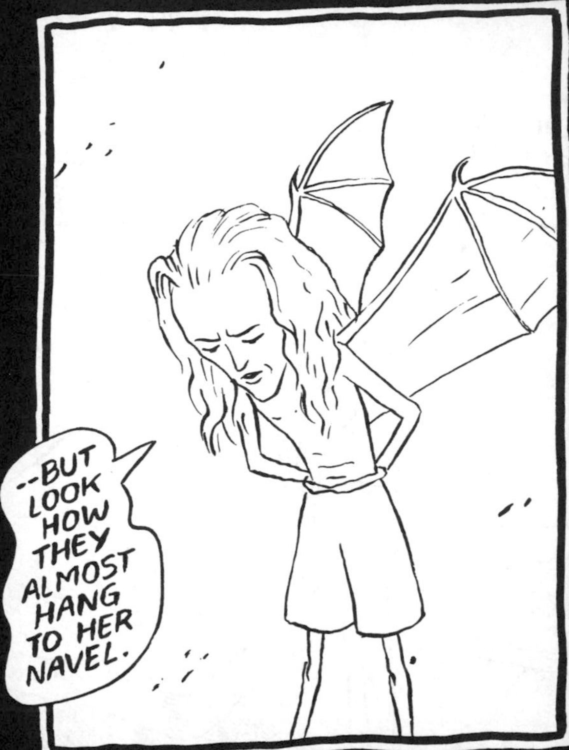
--BUT LOOK HOW THEY ALMOST HANG TO HER NAVEL.

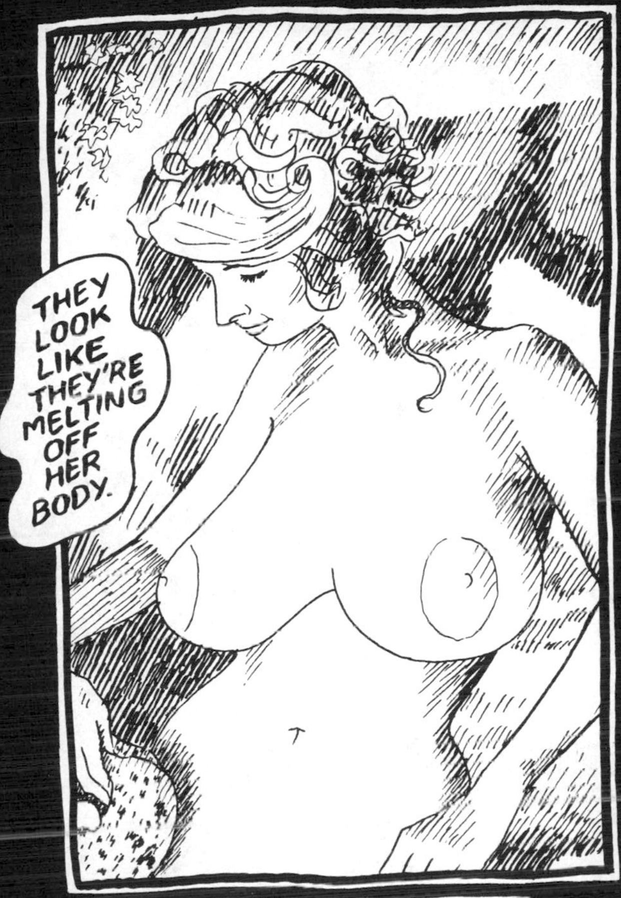
THEY LOOK LIKE THEY'RE MELTING OFF HER BODY.

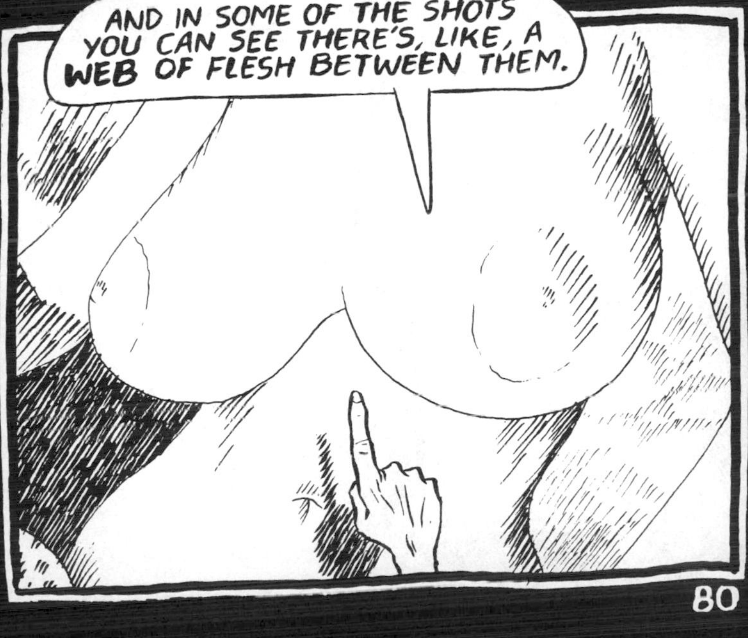
AND IN SOME OF THE SHOTS YOU CAN SEE THERE'S, LIKE, A WEB OF FLESH BETWEEN THEM.

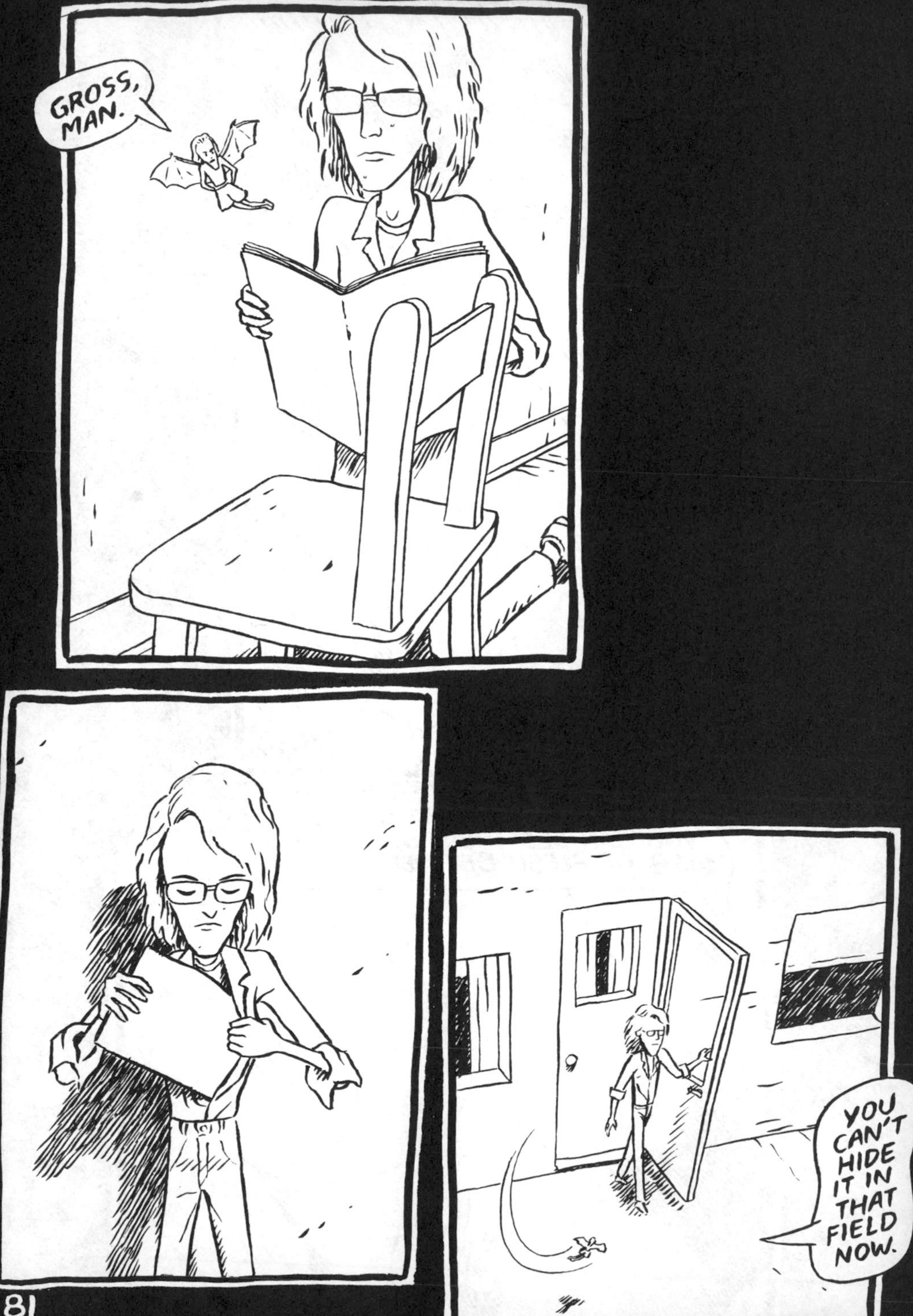
GROSS, MAN.
YOU CAN'T HIDE IT IN THAT FIELD NOW.

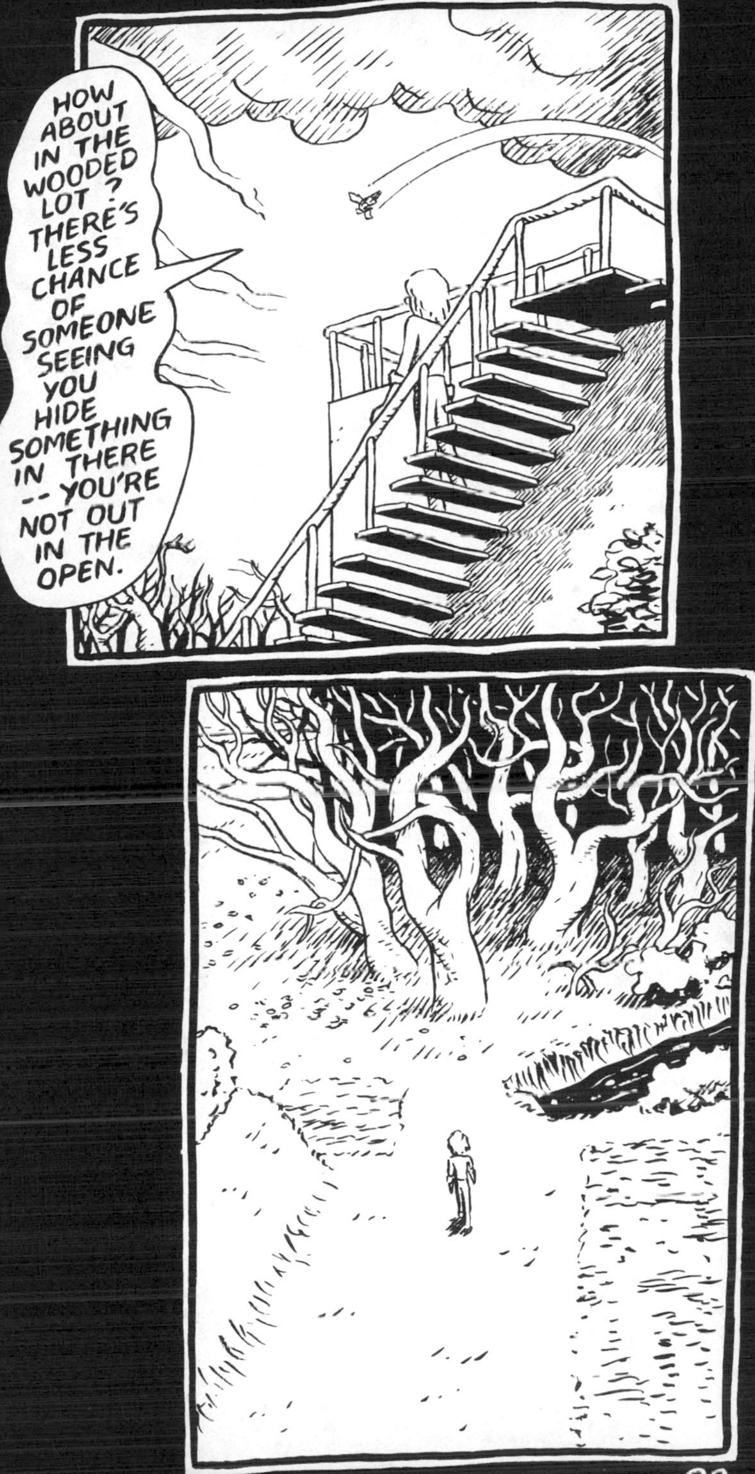
HOW ABOUT IN THE WOODED LOT ? THERE'S LESS CHANCE OF SOMEONE SEEING YOU HIDE SOMETHING IN THERE -- YOU'RE NOT OUT IN THE OPEN.

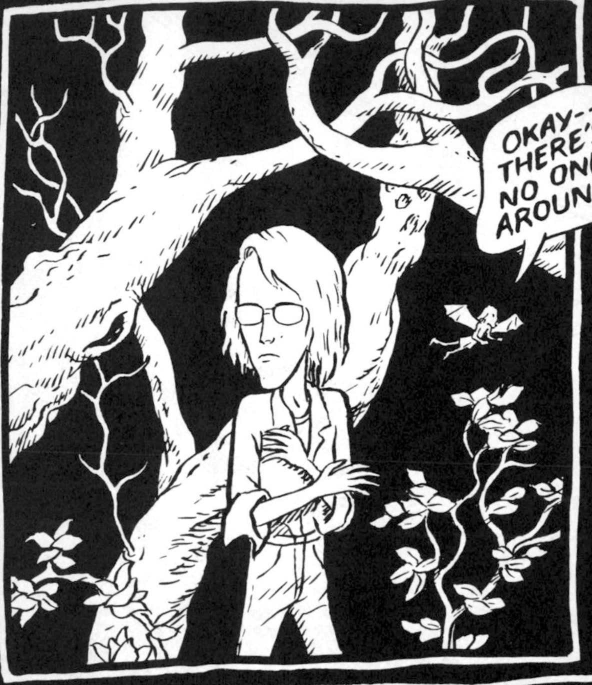
OKAY-- THERE'S NO ONE AROUND.

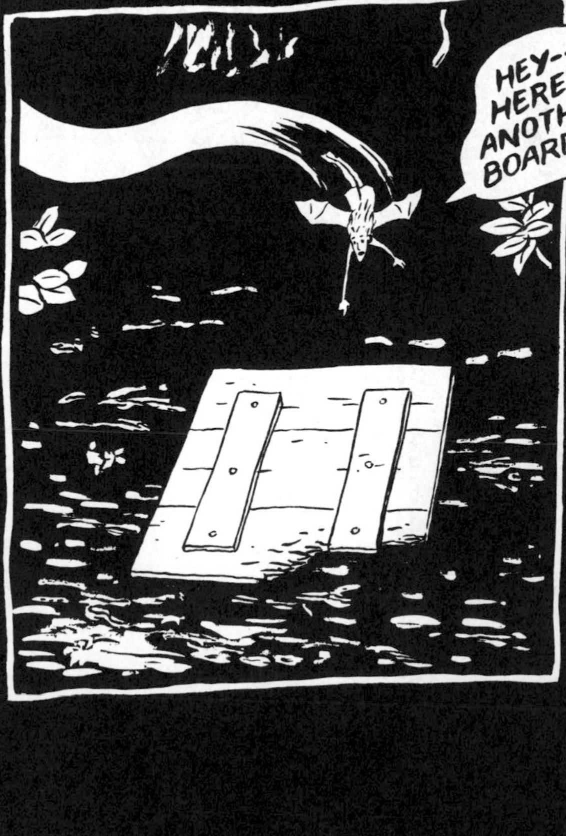
HEY-- HERE'S ANOTHER BOARD!

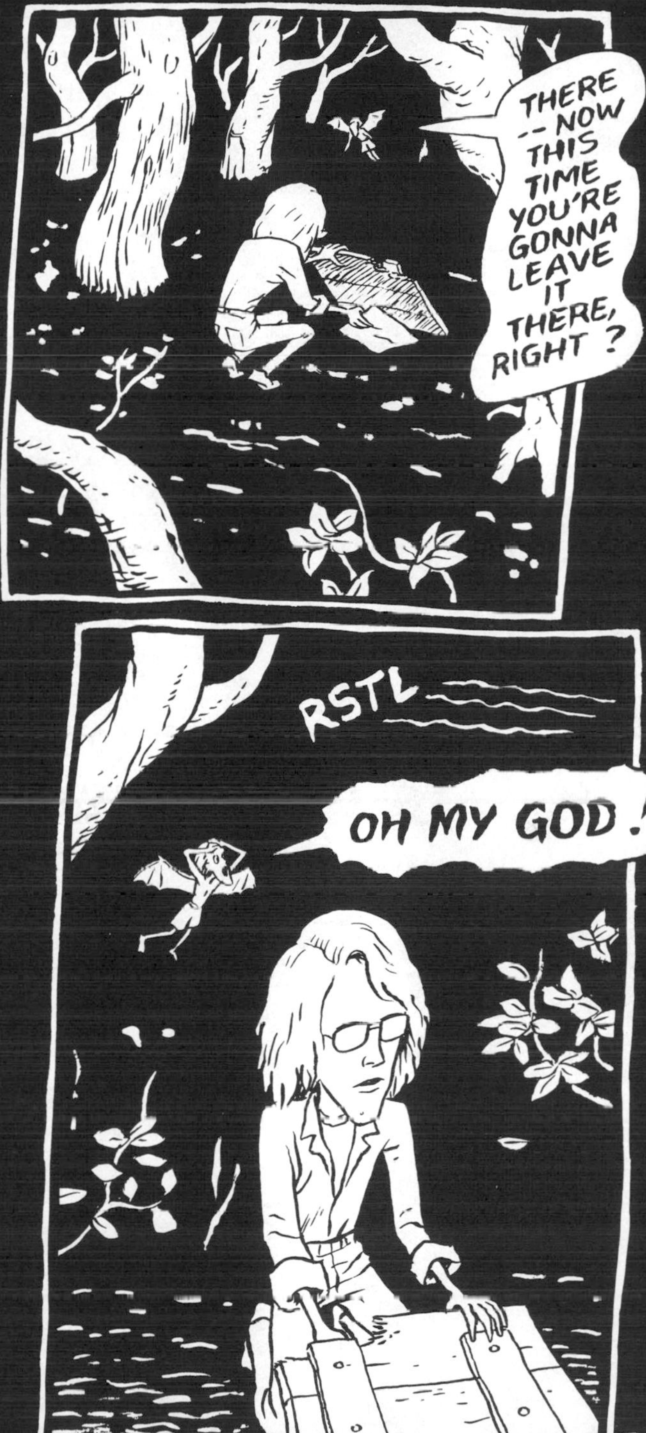
THERE -- NOW THIS TIME YOU'RE GONNA LEAVE IT THERE, RIGHT ?
RSTL
OH MY GOD !

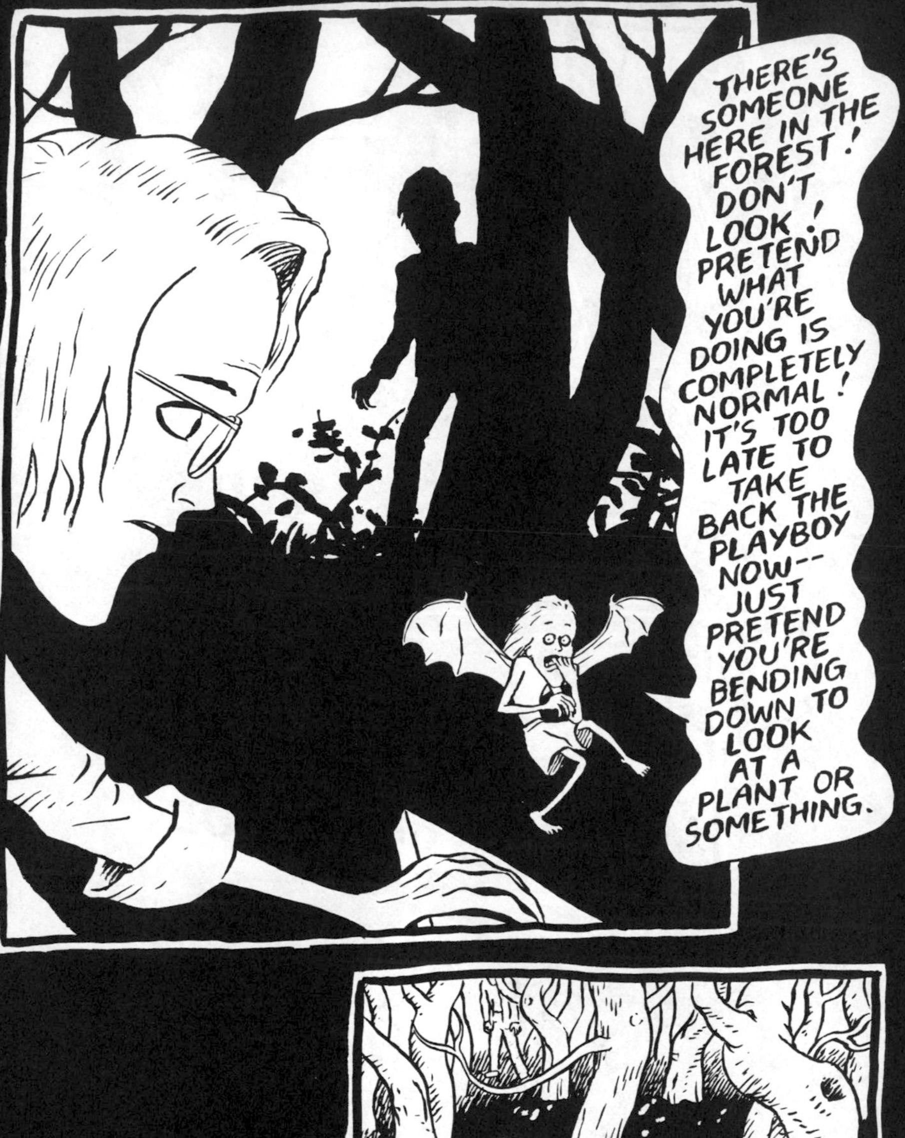
THERE'S SOMEONE HERE IN THE FOREST! DON'T LOOK, PRETEND WHAT YOU'RE DOING IS COMPLETELY NORMAL! IT'S TOO LATE TO TAKE BACK THE PLAYBOY NOW-- JUST PRETEND YOU'RE BENDING DOWN TO LOOK AT A PLANT OR SOMETHING.

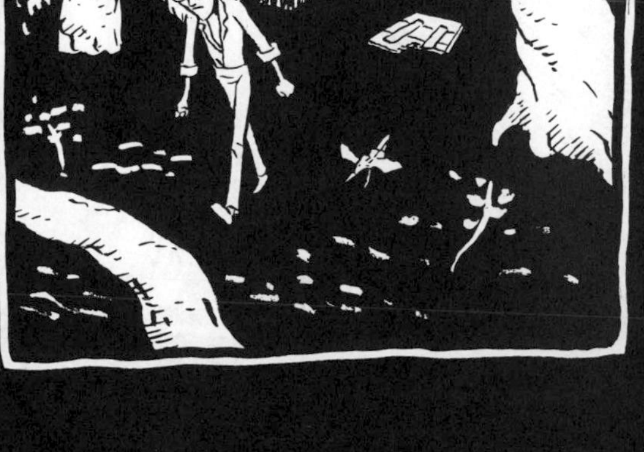

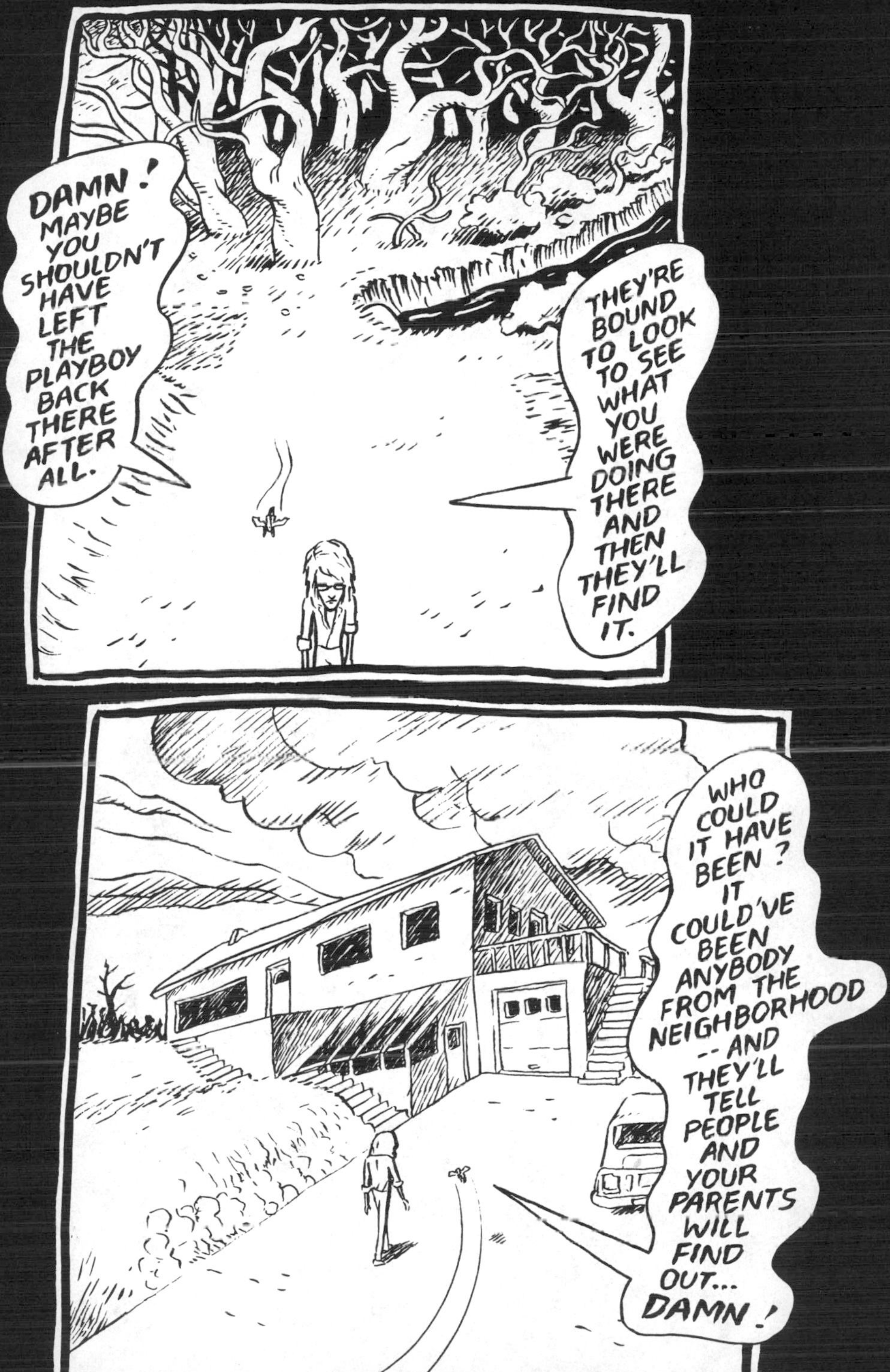
DAMN! MAYBE YOU SHOULDN'T HAVE LEFT THE PLAYBOY BACK THERE AFTER ALL.
THEY'RE BOUND TO LOOK TO SEE WHAT YOU WERE DOING THERE AND THEN THEY'LL FIND IT.
WHO COULD IT HAVE BEEN? IT COULD'VE BEEN ANYBODY FROM THE NEIGHBORHOOD -- AND THEY'LL TELL PEOPLE AND YOUR PARENTS WILL FIND OUT... DAMN!

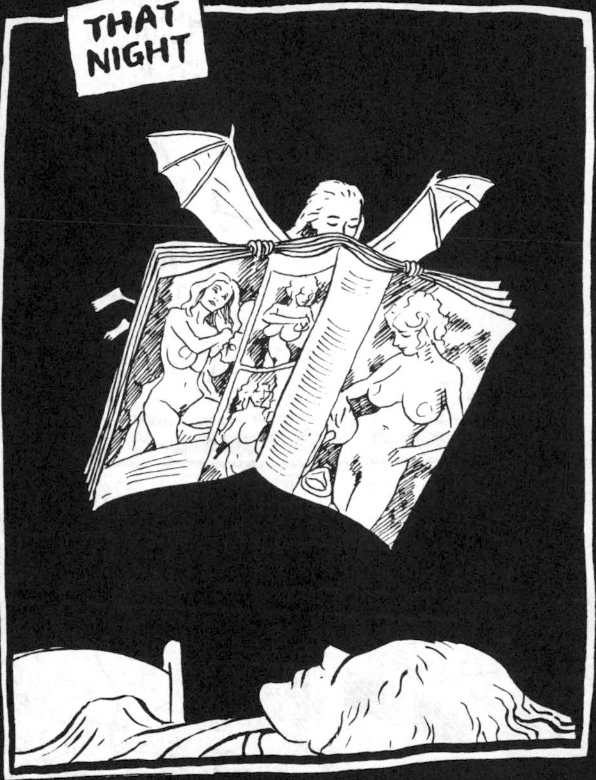
THAT NIGHT

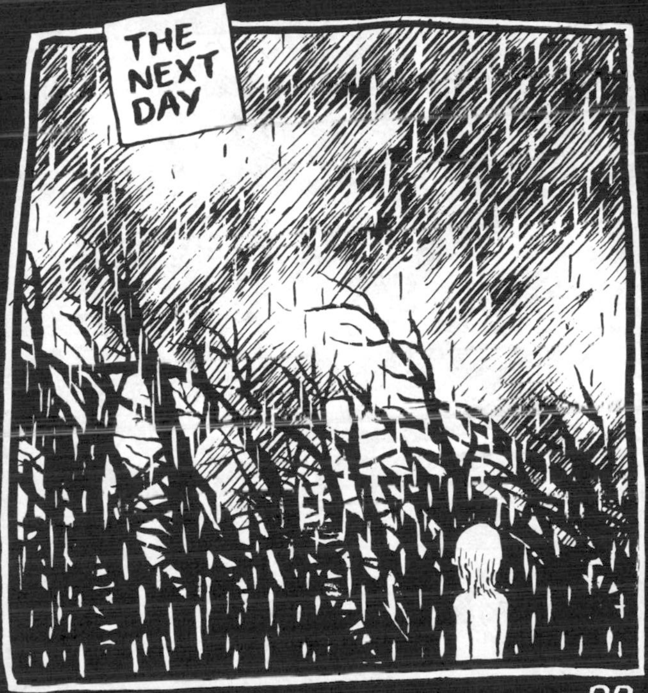
THE NEXT DAY

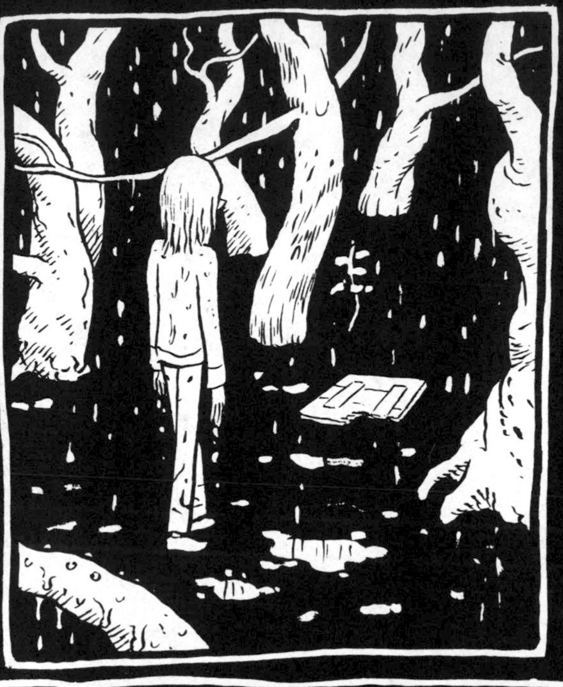

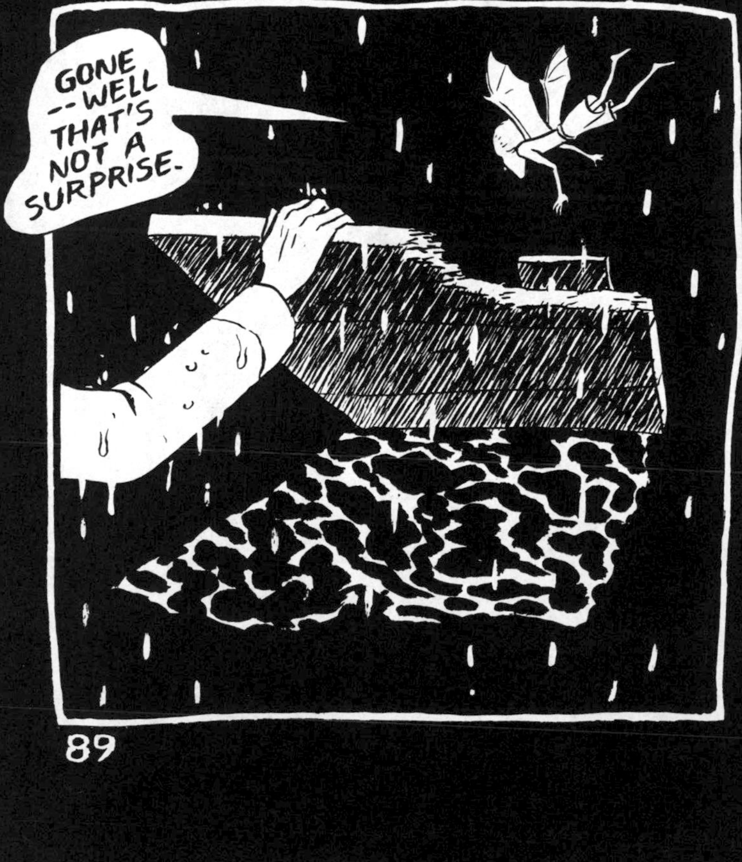
GONE --WELL THAT'S NOT A SURPRISE.

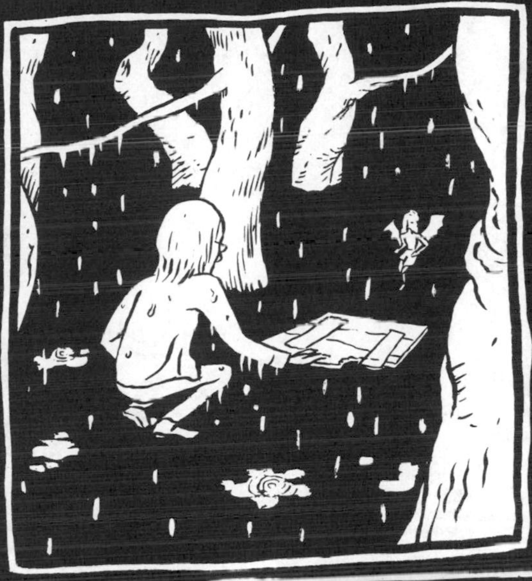

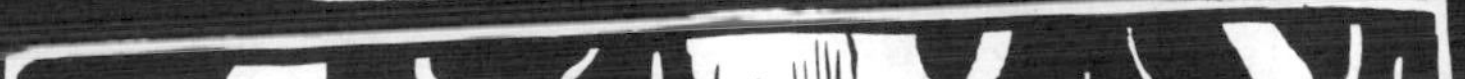
SAY WHAT'S THAT OVER THERE?

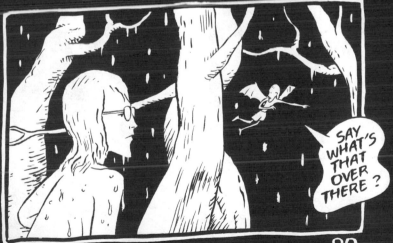

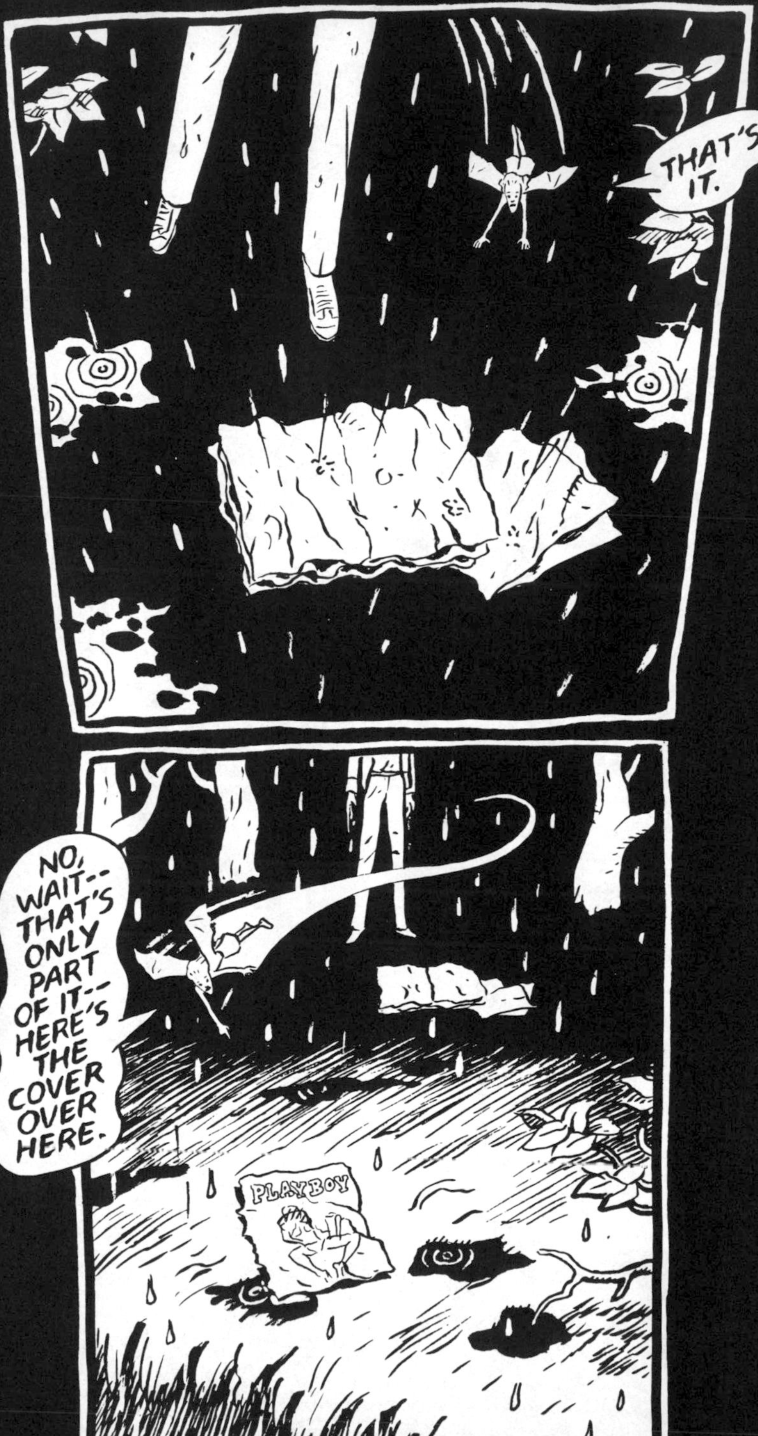
THAT'S IT.
NO, WAIT-- THAT'S ONLY PART OF IT-- HERE'S THE COVER OVER HERE.
PLAYBOY

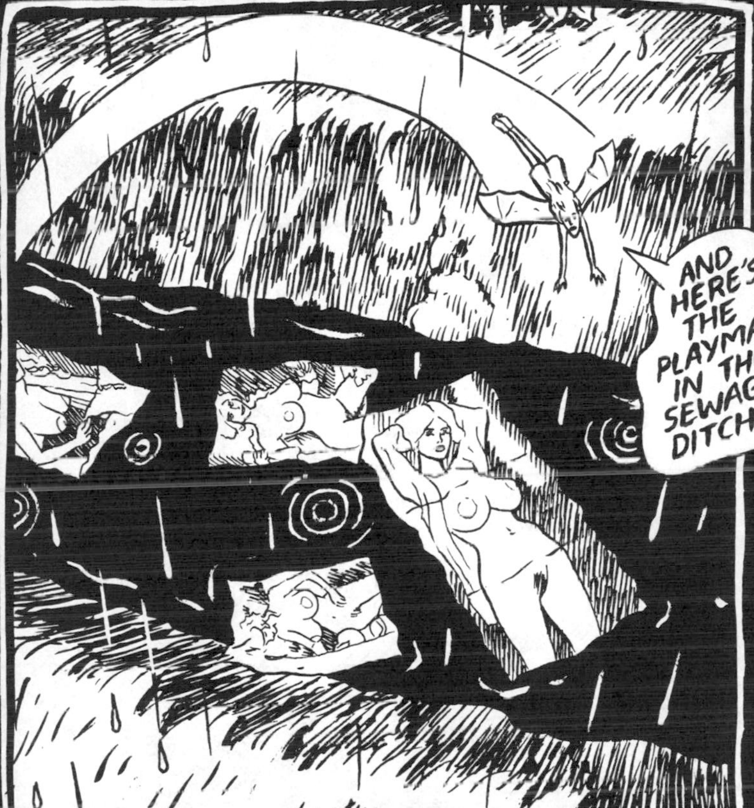
AND HERE'S THE PLAYMATE IN THE SEWAGE DITCH.

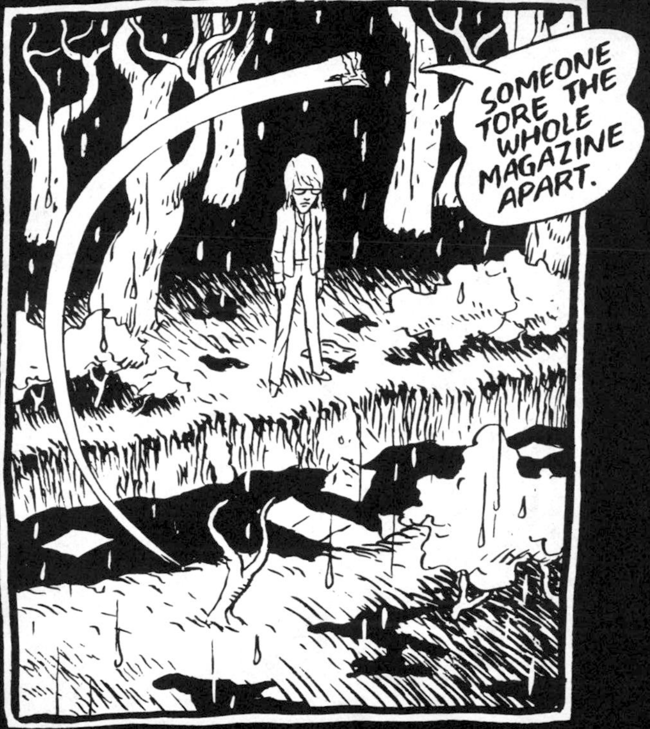
SOMEONE TORE THE WHOLE MAGAZINE APART.

PART
TWO

94

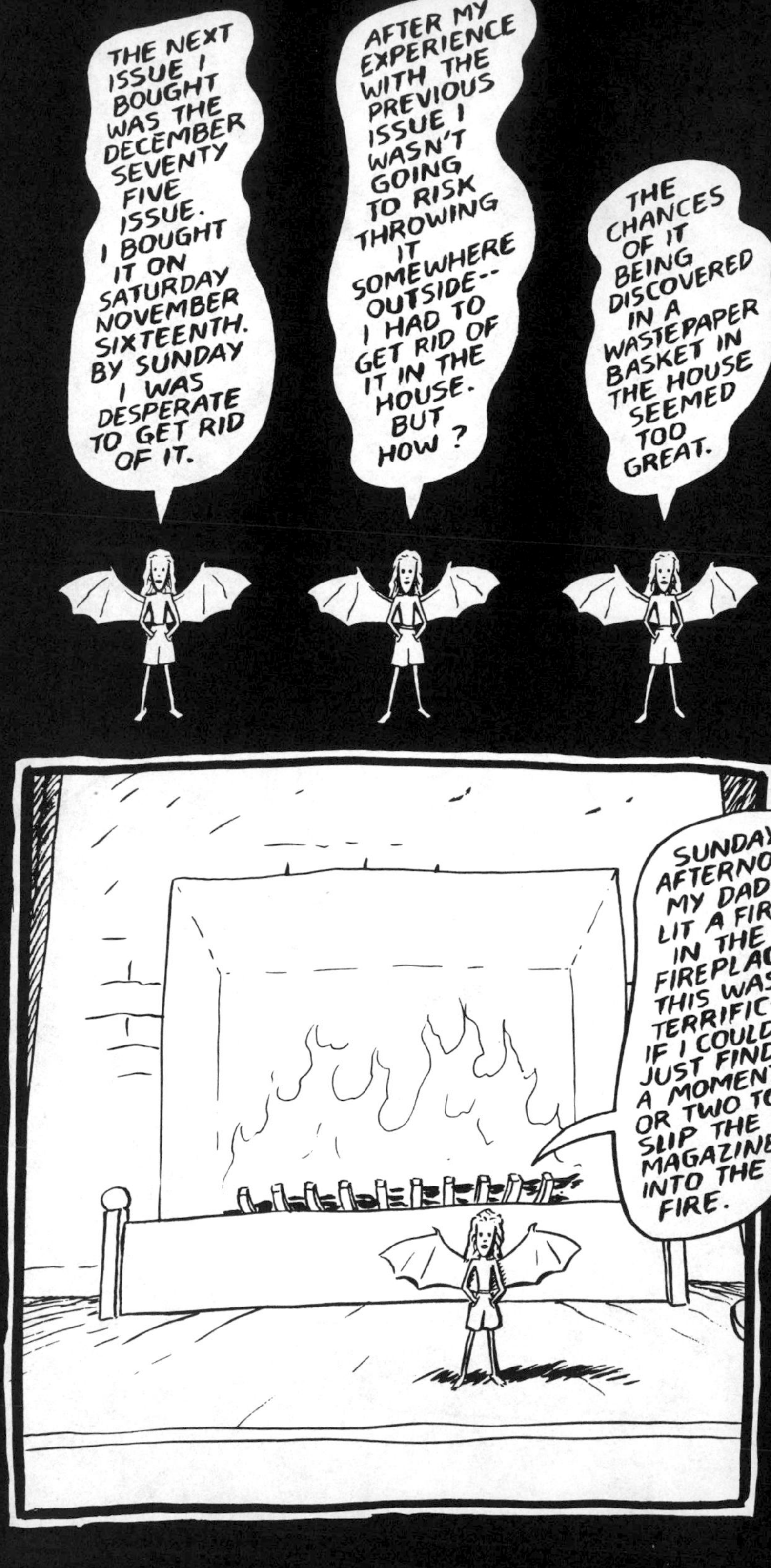
THE NEXT ISSUE I BOUGHT WAS THE DECEMBER SEVENTY FIVE ISSUE. I BOUGHT IT ON SATURDAY NOVEMBER SIXTEENTH. BY SUNDAY I WAS DESPERATE TO GET RID OF IT.
AFTER MY EXPERIENCE WITH THE PREVIOUS ISSUE I WASN'T GOING TO RISK THROWING IT SOMEWHERE OUTSIDE-- I HAD TO GET RID OF IT IN THE HOUSE. BUT HOW ?
THE CHANCES OF IT BEING DISCOVERED IN A WASTEPAPER BASKET IN THE HOUSE SEEMED TOO GREAT.
SUNDAY AFTERNOON MY DAD LIT A FIRE IN THE FIREPLACE. THIS WAS TERRIFIC-- IF I COULD JUST FIND A MOMENT OR TWO TO SLIP THE MAGAZINE INTO THE FIRE.

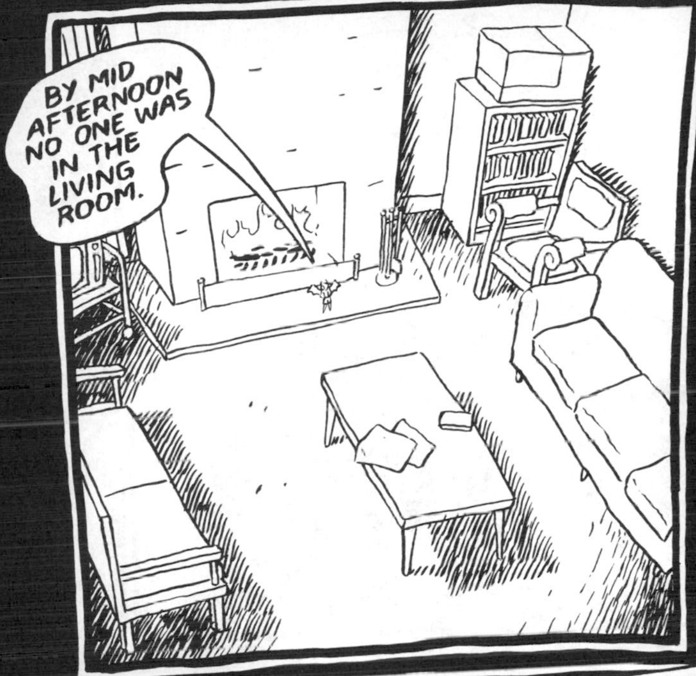
BY MID AFTERNOON NO ONE WAS IN THE LIVING ROOM.

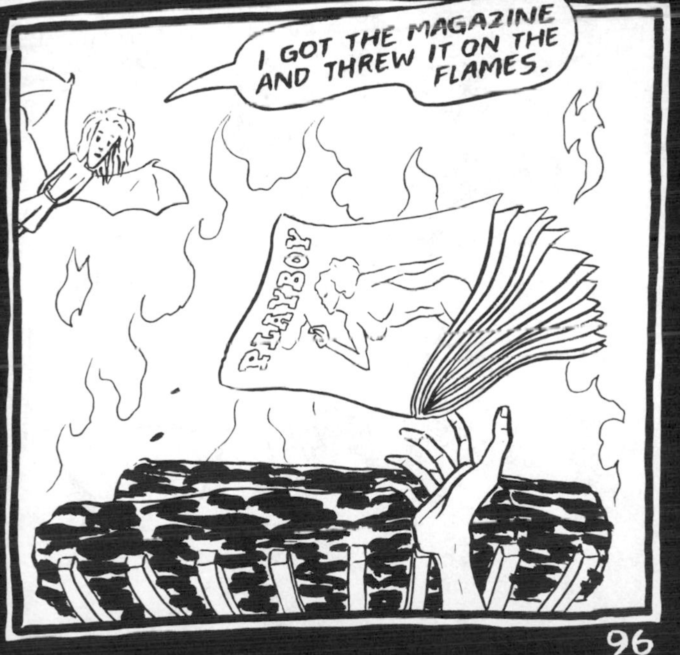
I GOT THE MAGAZINE AND THREW IT ON THE FLAMES.
PLAYBOY

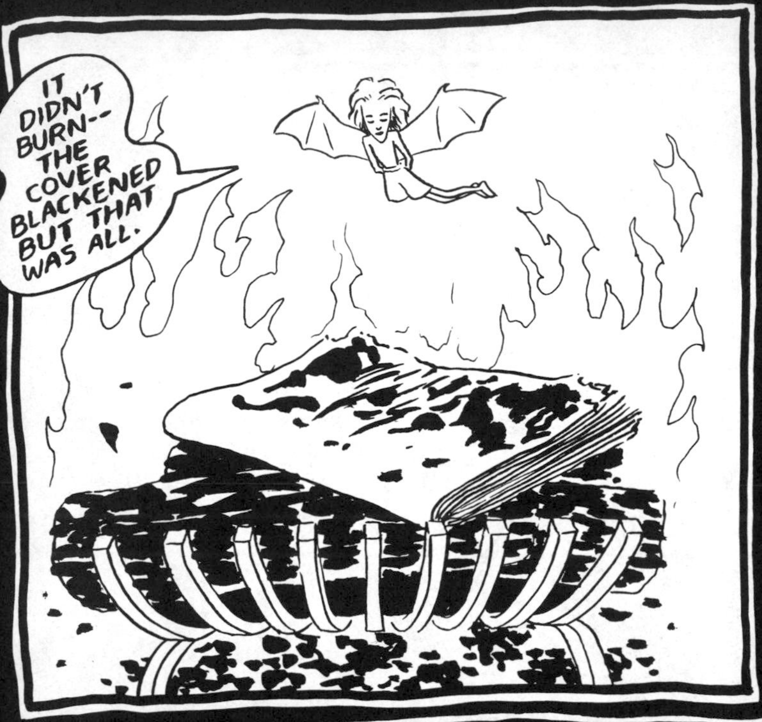
IT DIDN'T BURN-- THE COVER BLACKENED BUT THAT WAS ALL.

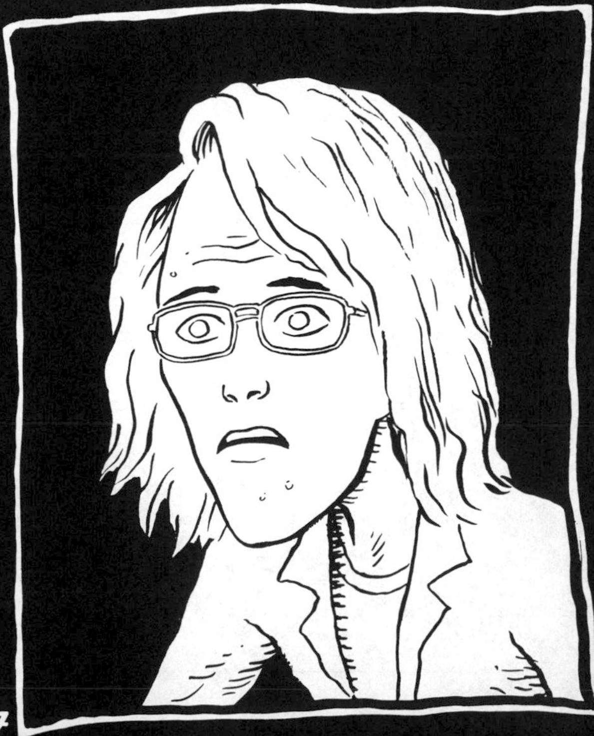

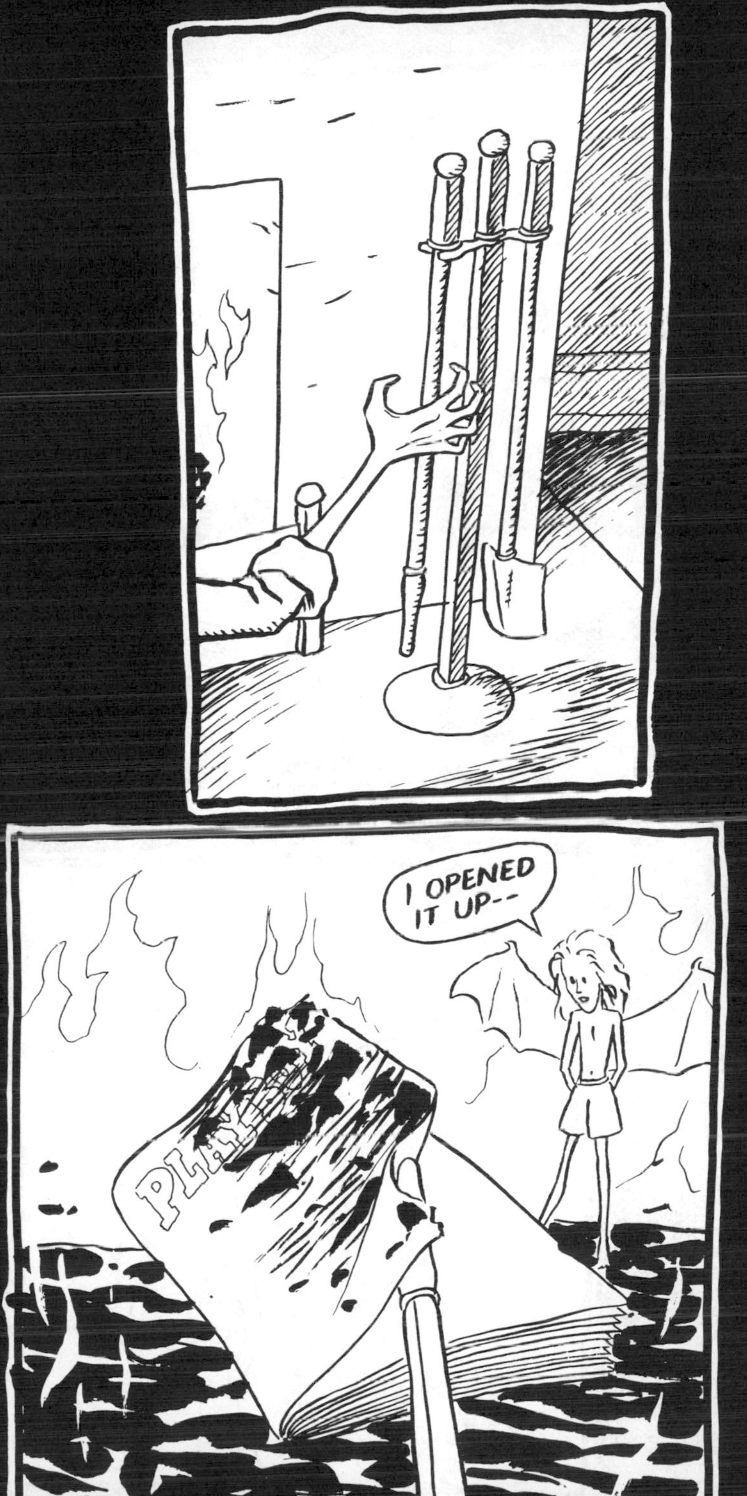
I OPENED IT UP--

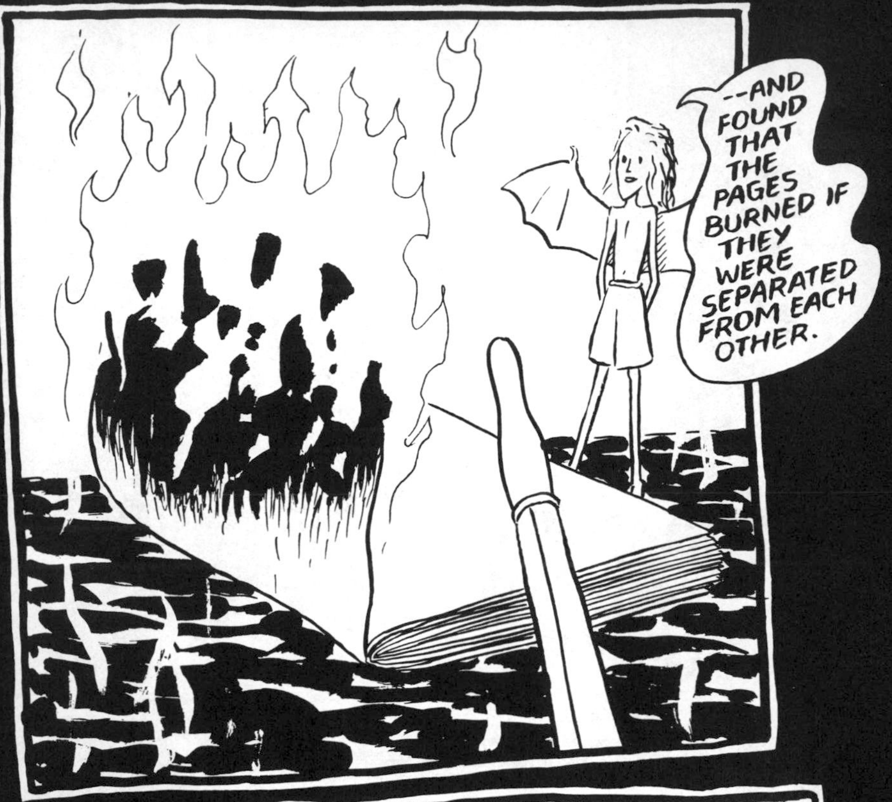
--AND FOUND THAT THE PAGES BURNED IF THEY WERE SEPARATED FROM EACH OTHER.

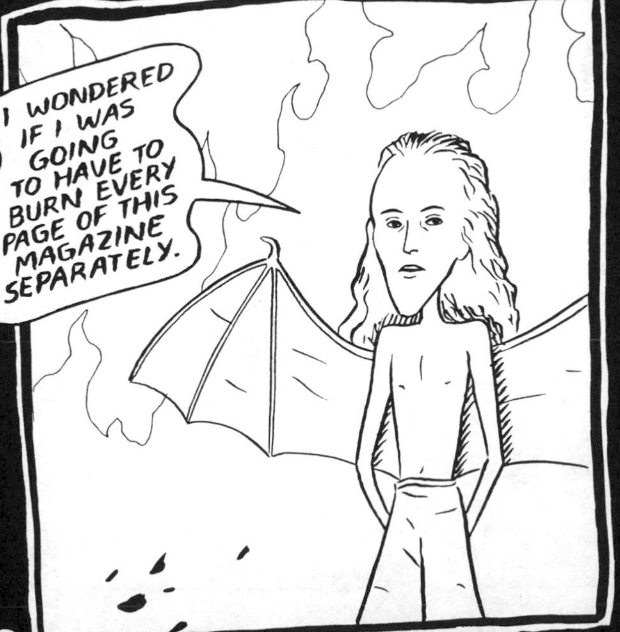
I WONDERED IF I WAS GOING TO HAVE TO BURN EVERY PAGE OF THIS MAGAZINE SEPARATELY.

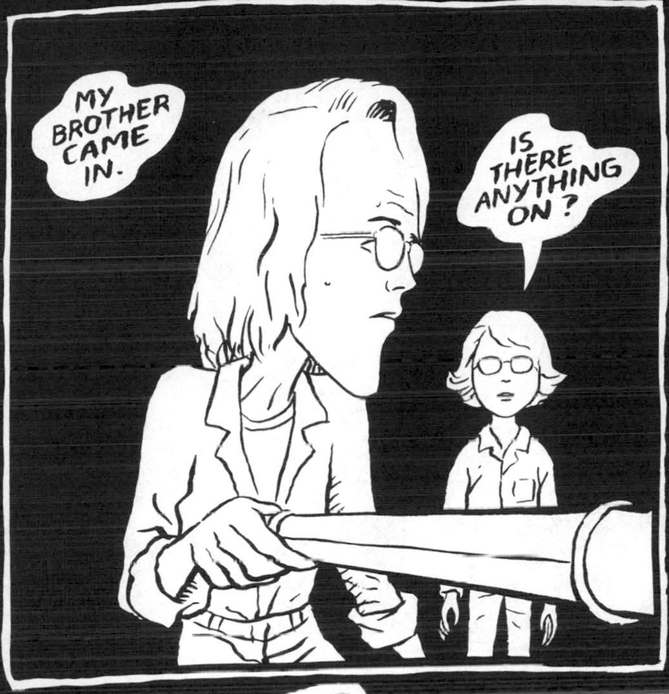
MY BROTHER CAME IN.
IS THERE ANYTHING ON?

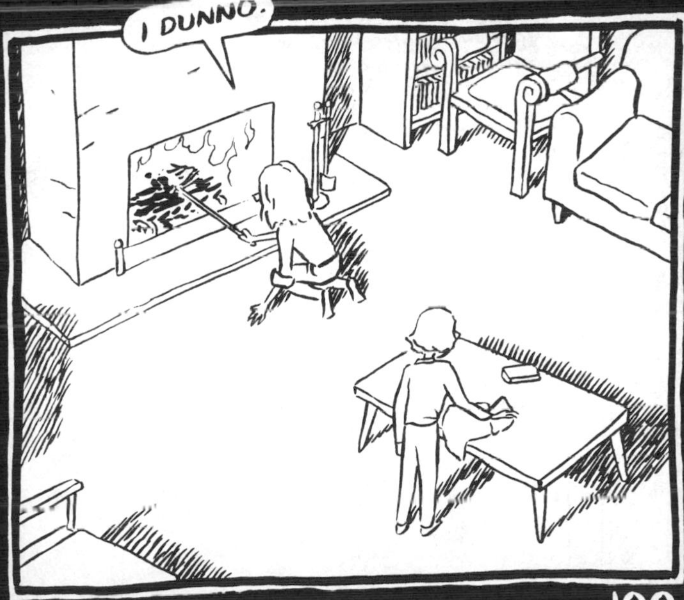
I DUNNO.

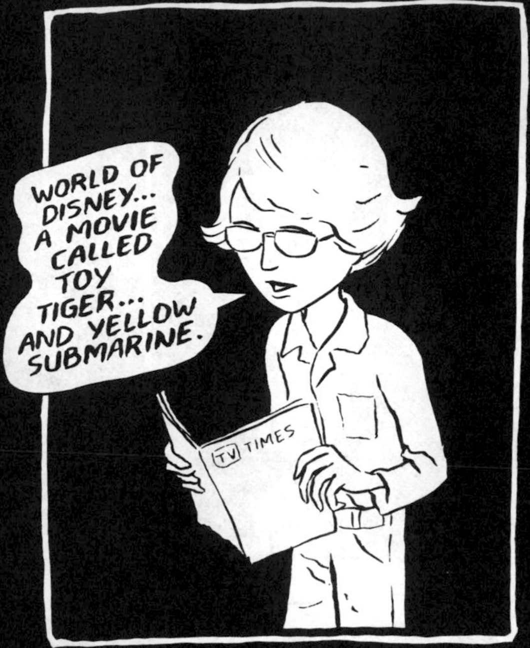
WORLD OF DISNEY... A MOVIE CALLED TOY TIGER... AND YELLOW SUBMARINE.
TV TIMES

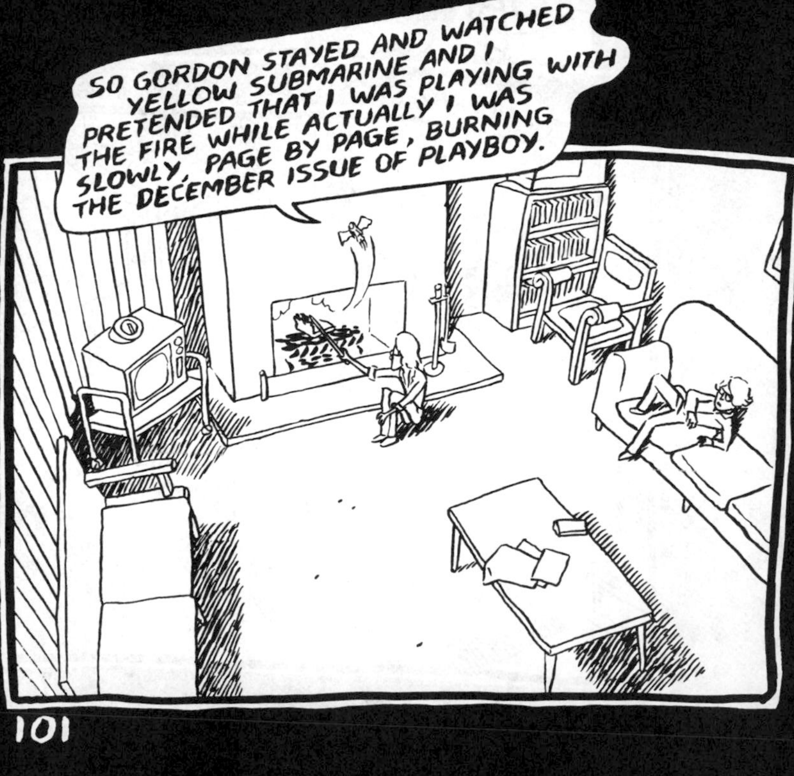
SO GORDON STAYED AND WATCHED YELLOW SUBMARINE AND I PRETENDED THAT I WAS PLAYING WITH THE FIRE WHILE ACTUALLY I WAS SLOWLY, PAGE BY PAGE, BURNING THE DECEMBER ISSUE OF PLAYBOY.

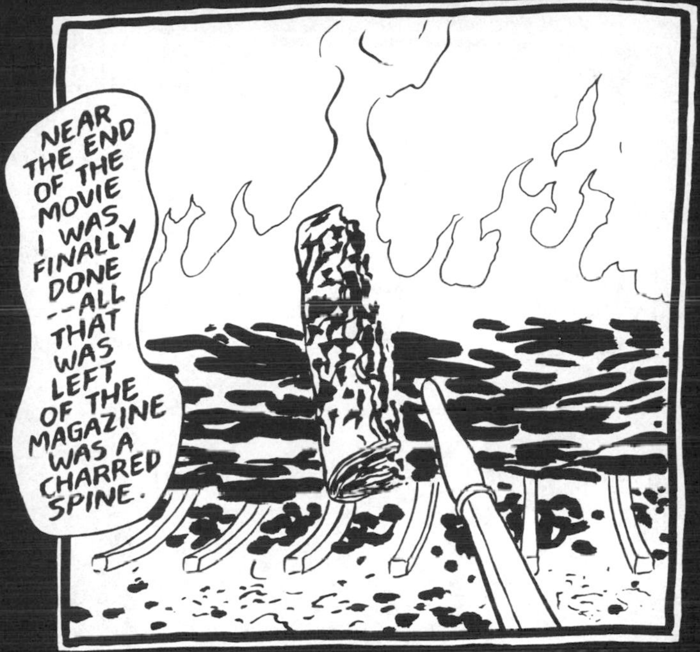
NEAR THE END OF THE MOVIE I WAS FINALLY DONE --ALL THAT WAS LEFT OF THE MAGAZINE WAS A CHARRED SPINE.

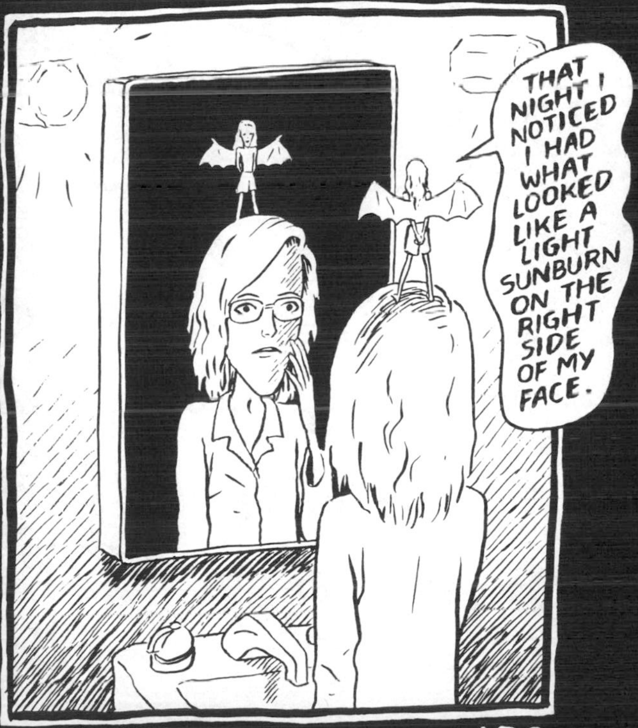
THAT NIGHT I NOTICED I HAD WHAT LOOKED LIKE A LIGHT SUNBURN ON THE RIGHT SIDE OF MY FACE.

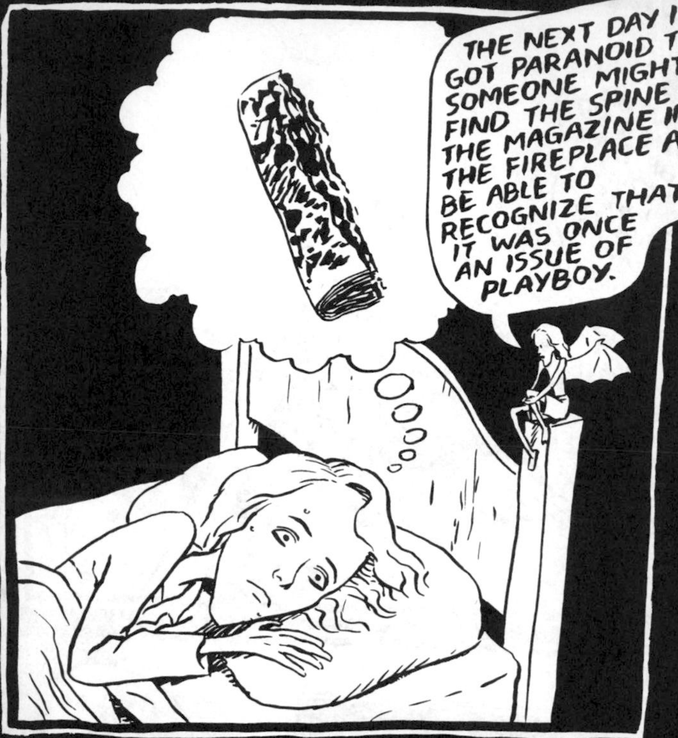
THE NEXT DAY I GOT PARANOID THAT SOMEONE MIGHT FIND THE SPINE OF THE MAGAZINE IN THE FIREPLACE AND BE ABLE TO RECOGNIZE THAT IT WAS ONCE AN ISSUE OF PLAYBOY.

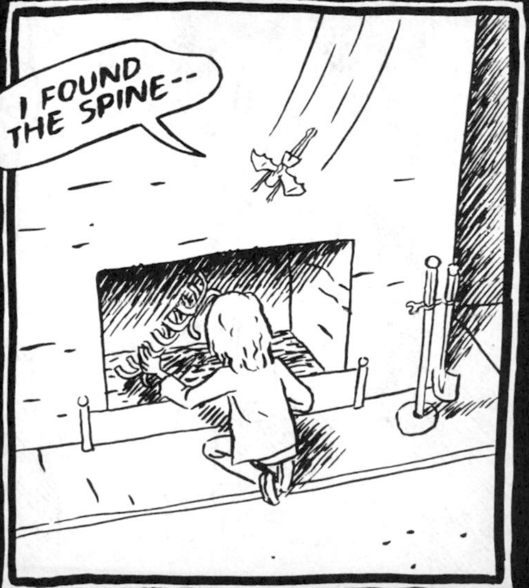
I FOUND THE SPINE--

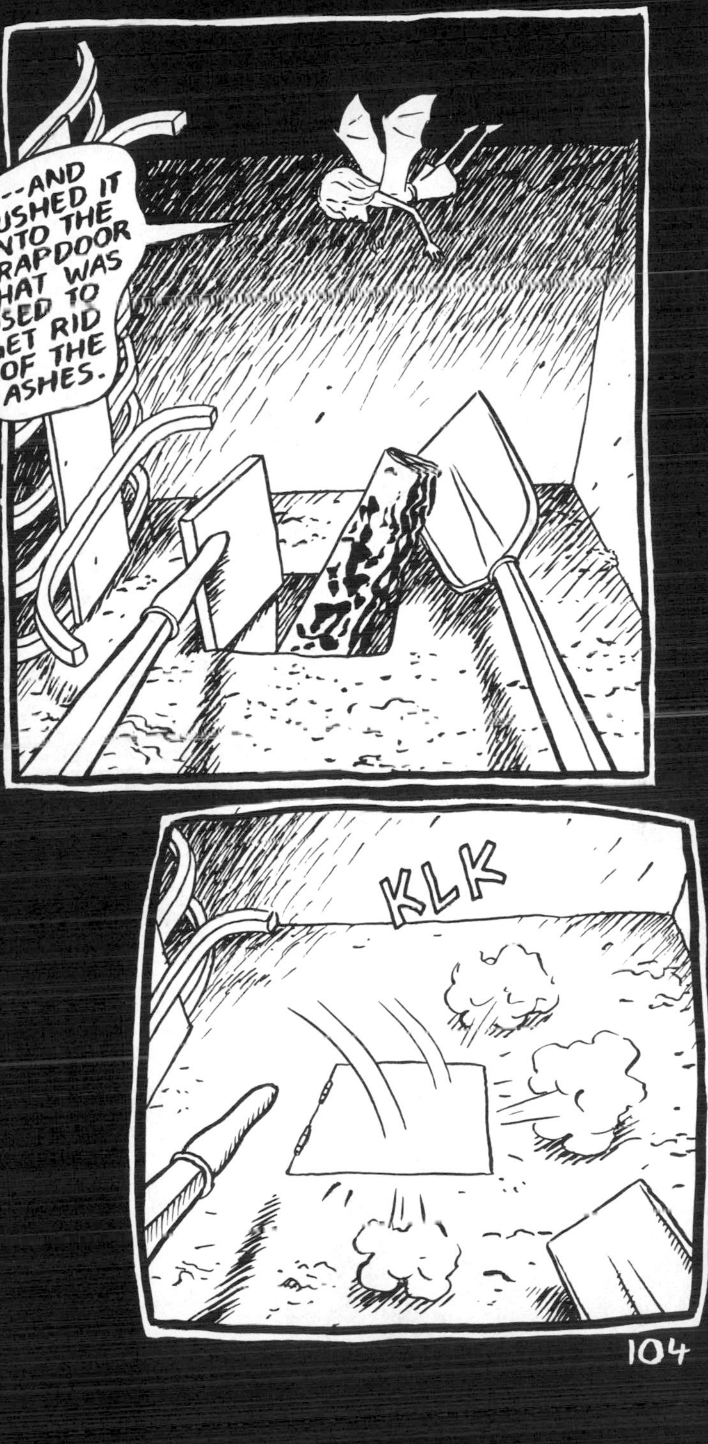
--AND PUSHED IT INTO THE TRAPDOOR THAT WAS USED TO GET RID OF THE ASHES.
KLK

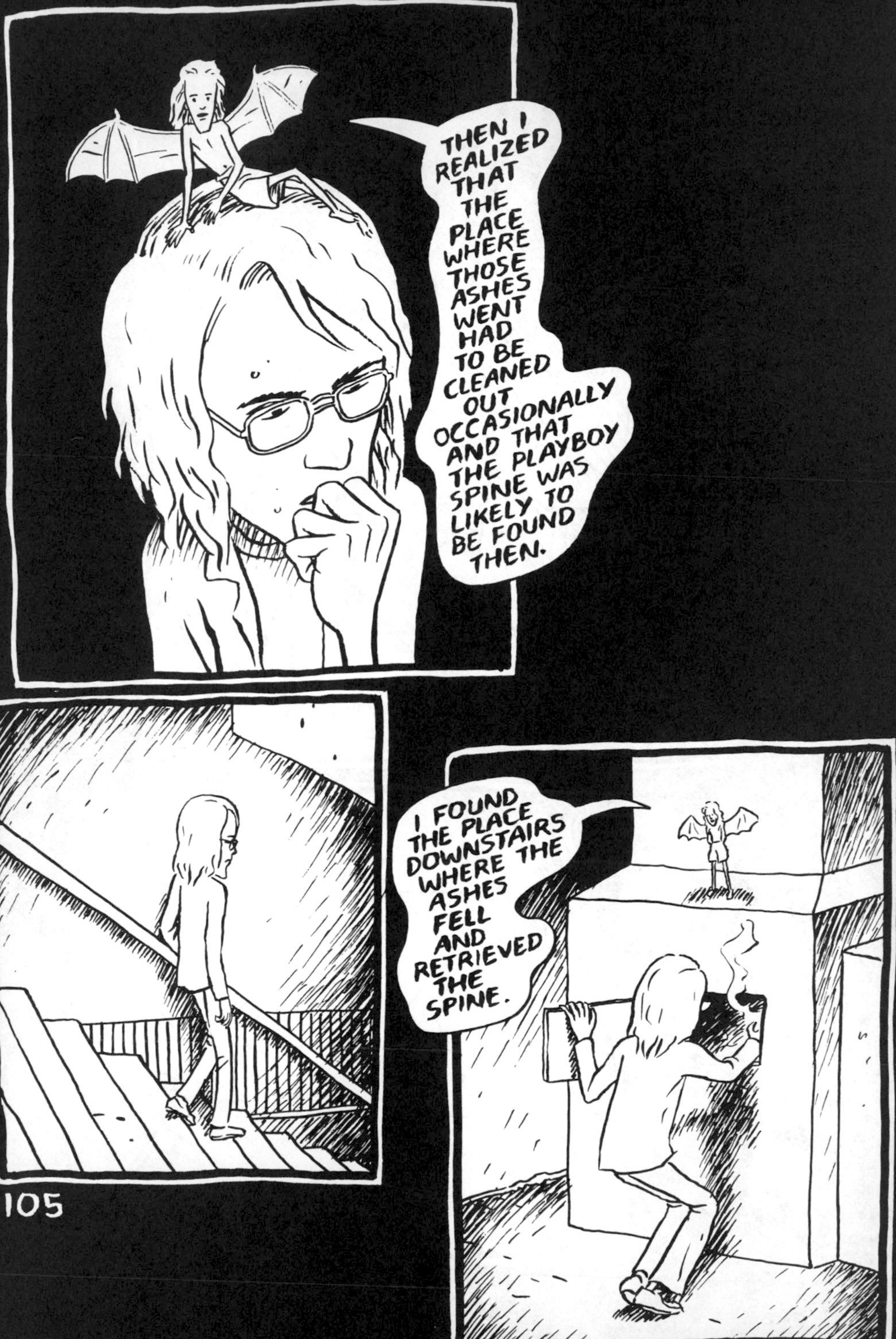
THEN I REALIZED THAT THE PLACE WHERE THOSE ASHES WENT HAD TO BE CLEANED OUT OCCASIONALLY AND THAT THE PLAYBOY SPINE WAS LIKELY TO BE FOUND THEN.
I FOUND THE PLACE DOWNSTAIRS WHERE THE ASHES FELL AND RETRIEVED THE SPINE.

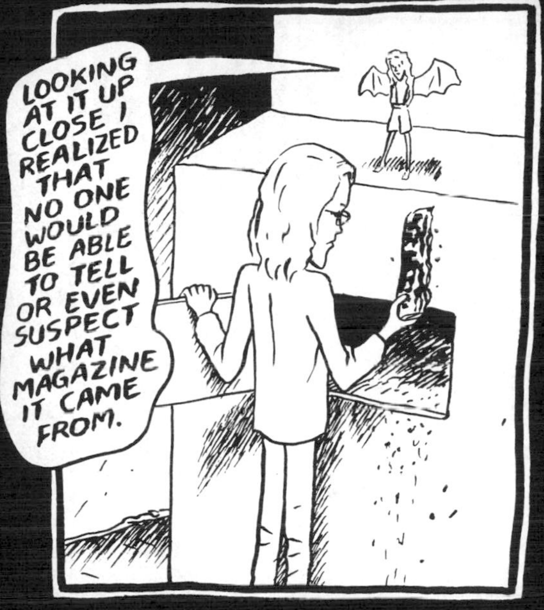
LOOKING AT IT UP CLOSE I REALIZED THAT NO ONE WOULD BE ABLE TO TELL OR EVEN SUSPECT WHAT MAGAZINE IT CAME FROM.

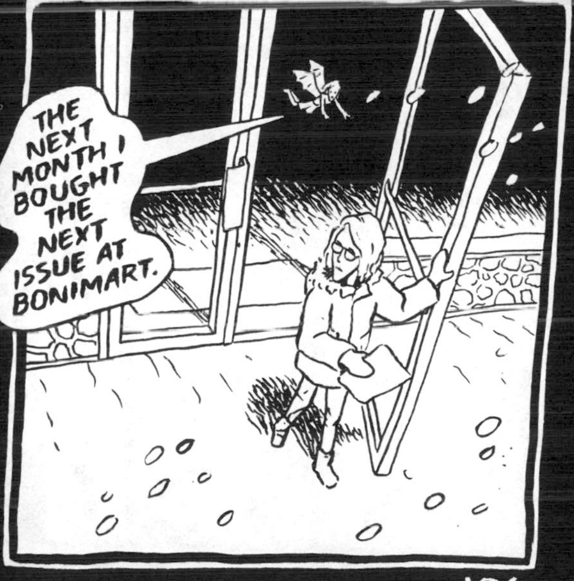
THE NEXT MONTH I BOUGHT THE NEXT ISSUE AT BONIMART.

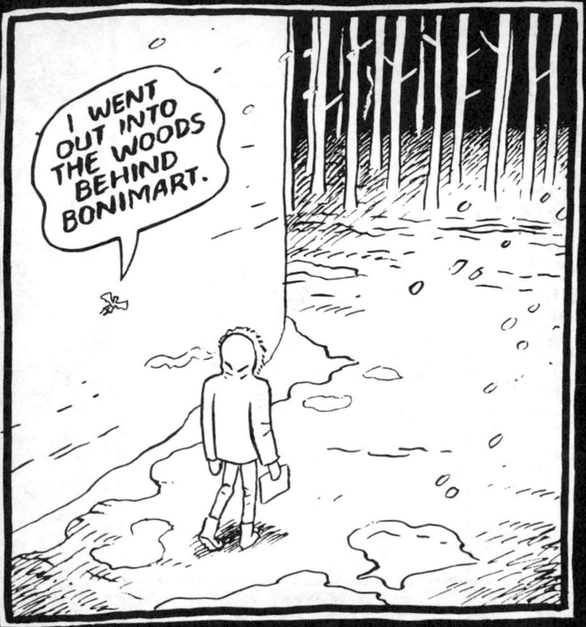
I WENT OUT INTO THE WOODS BEHIND BONIMART.

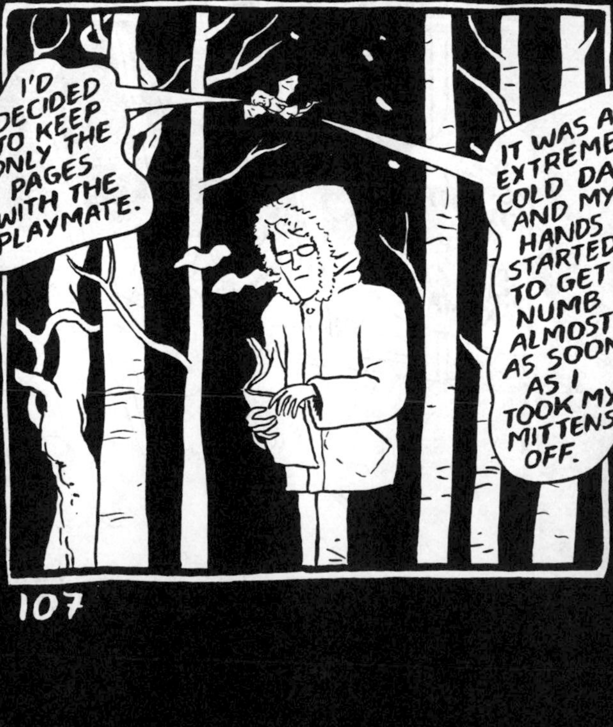
I'D DECIDED TO KEEP ONLY THE PAGES WITH THE PLAYMATE.
IT WAS AN EXTREMELY COLD DAY AND MY HANDS STARTED TO GET NUMB ALMOST AS SOON AS I TOOK MY MITTENS OFF.

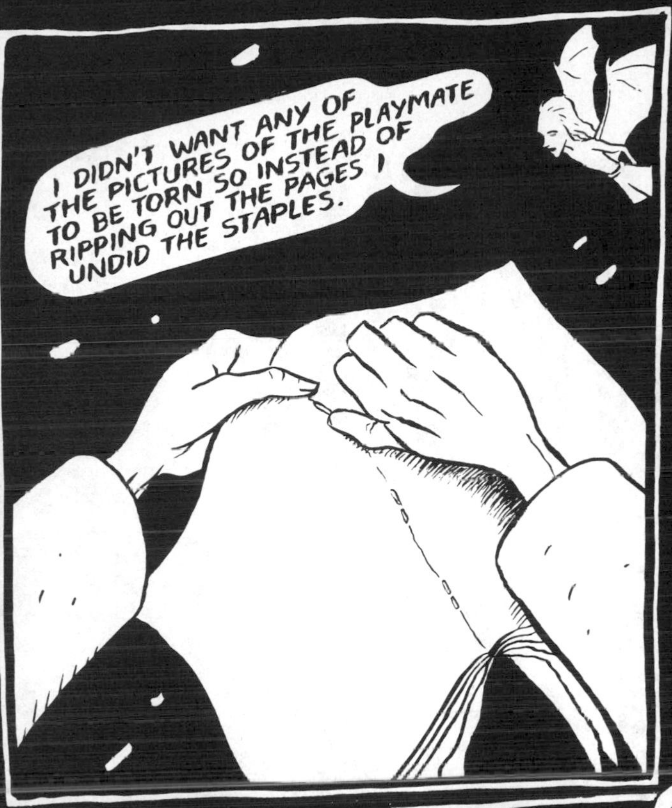
I DIDN'T WANT ANY OF THE PICTURES OF THE PLAYMATE TO BE TORN SO INSTEAD OF RIPPING OUT THE PAGES I UNDID THE STAPLES.

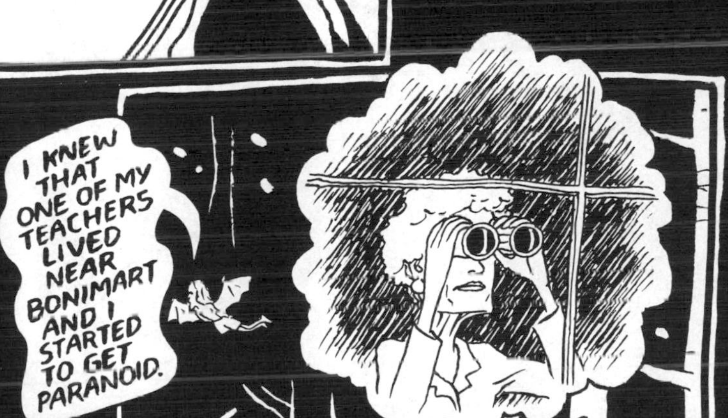
I KNEW THAT ONE OF MY TEACHERS LIVED NEAR BONIMART AND I STARTED TO GET PARANOID.

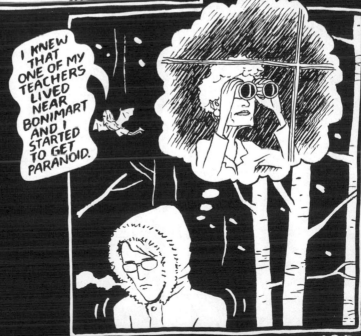

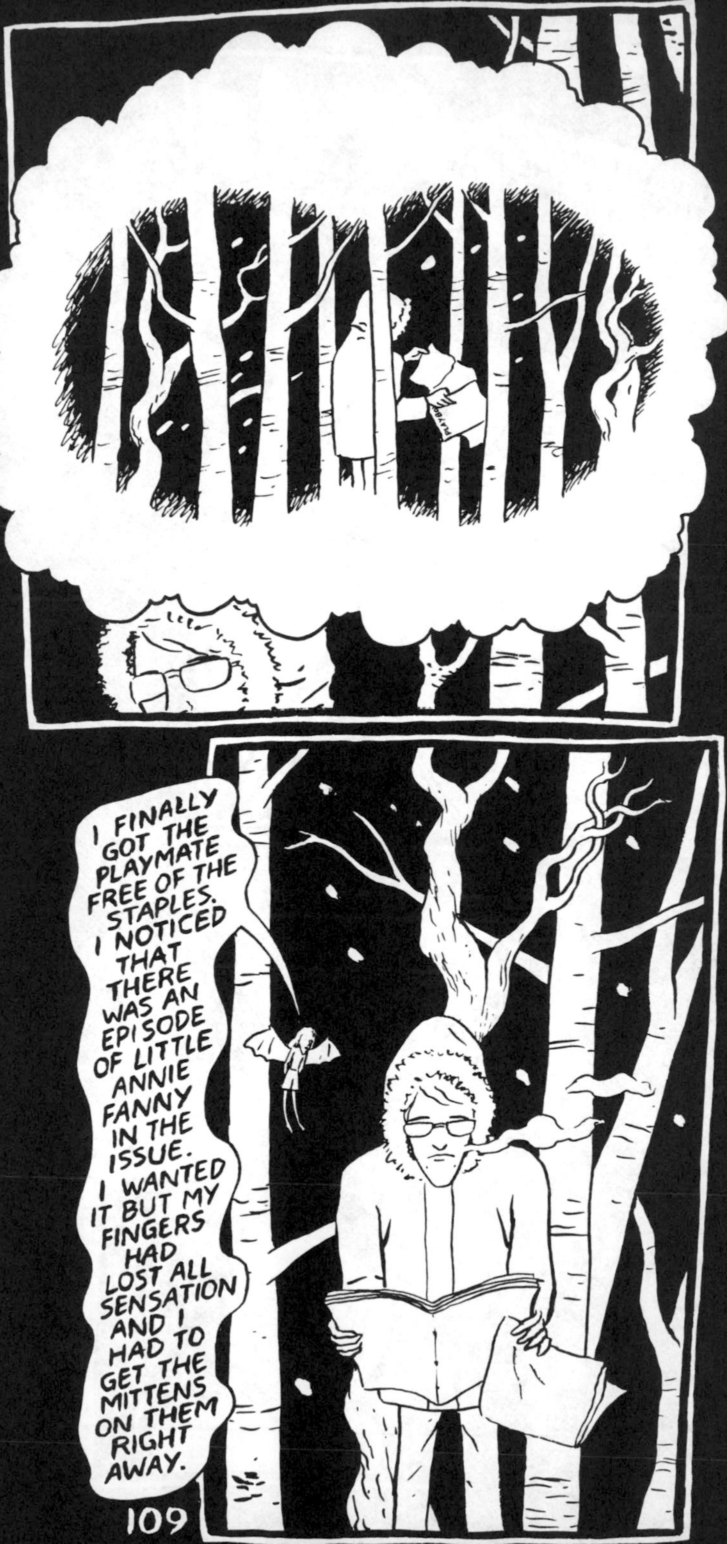
I FINALLY GOT THE PLAYMATE FREE OF THE STAPLES. I NOTICED THAT THERE WAS AN EPISODE OF LITTLE ANNIE FANNY IN THE ISSUE. I WANTED IT BUT MY FINGERS HAD LOST ALL SENSATION AND I HAD TO GET THE MITTENS ON THEM RIGHT AWAY.

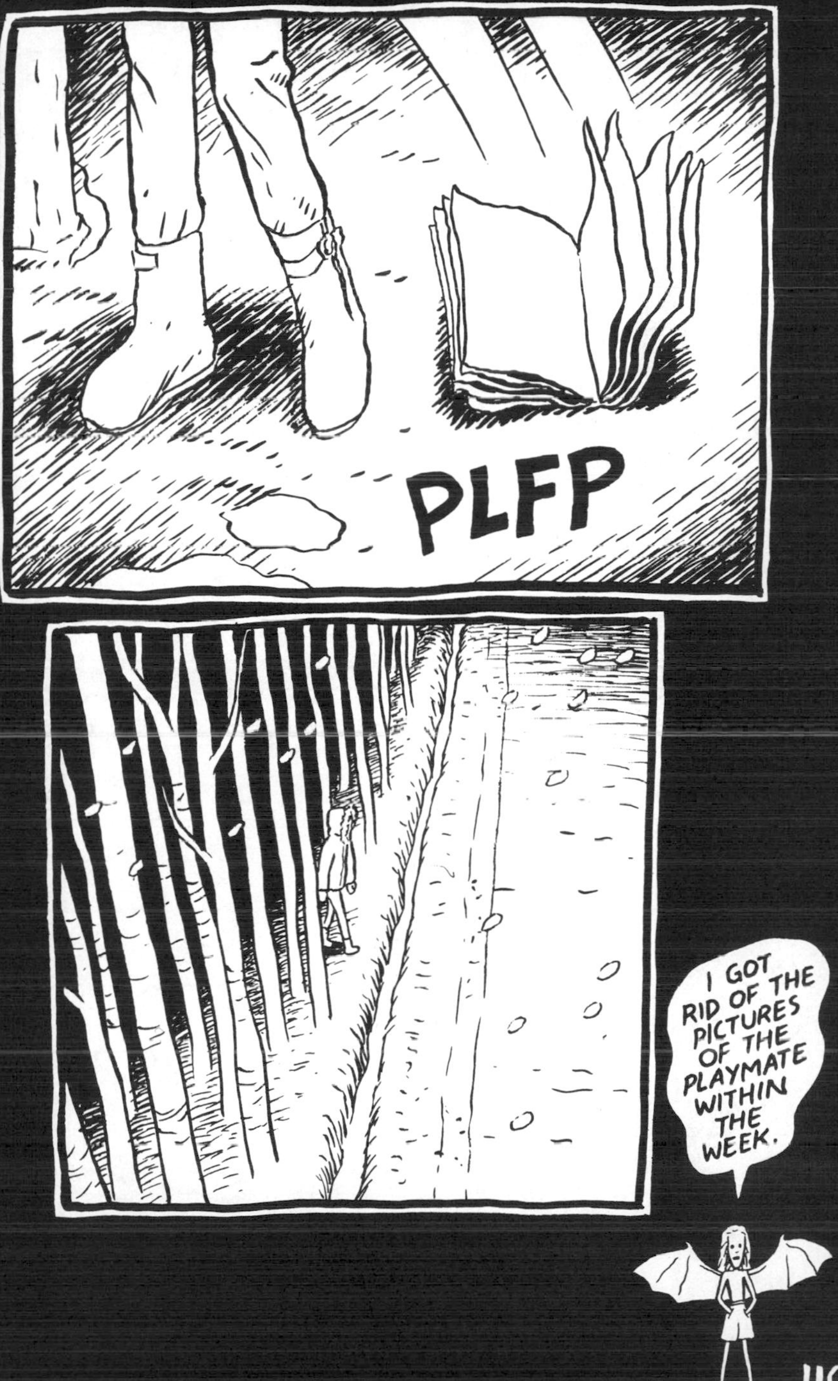
PLFP
I GOT RID OF THE PICTURES OF THE PLAYMATE WITHIN THE WEEK.

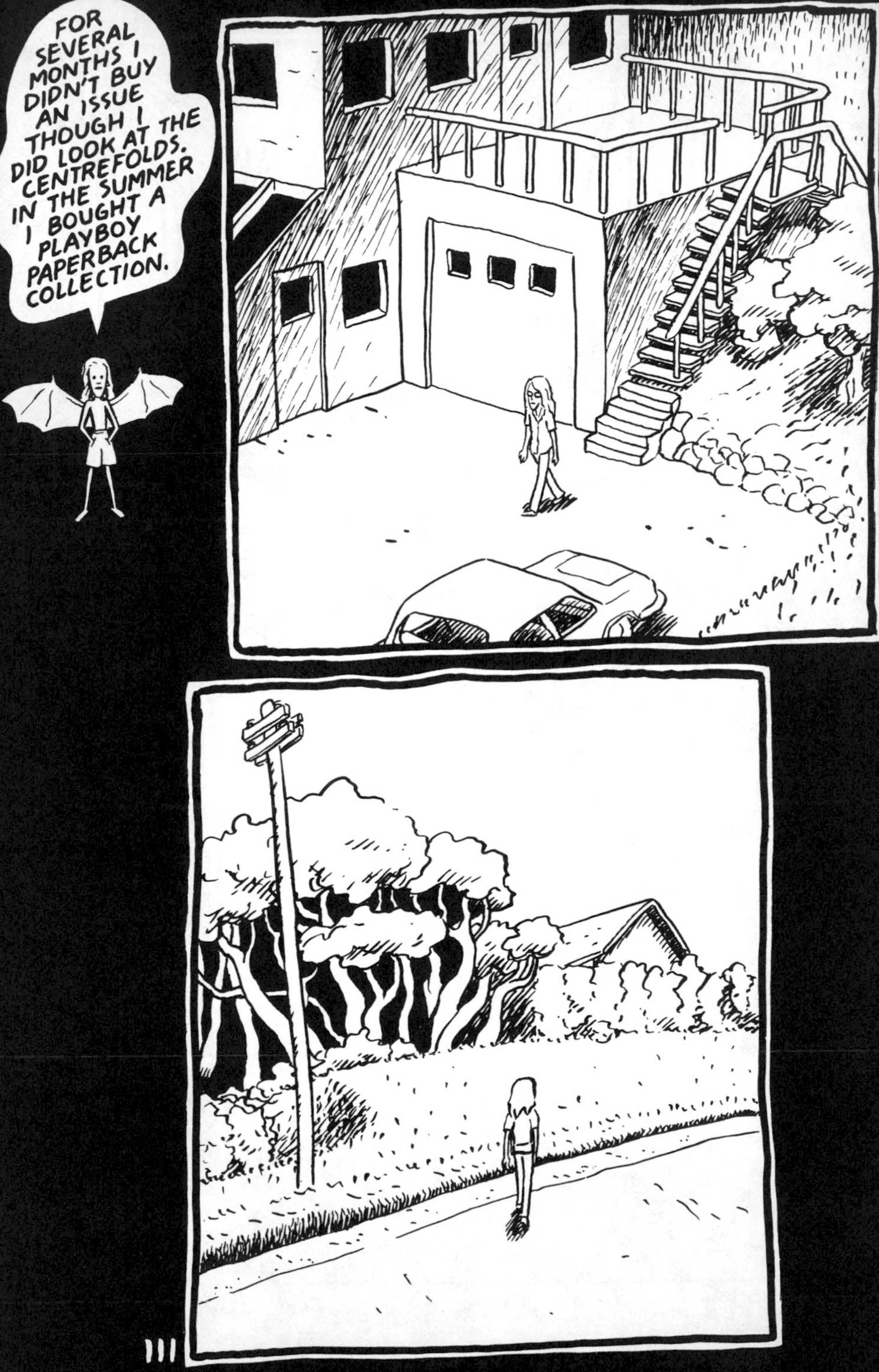
FOR SEVERAL MONTHS I DIDN'T BUY AN ISSUE THOUGH I DID LOOK AT THE CENTREFOLDS. IN THE SUMMER I BOUGHT A PLAYBOY PAPERBACK COLLECTION.

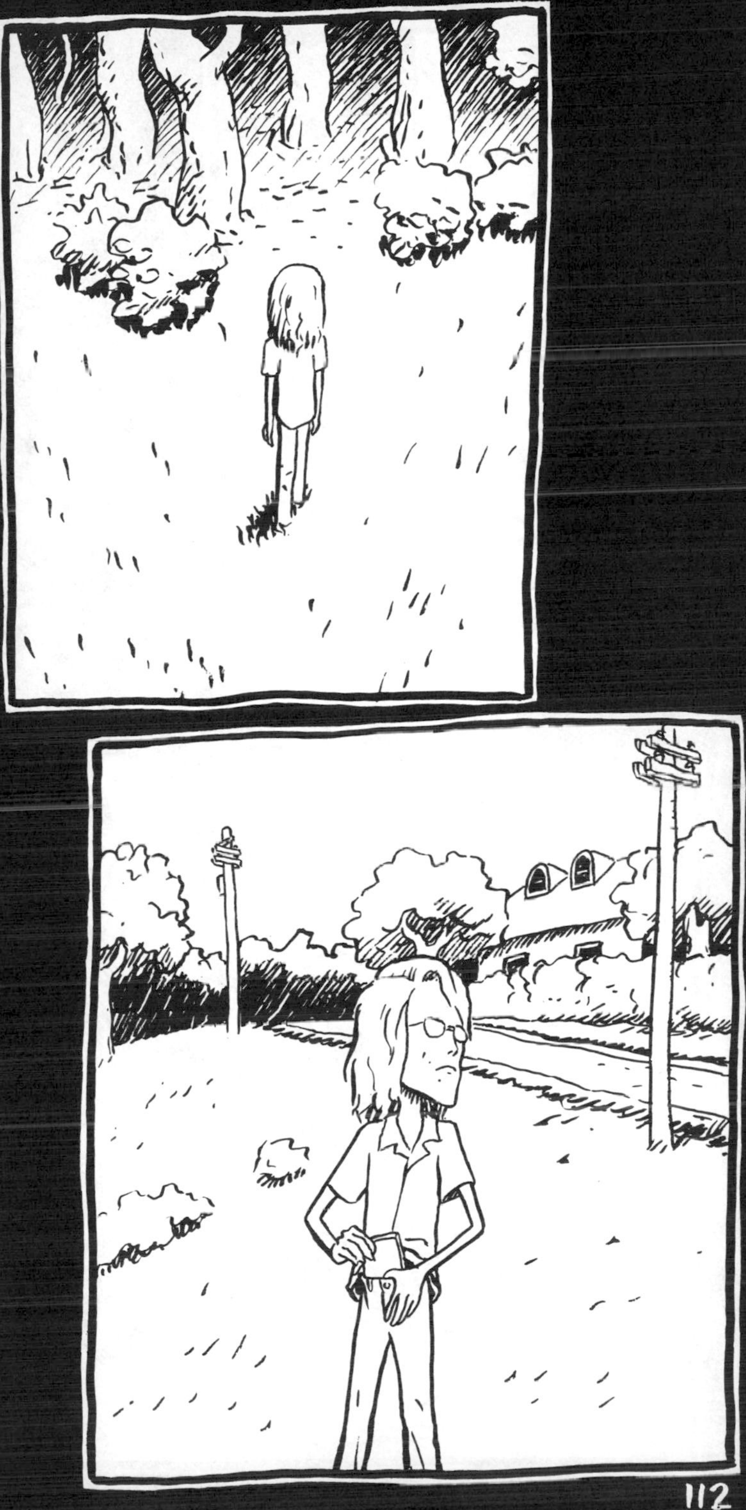

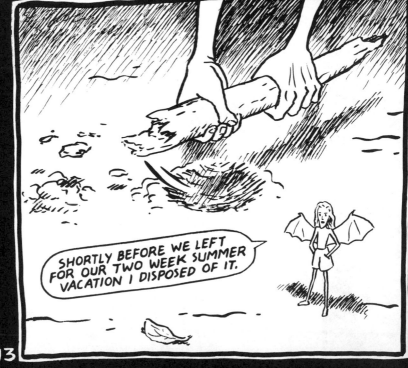

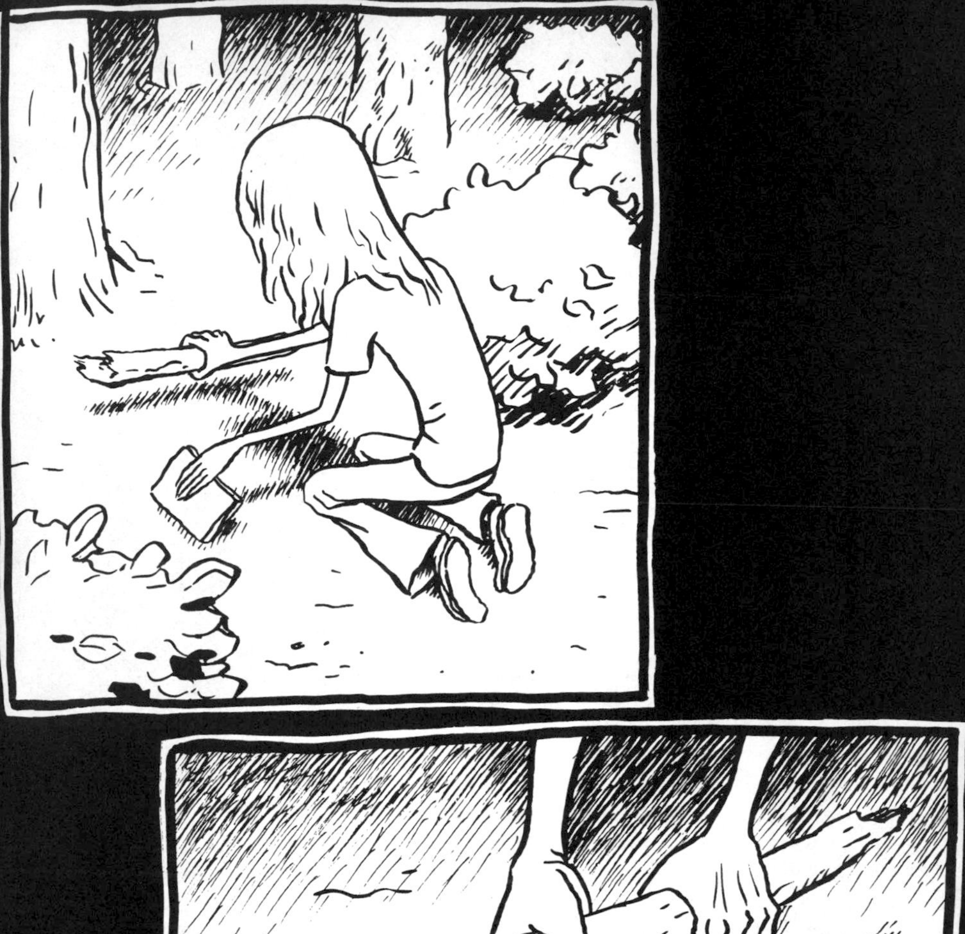
SHORTLY BEFORE WE LEFT FOR OUR TWO WEEK SUMMER VACATION I DISPOSED OF IT.

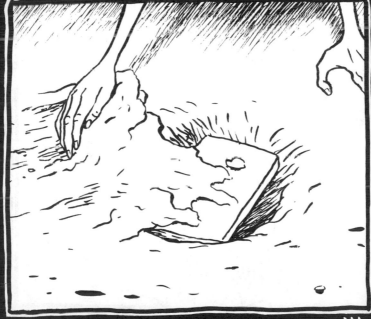

114

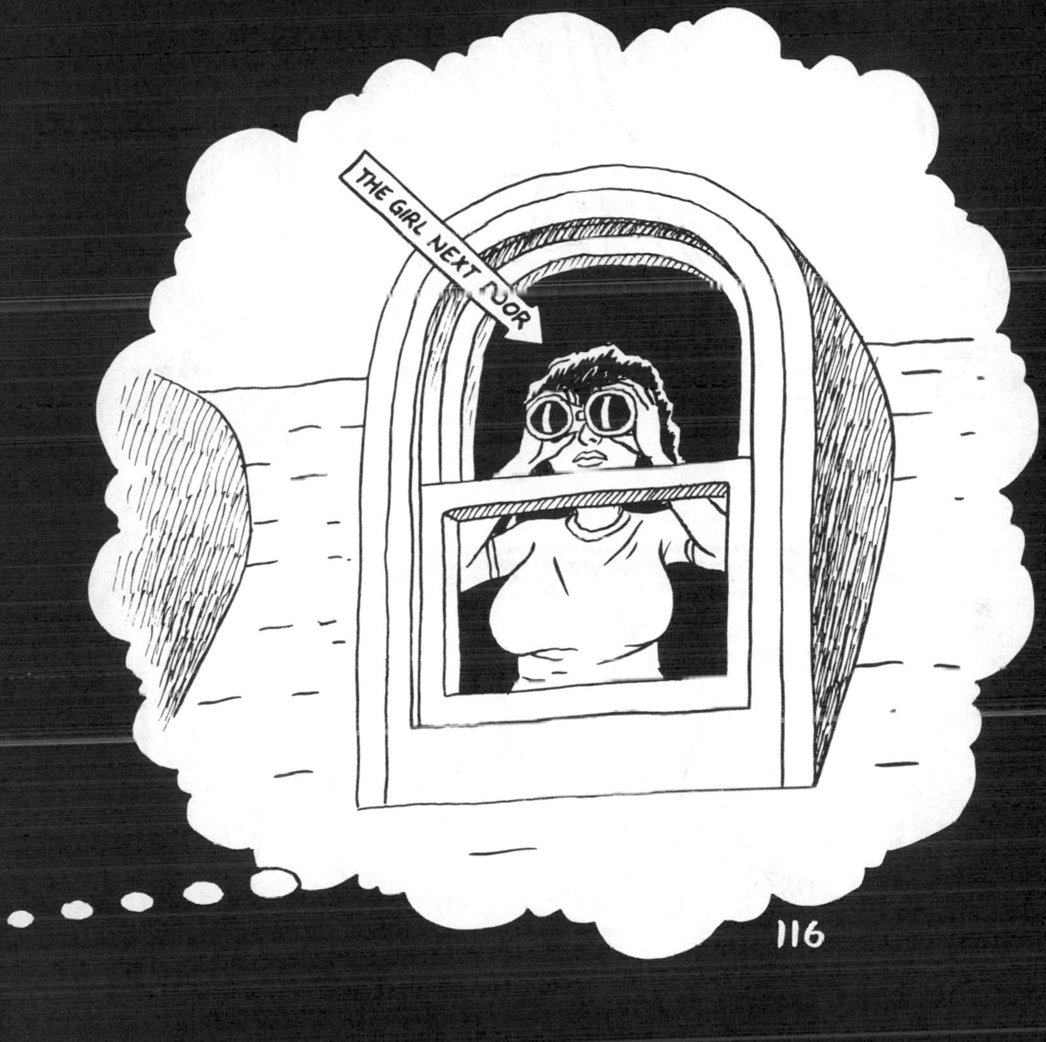
THE GIRL NEXT DOOR

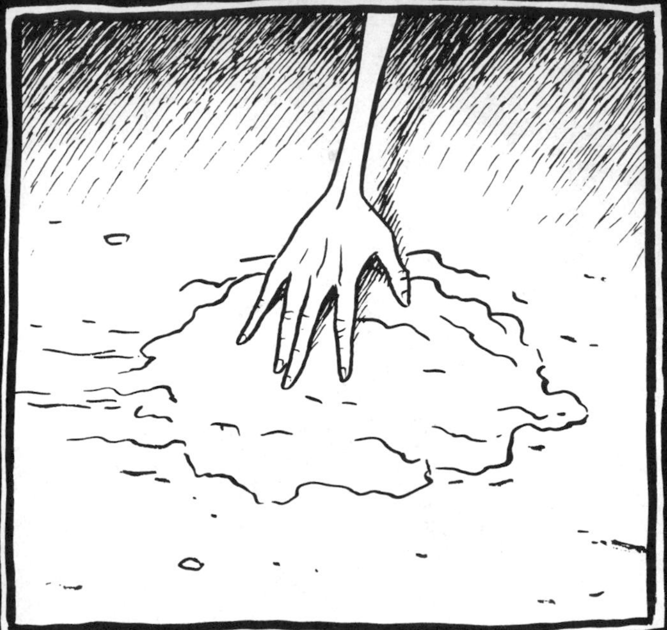

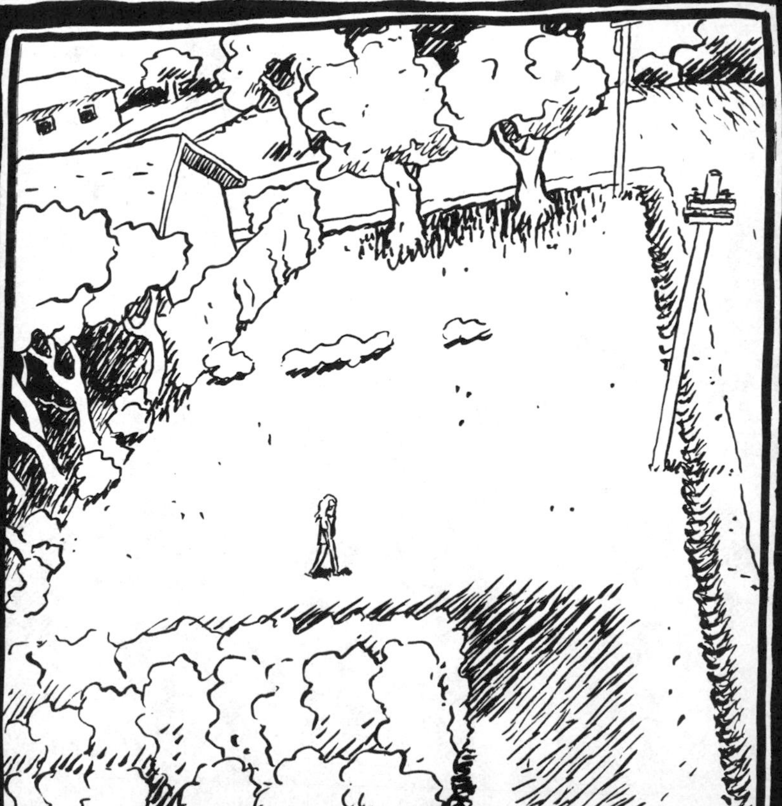

THE VACATION WAS NOT A HAPPY ONE. MY MOTHER DIED WHILE WE WERE AWAY.

AS SOON AS WE GOT BACK FROM THE VACATION I RETURNED TO THIS SPOT.

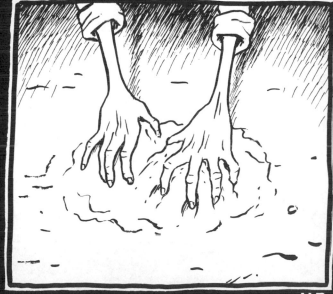

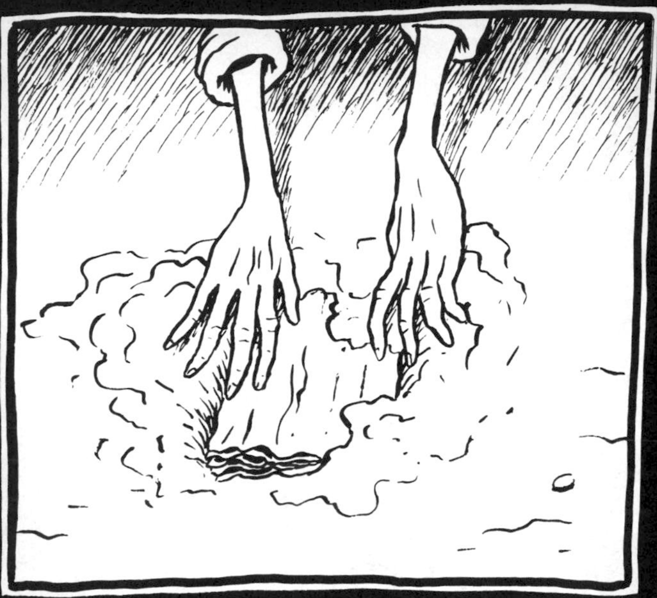

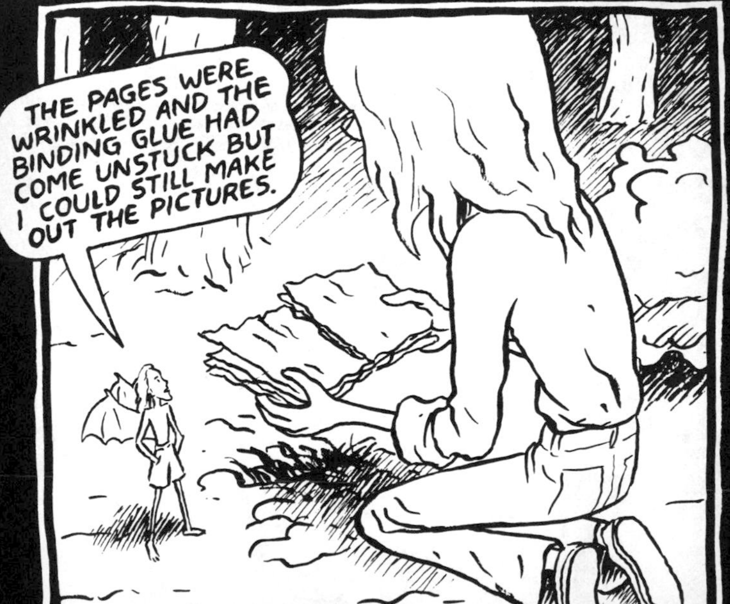
THE PAGES WERE WRINKLED AND THE BINDING GLUE HAD COME UNSTUCK BUT I COULD STILL MAKE OUT THE PICTURES.

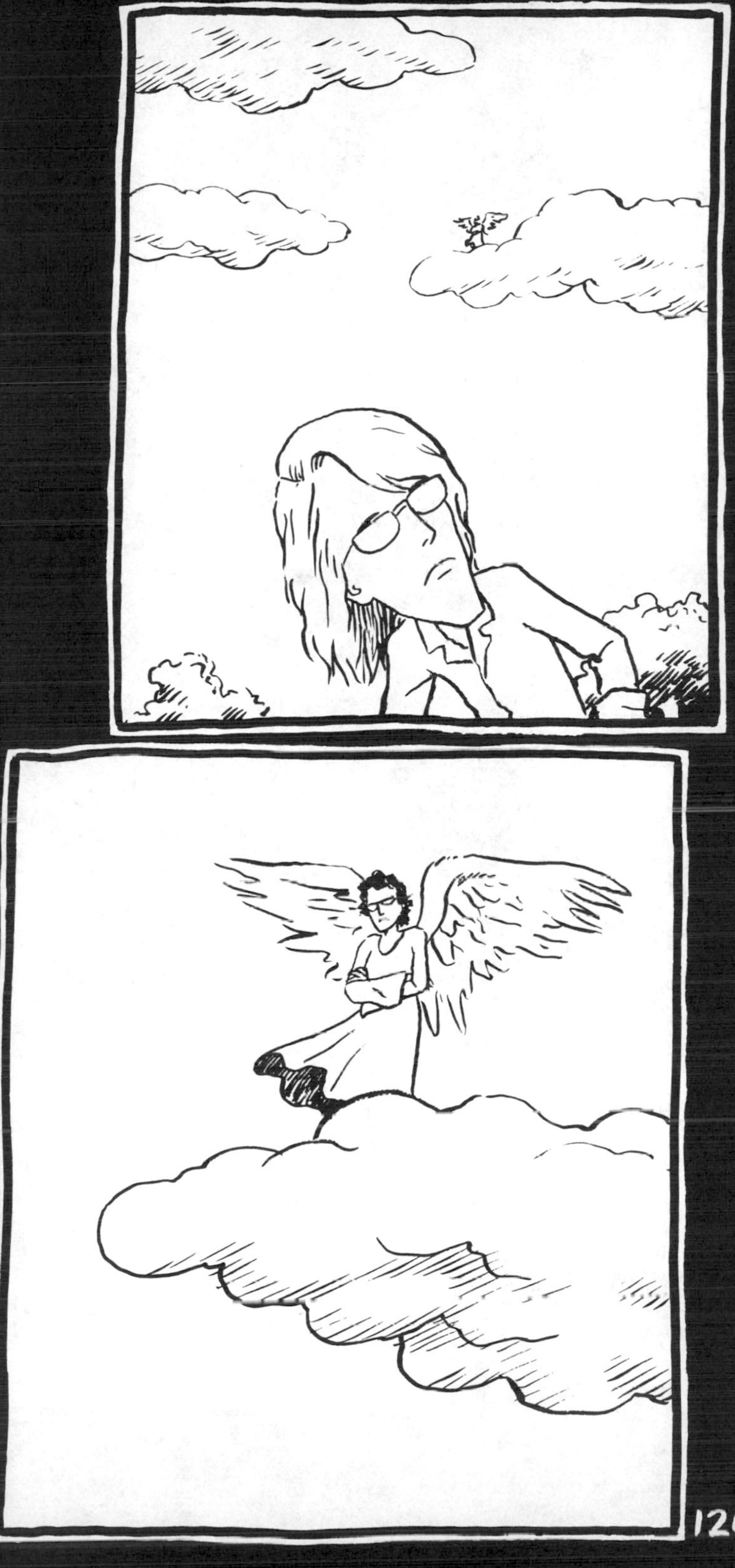

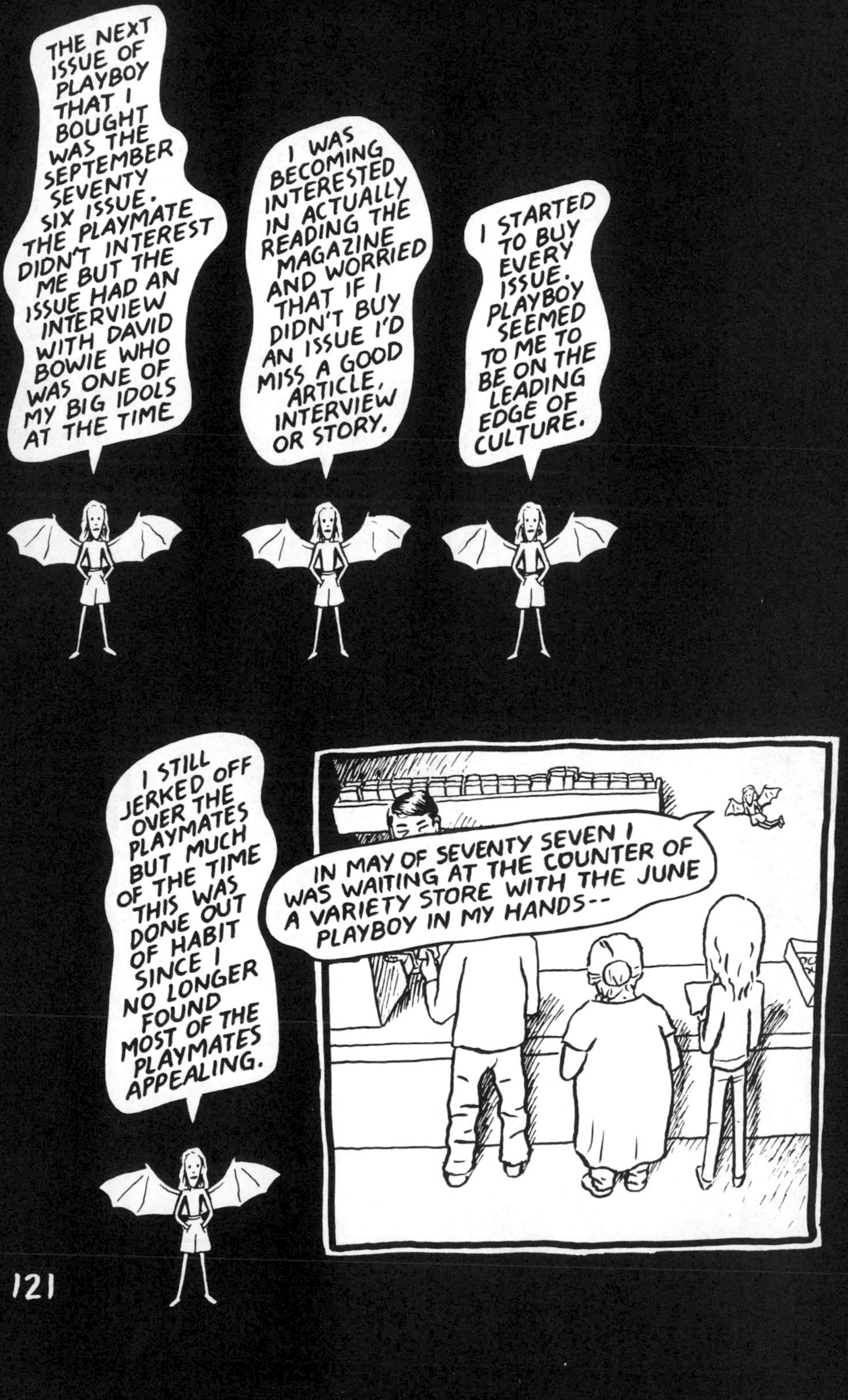
THE NEXT ISSUE OF PLAYBOY THAT I BOUGHT WAS THE SEPTEMBER SEVENTY SIX ISSUE. THE PLAYMATE DIDN'T INTEREST ME BUT THE ISSUE HAD AN INTERVIEW WITH DAVID BOWIE WHO WAS ONE OF MY BIG IDOLS AT THE TIME
I WAS BECOMING INTERESTED IN ACTUALLY READING THE MAGAZINE AND WORRIED THAT IF I DIDN'T BUY AN ISSUE I'D MISS A GOOD ARTICLE, INTERVIEW OR STORY.
I STARTED TO BUY EVERY ISSUE. PLAYBOY SEEMED TO ME TO BE ON THE LEADING EDGE OF CULTURE.
I STILL JERKED OFF OVER THE PLAYMATES BUT MUCH OF THE TIME THIS WAS DONE OUT OF HABIT SINCE I NO LONGER FOUND MOST OF THE PLAYMATES APPEALING.
IN MAY OF SEVENTY SEVEN I WAS WAITING AT THE COUNTER OF A VARIETY STORE WITH THE JUNE PLAYBOY IN MY HANDS--

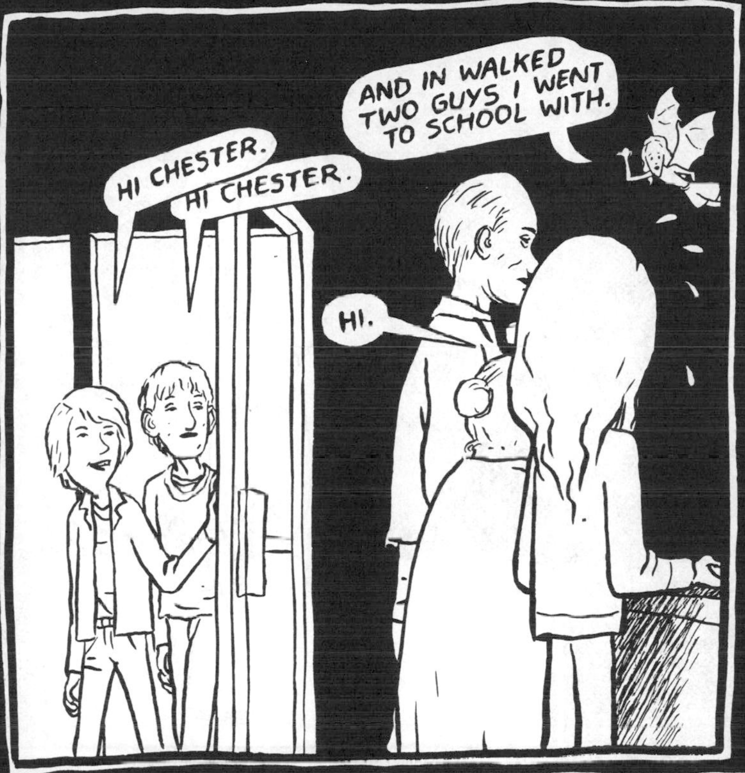
HI CHESTER.
HI CHESTER.
AND IN WALKED TWO GUYS I WENT TO SCHOOL WITH.
HI.

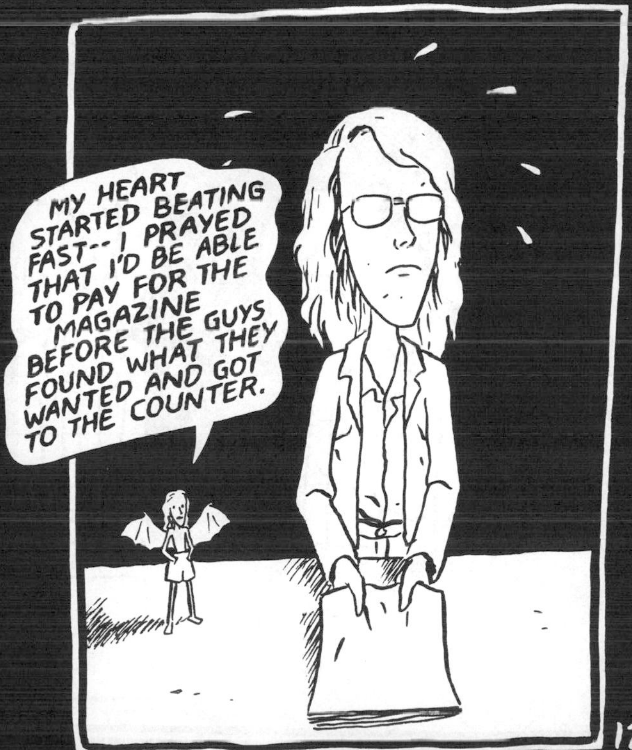
MY HEART STARTED BEATING FAST-- I PRAYED THAT I'D BE ABLE TO PAY FOR THE MAGAZINE BEFORE THE GUYS FOUND WHAT THEY WANTED AND GOT TO THE COUNTER.

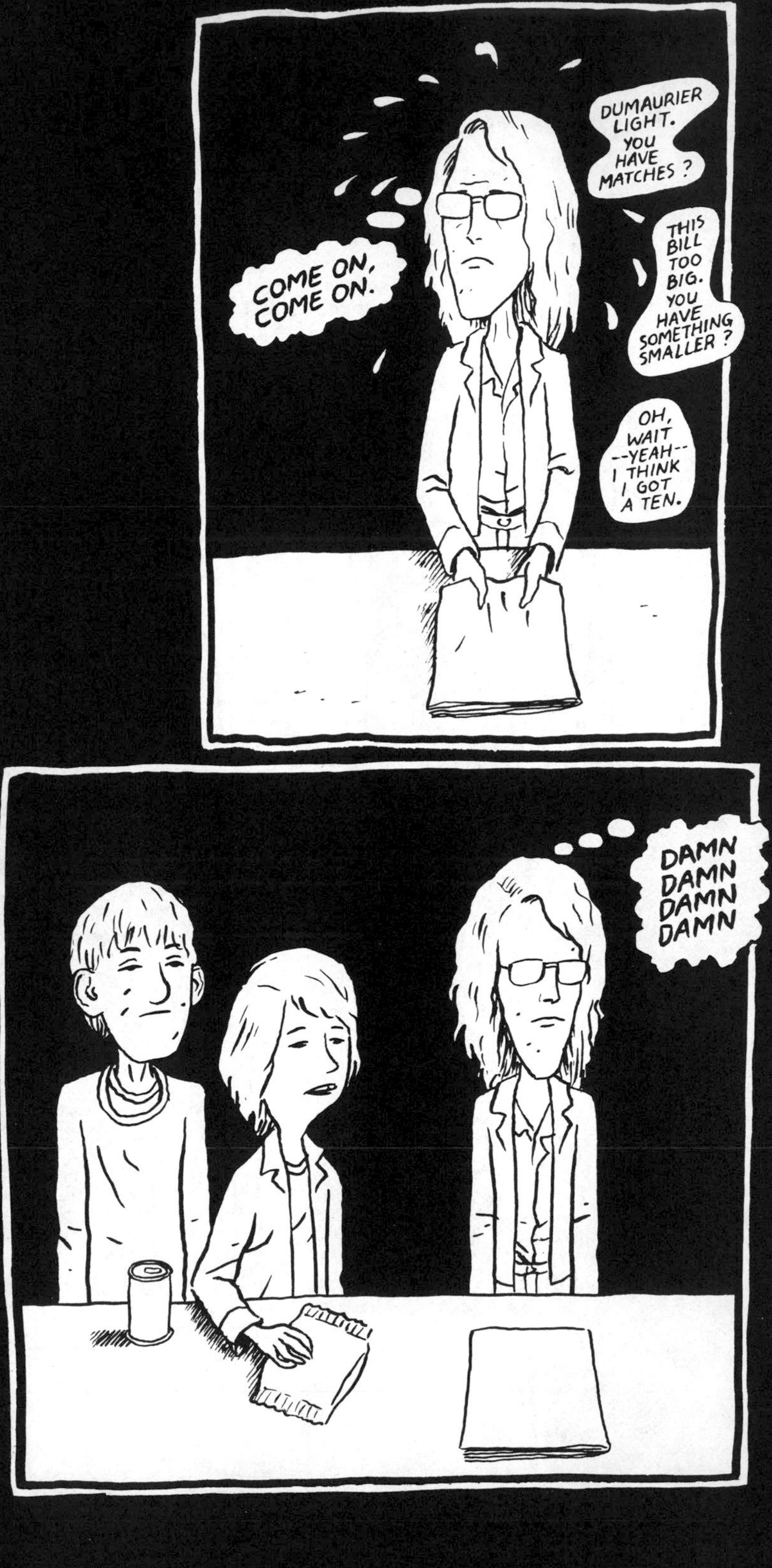
DUMAURIER LIGHT. YOU HAVE MATCHES ?
COME ON, COME ON.
THIS BILL TOO BIG. YOU HAVE SOMETHING SMALLER ?
OH, WAIT --YEAH-- I THINK I GOT A TEN.
DAMN DAMN DAMN DAMN

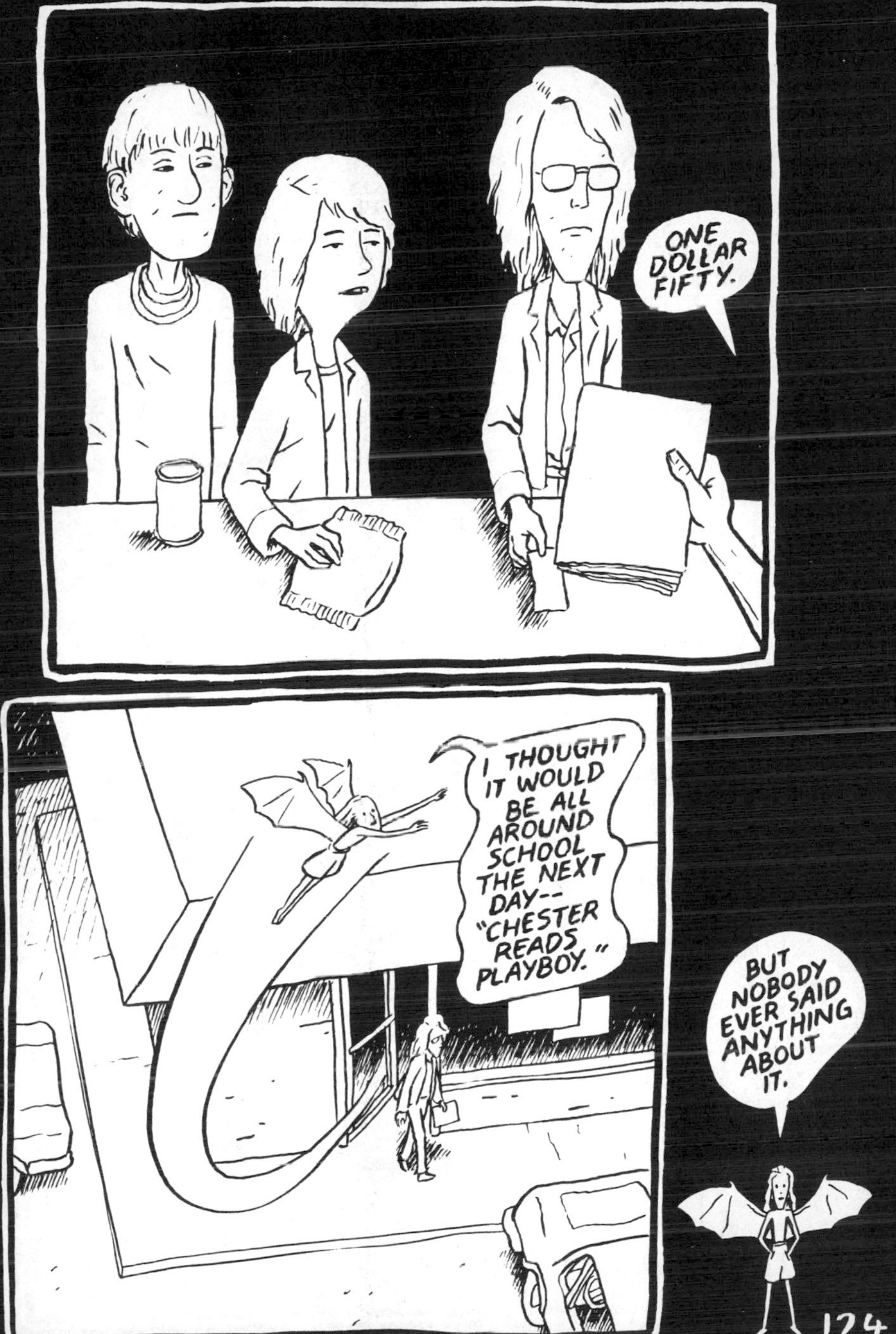
ONE DOLLAR FIFTY.
I THOUGHT IT WOULD BE ALL AROUND SCHOOL THE NEXT DAY-- "CHESTER READS PLAYBOY."
BUT NOBODY EVER SAID ANYTHING ABOUT IT.

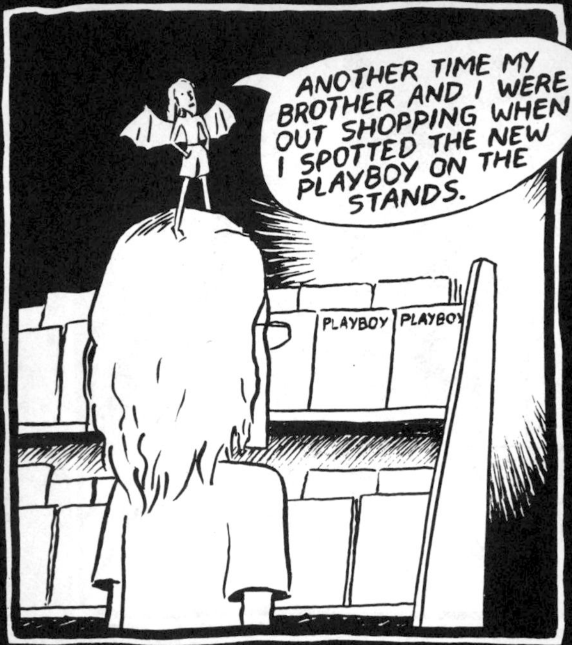
ANOTHER TIME MY BROTHER AND I WERE OUT SHOPPING WHEN I SPOTTED THE NEW PLAYBOY ON THE STANDS.
PLAYBOY
PLAYBOY

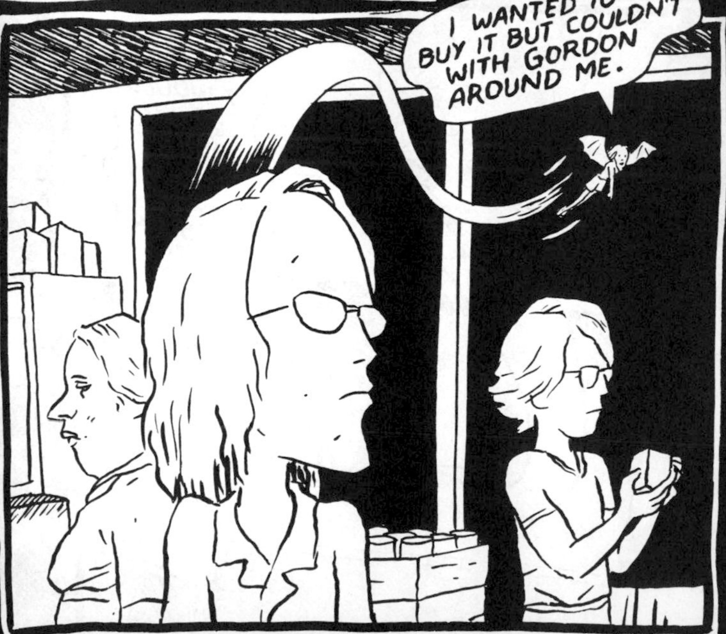
I WANTED TO BUY IT BUT COULDN'T WITH GORDON AROUND ME.

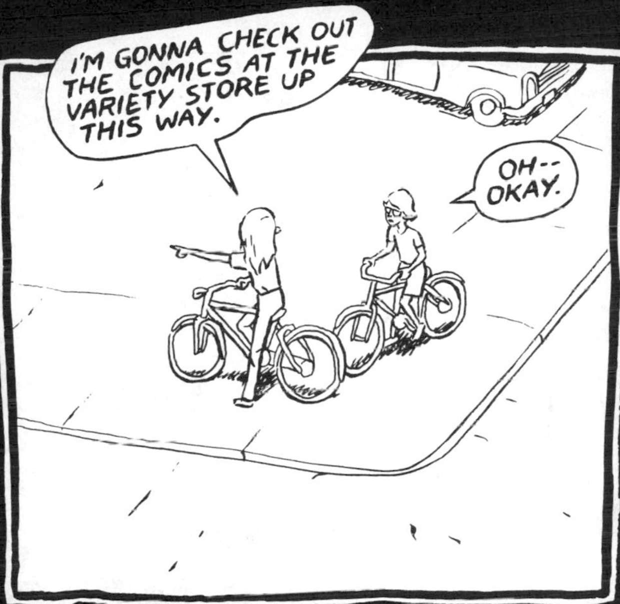
I'M GONNA CHECK OUT THE COMICS AT THE VARIETY STORE UP THIS WAY.
OH-- OKAY.

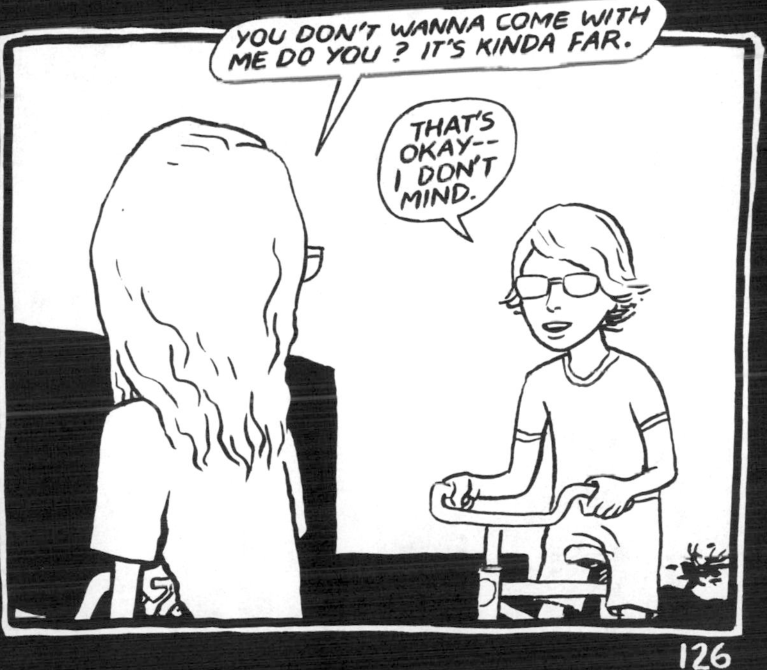
YOU DON'T WANNA COME WITH ME DO YOU ? IT'S KINDA FAR.
THAT'S OKAY-- I DON'T MIND.

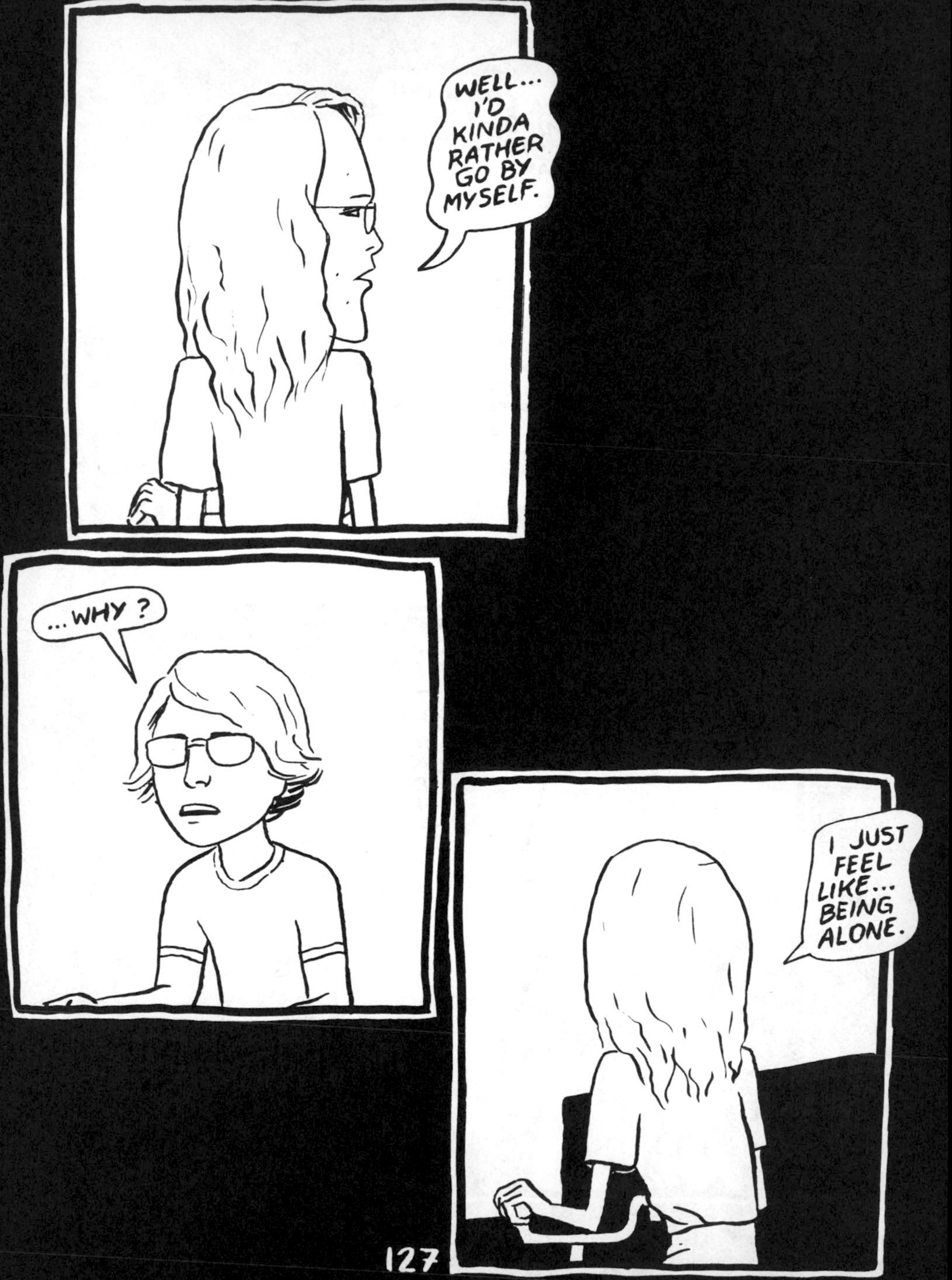
WELL... I'D KINDA RATHER GO BY MYSELF.
...WHY ?
I JUST FEEL LIKE... BEING ALONE.

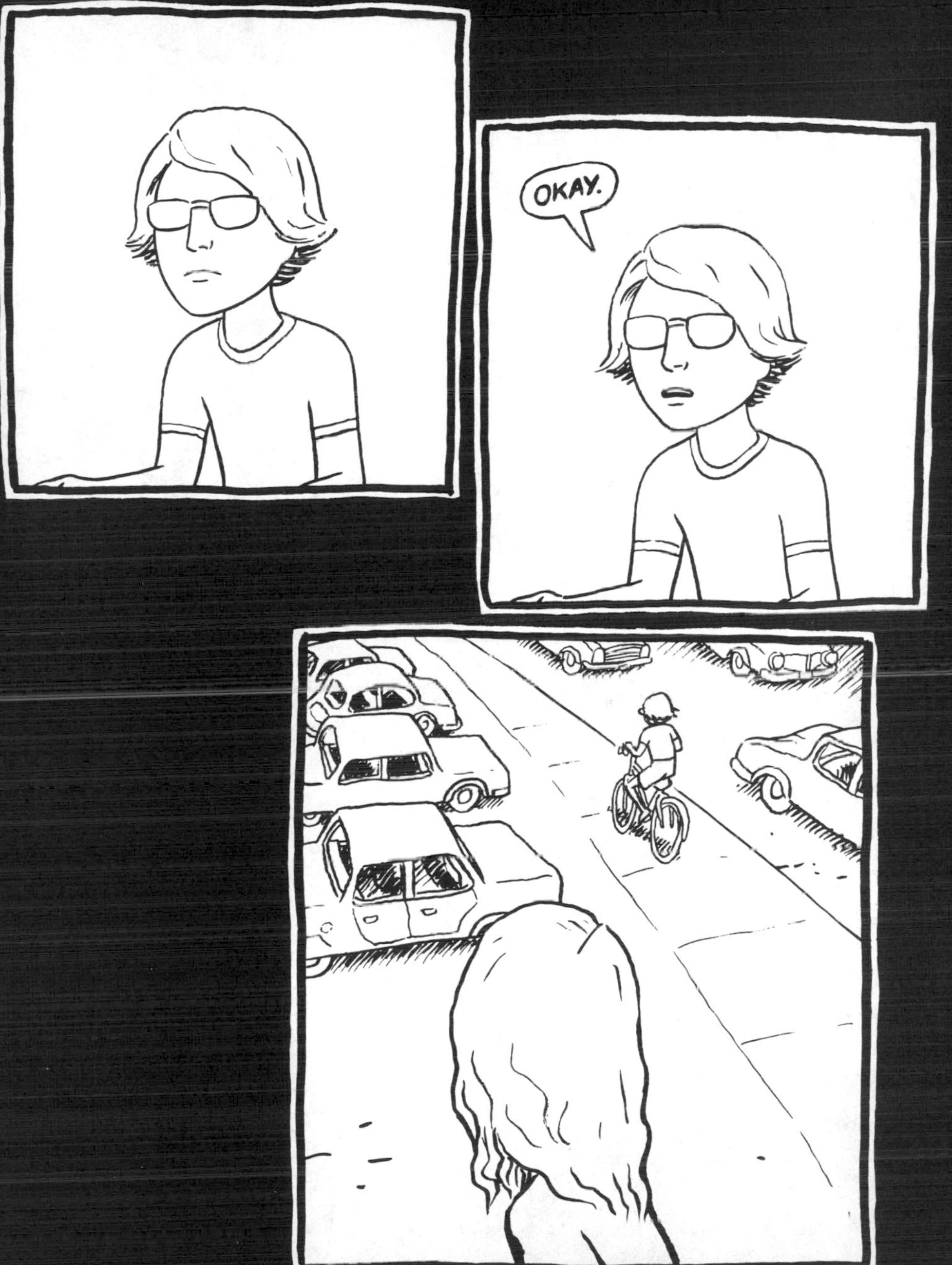
OKAY.

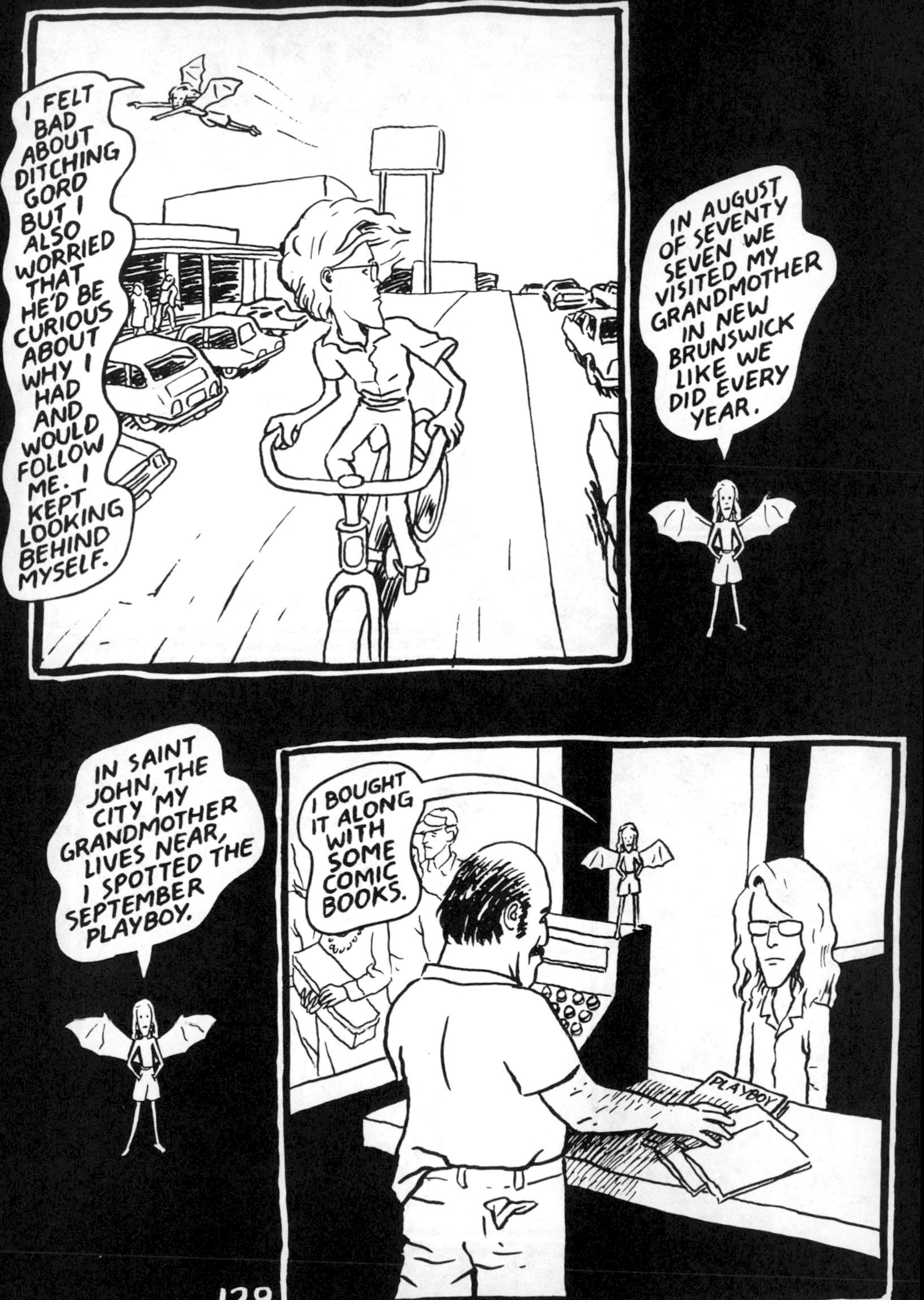
I FELT BAD ABOUT DITCHING GORD BUT I ALSO WORRIED THAT HE'D BE CURIOUS ABOUT WHY I HAD AND WOULD FOLLOW ME. I KEPT LOOKING BEHIND MYSELF.
IN AUGUST OF SEVENTY SEVEN WE VISITED MY GRANDMOTHER IN NEW BRUNSWICK LIKE WE DID EVERY YEAR.
IN SAINT JOHN, THE CITY MY GRANDMOTHER LIVES NEAR, I SPOTTED THE SEPTEMBER PLAYBOY.
I BOUGHT IT ALONG WITH SOME COMIC BOOKS.
PLAYBOY

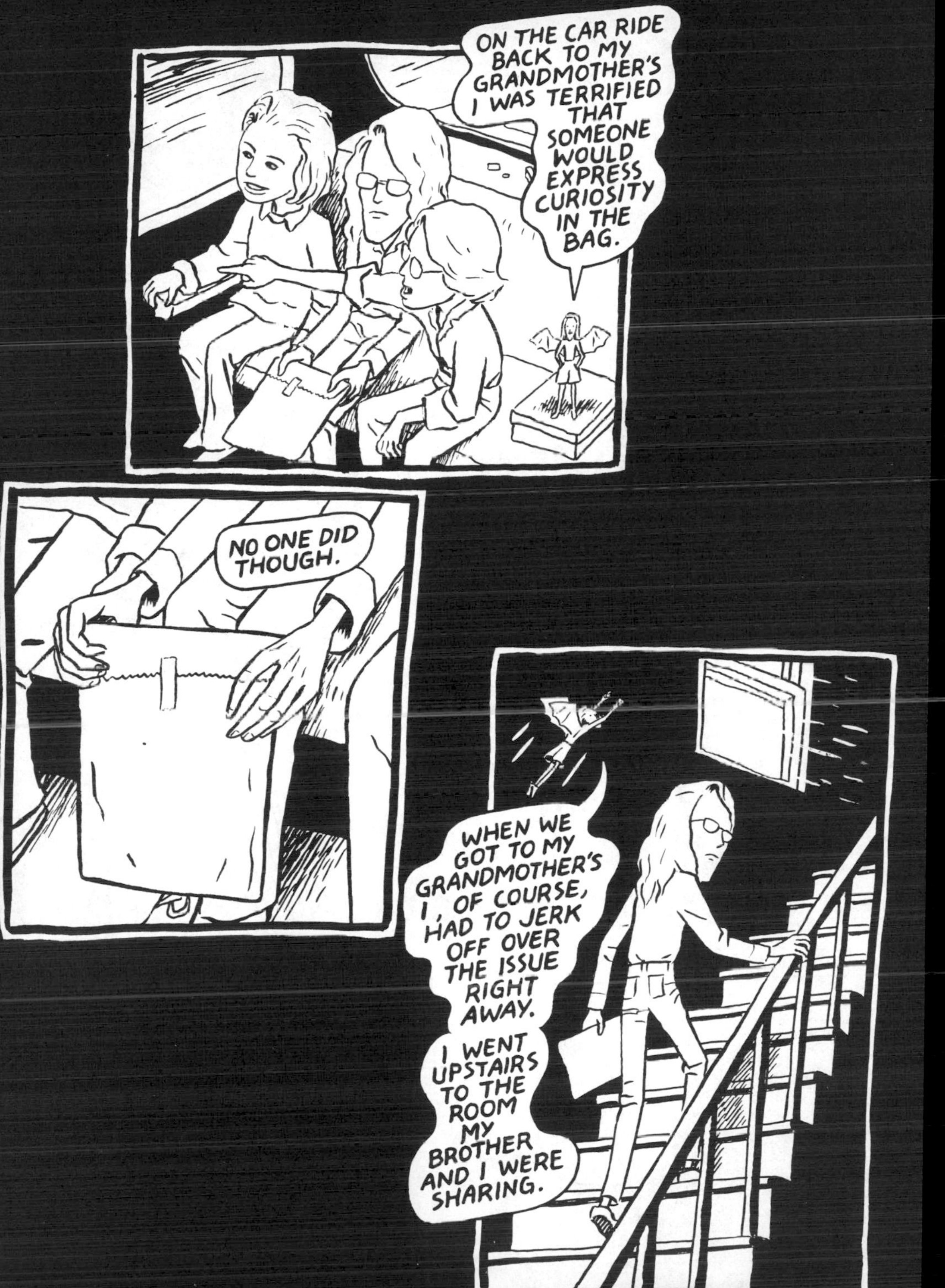
ON THE CAR RIDE BACK TO MY GRANDMOTHER'S I WAS TERRIFIED THAT SOMEONE WOULD EXPRESS CURIOSITY IN THE BAG.
NO ONE DID THOUGH.
WHEN WE GOT TO MY GRANDMOTHER'S I, OF COURSE, HAD TO JERK OFF OVER THE ISSUE RIGHT AWAY.
I WENT UPSTAIRS TO THE ROOM MY BROTHER AND I WERE SHARING.

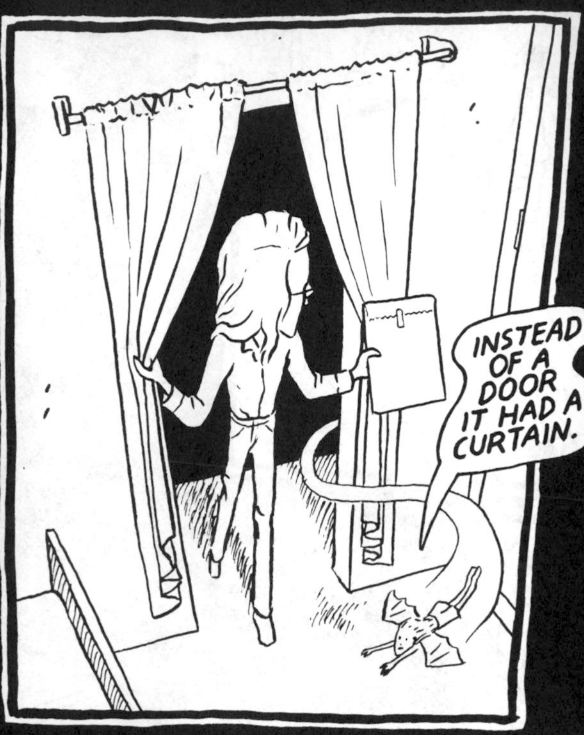
INSTEAD OF A DOOR IT HAD A CURTAIN.

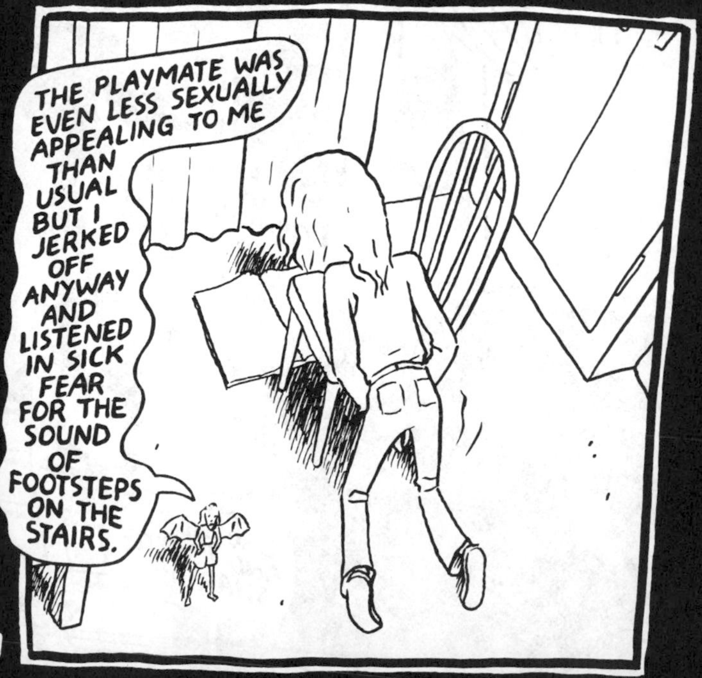
THE PLAYMATE WAS EVEN LESS SEXUALLY APPEALING TO ME THAN USUAL BUT I JERKED OFF ANYWAY AND LISTENED IN SICK FEAR FOR THE SOUND OF FOOTSTEPS ON THE STAIRS.

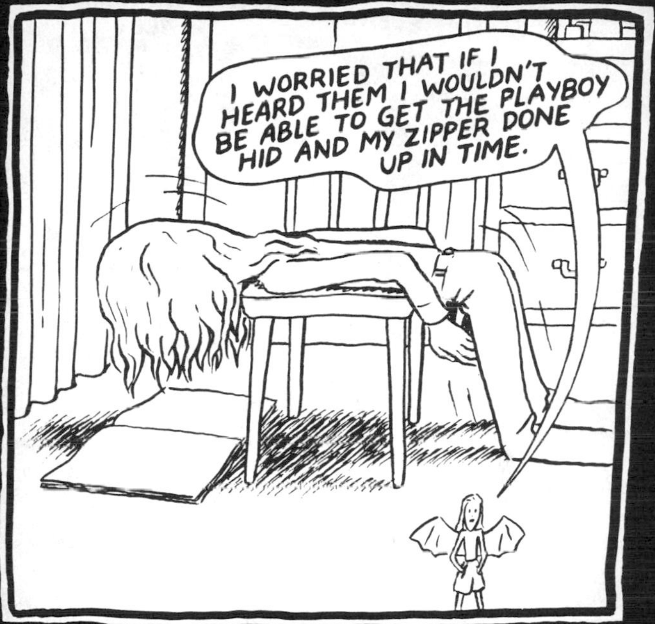
I WORRIED THAT IF I HEARD THEM I WOULDN'T BE ABLE TO GET THE PLAYBOY HID AND MY ZIPPER DONE UP IN TIME.

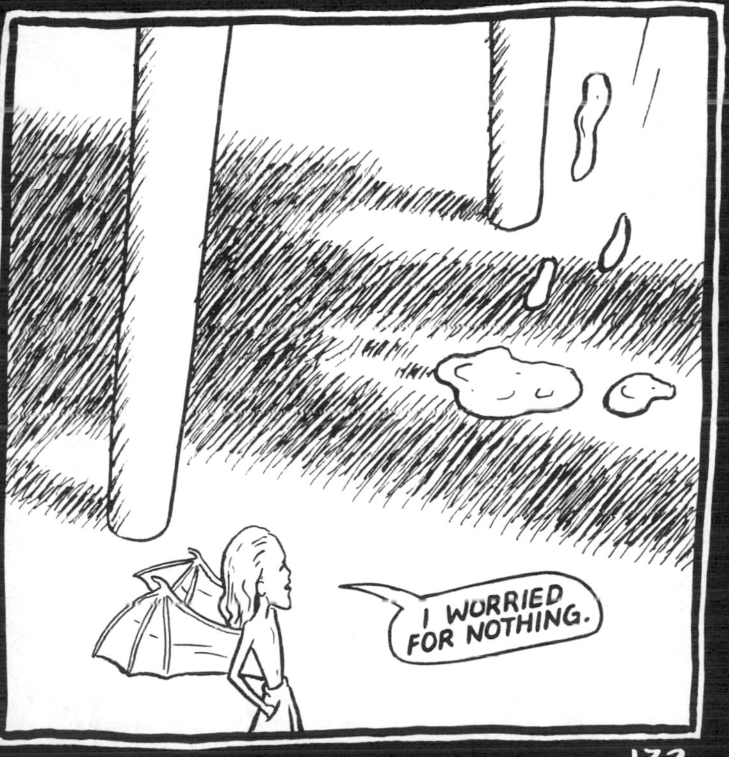
I WORRIED FOR NOTHING.

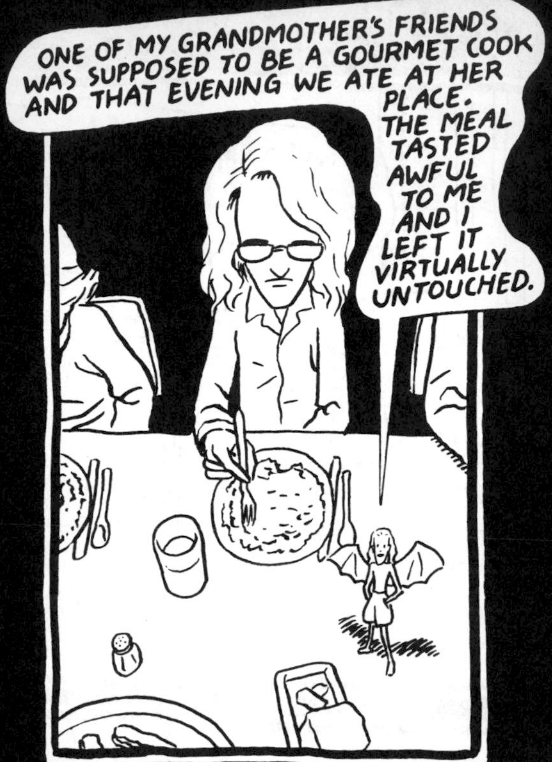
ONE OF MY GRANDMOTHER'S FRIENDS WAS SUPPOSED TO BE A GOURMET COOK AND THAT EVENING WE ATE AT HER PLACE. THE MEAL TASTED AWFUL TO ME AND I LEFT IT VIRTUALLY UNTOUCHED.

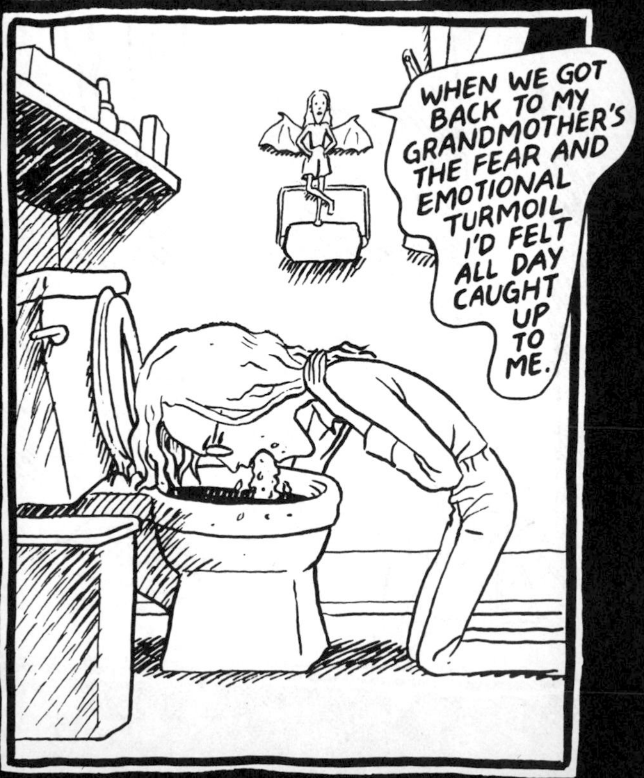
WHEN WE GOT BACK TO MY GRANDMOTHER'S THE FEAR AND EMOTIONAL TURMOIL I'D FELT ALL DAY CAUGHT UP TO ME.

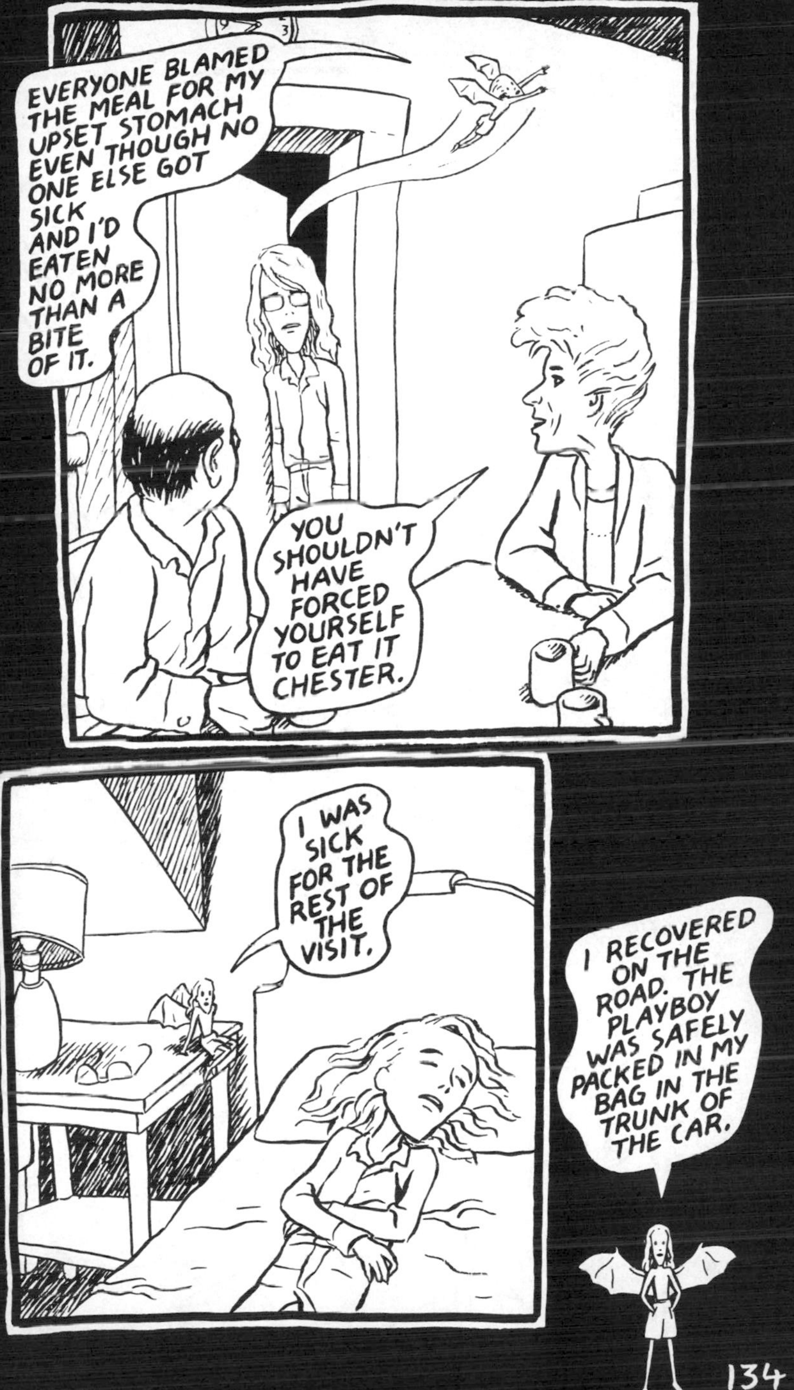
EVERYONE BLAMED THE MEAL FOR MY UPSET STOMACH EVEN THOUGH NO ONE ELSE GOT SICK AND I'D EATEN NO MORE THAN A BITE OF IT.
YOU SHOULDN'T HAVE FORCED YOURSELF TO EAT IT CHESTER.
I WAS SICK FOR THE REST OF THE VISIT.
I RECOVERED ON THE ROAD. THE PLAYBOY WAS SAFELY PACKED IN MY BAG IN THE TRUNK OF THE CAR.

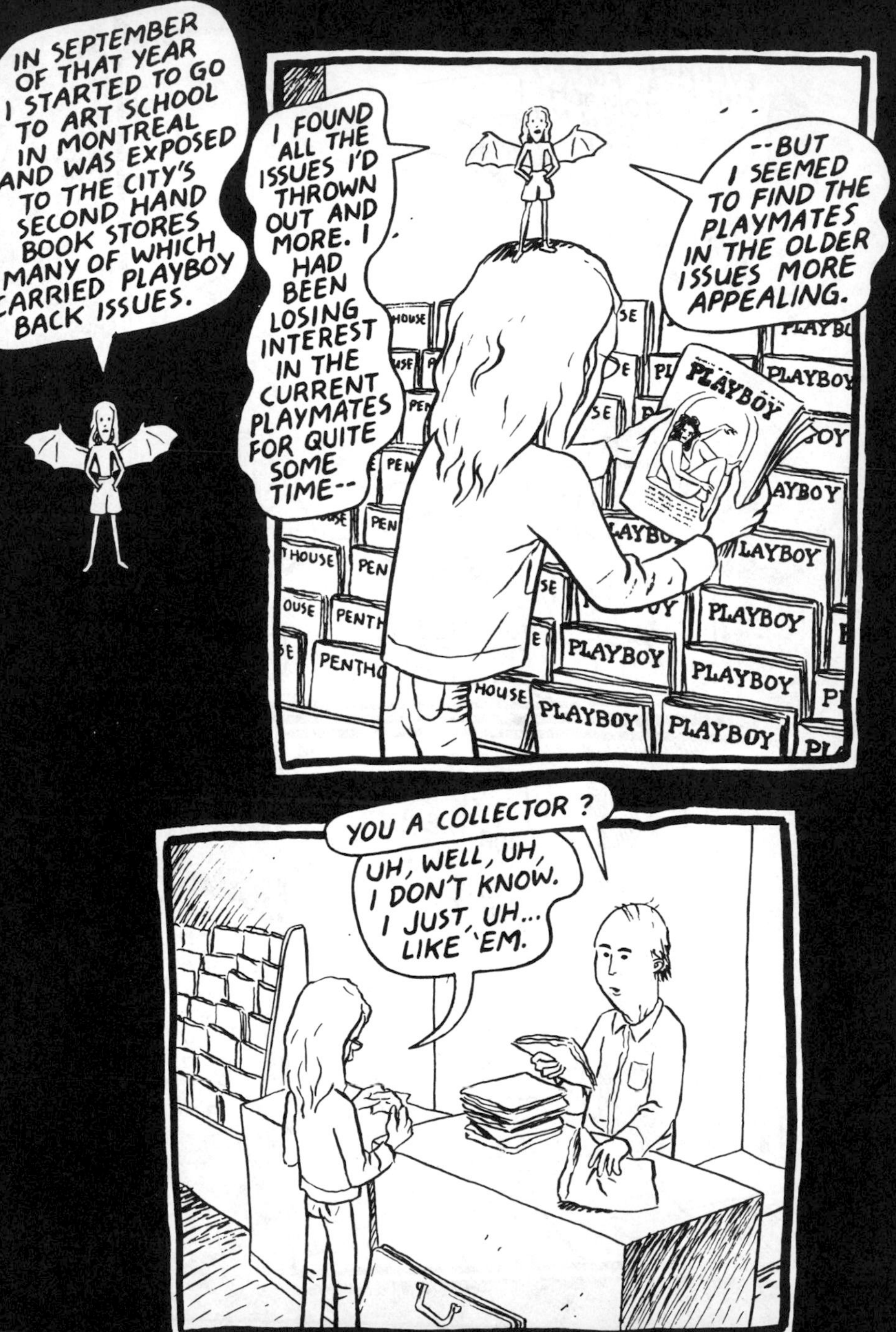
IN SEPTEMBER OF THAT YEAR I STARTED TO GO TO ART SCHOOL IN MONTREAL AND WAS EXPOSED TO THE CITY'S SECOND HAND BOOK STORES MANY OF WHICH CARRIED PLAYBOY BACK ISSUES.
I FOUND ALL THE ISSUES I'D THROWN OUT AND MORE. I HAD BEEN LOSING INTEREST IN THE CURRENT PLAYMATES FOR QUITE SOME TIME--
--BUT I SEEMED TO FIND THE PLAYMATES IN THE OLDER ISSUES MORE APPEALING.
PLAYBOY
PENTHOUSE
YOU A COLLECTOR ?
UH, WELL, UH, I DON'T KNOW. I JUST, UH... LIKE 'EM.

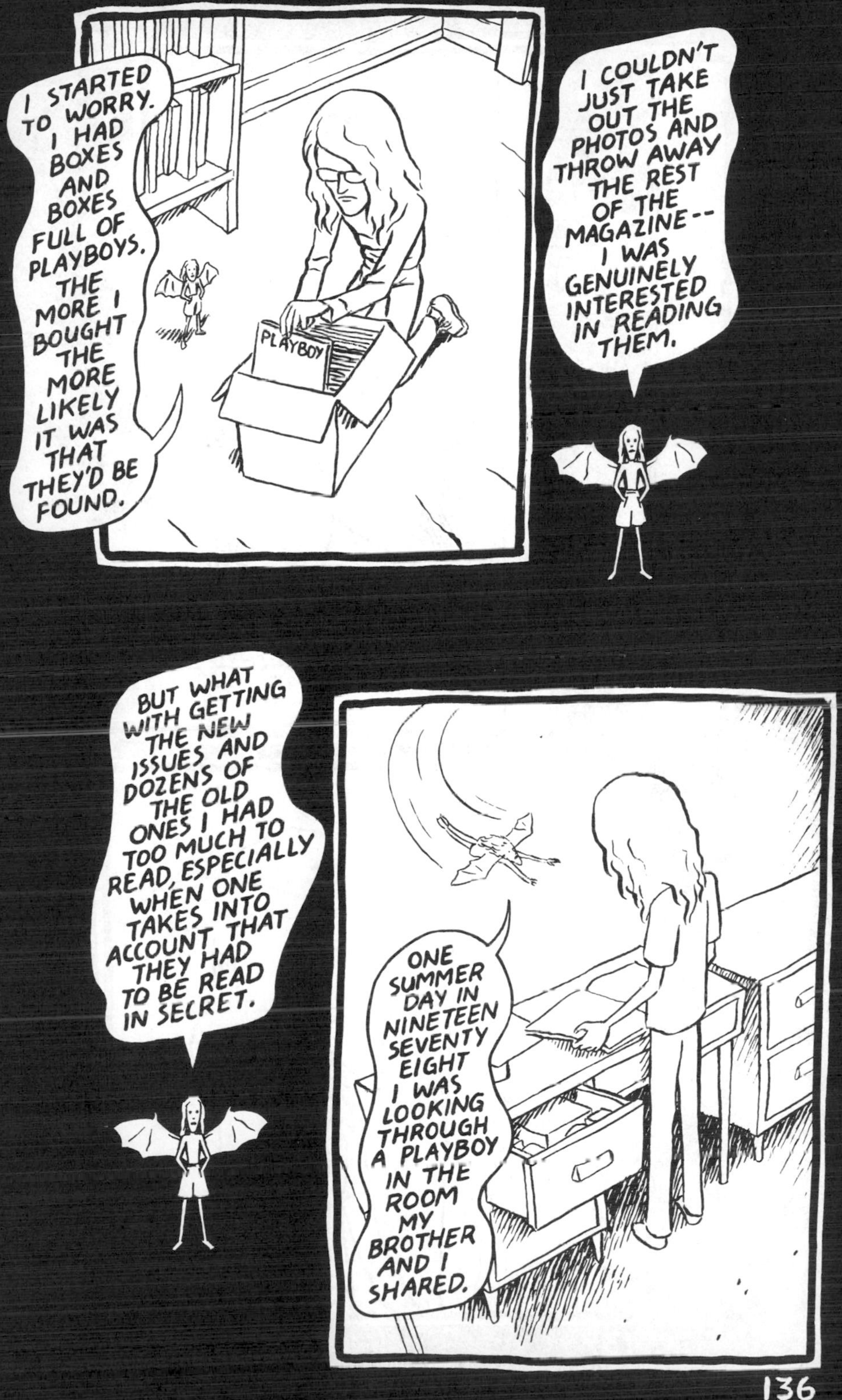

I STARTED TO WORRY. I HAD BOXES AND BOXES FULL OF PLAYBOYS. THE MORE I BOUGHT THE MORE LIKELY IT WAS THAT THEY'D BE FOUND.
PLAYBOY
I COULDN'T JUST TAKE OUT THE PHOTOS AND THROW AWAY THE REST OF THE MAGAZINE-- I WAS GENUINELY INTERESTED IN READING THEM.
BUT WHAT WITH GETTING THE NEW ISSUES AND DOZENS OF THE OLD ONES I HAD TOO MUCH TO READ, ESPECIALLY WHEN ONE TAKES INTO ACCOUNT THAT THEY HAD TO BE READ IN SECRET.
ONE SUMMER DAY IN NINETEEN SEVENTY EIGHT I WAS LOOKING THROUGH A PLAYBOY IN THE ROOM MY BROTHER AND I SHARED.

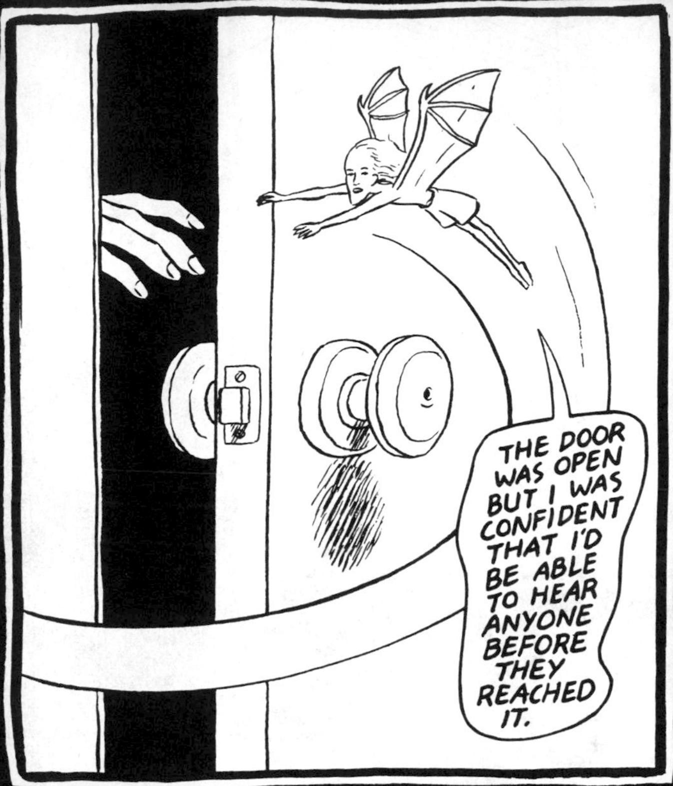
THE DOOR WAS OPEN BUT I WAS CONFIDENT THAT I'D BE ABLE TO HEAR ANYONE BEFORE THEY REACHED IT.

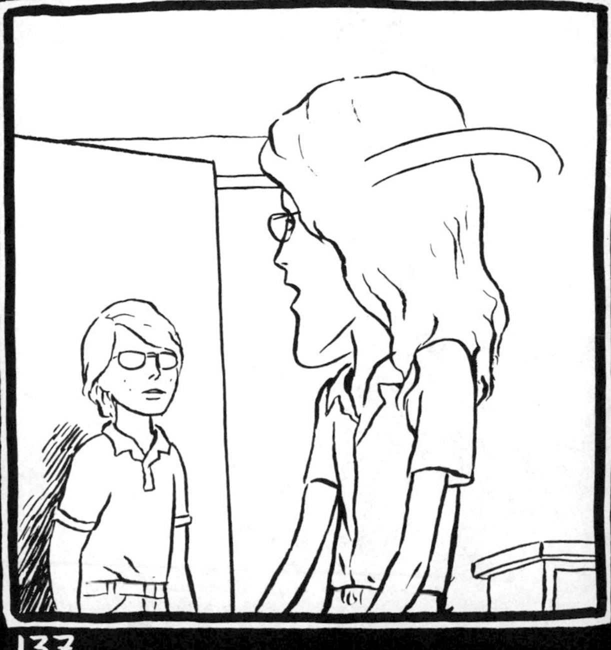

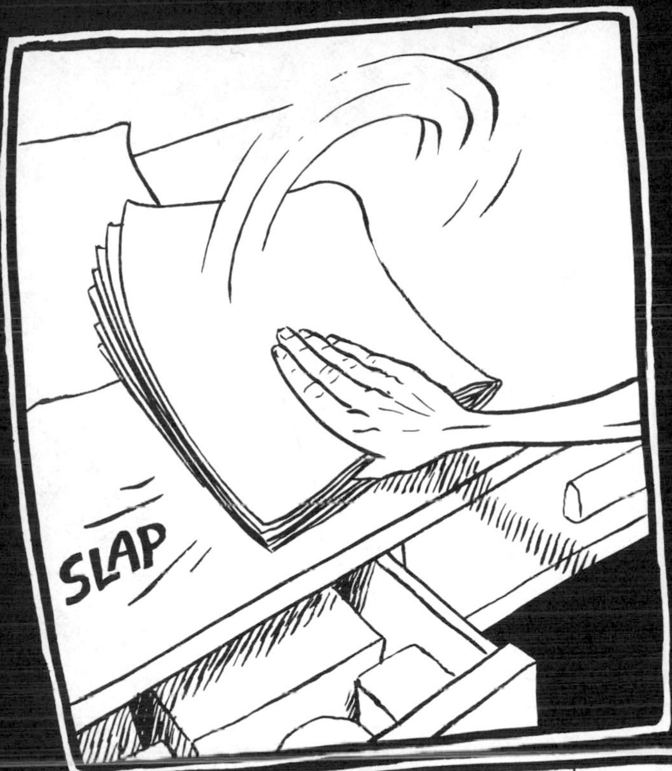
SLAP
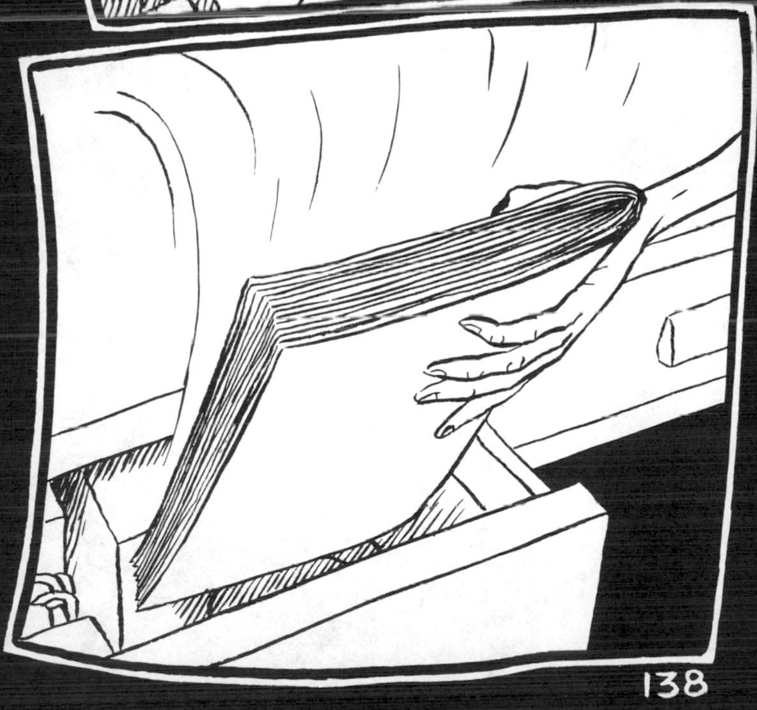

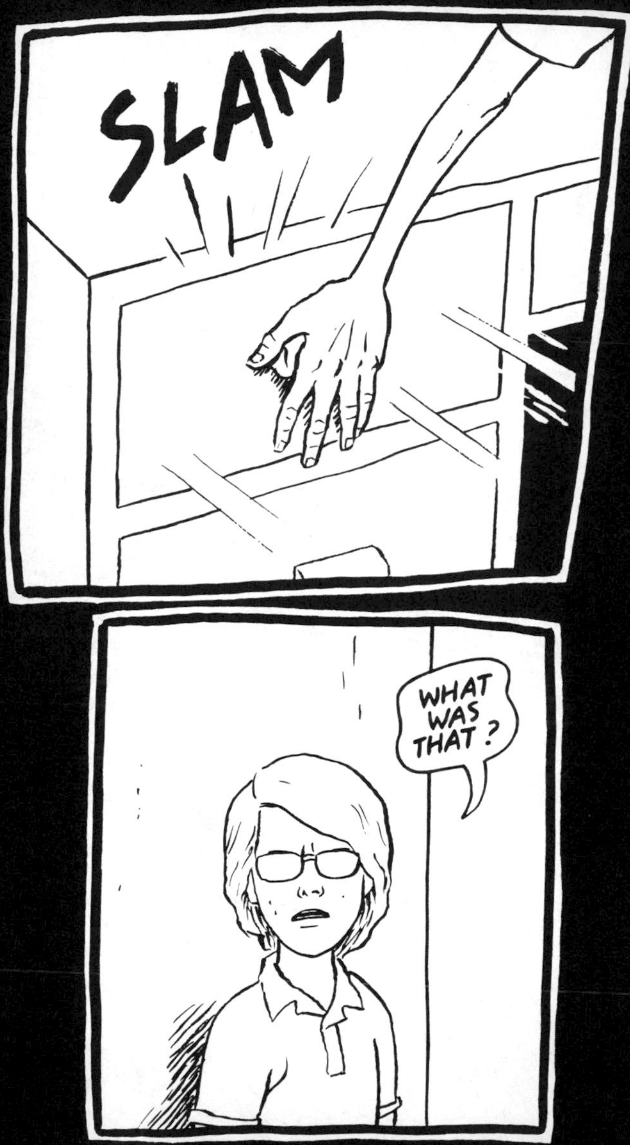
SLAM
WHAT WAS THAT?

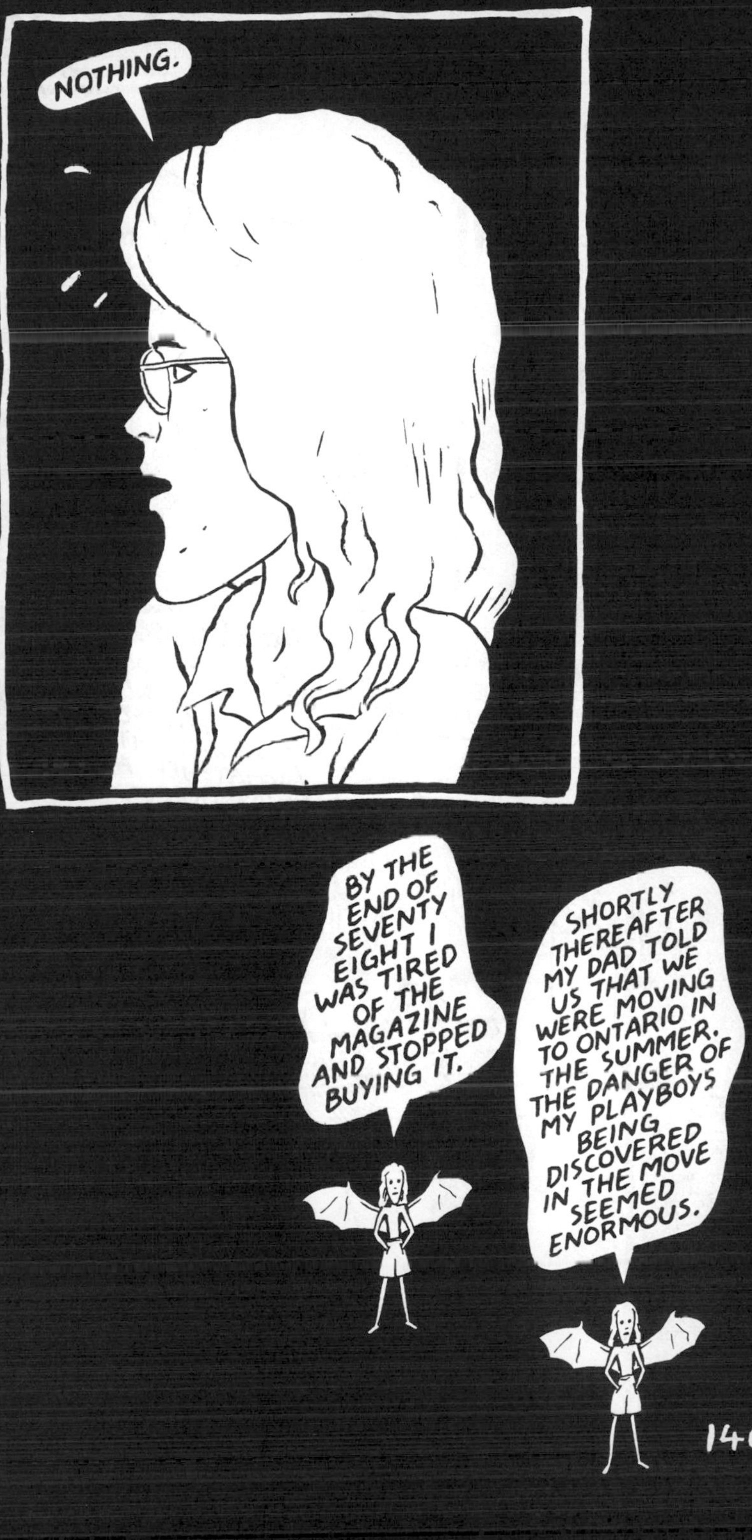
NOTHING.
BY THE END OF SEVENTY EIGHT I WAS TIRED OF THE MAGAZINE AND STOPPED BUYING IT.
SHORTLY THEREAFTER MY DAD TOLD US THAT WE WERE MOVING TO ONTARIO IN THE SUMMER. THE DANGER OF MY PLAYBOYS BEING DISCOVERED IN THE MOVE SEEMED ENORMOUS.

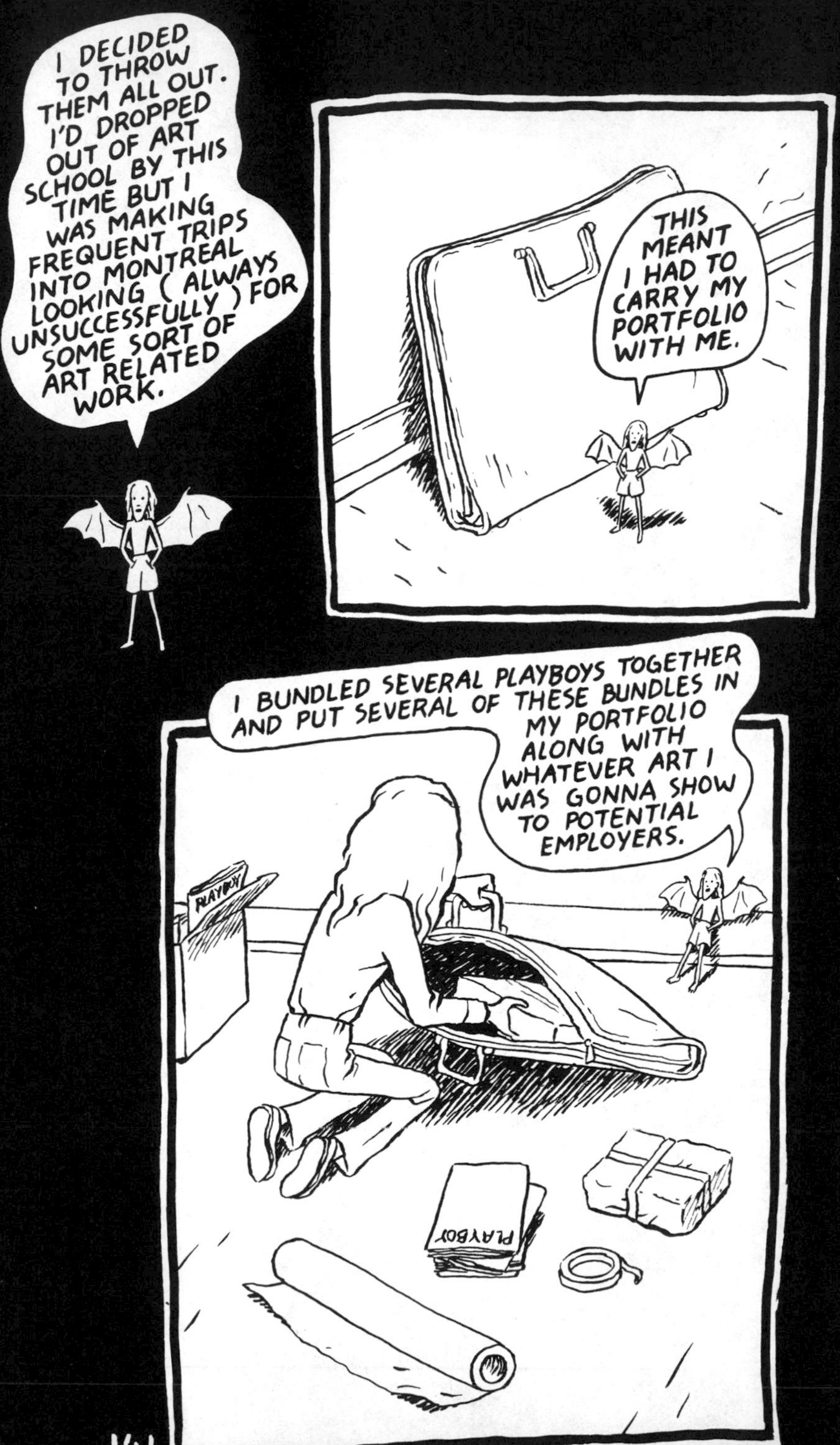
I DECIDED TO THROW THEM ALL OUT. I'D DROPPED OUT OF ART SCHOOL BY THIS TIME BUT I WAS MAKING FREQUENT TRIPS INTO MONTREAL LOOKING (ALWAYS UNSUCCESSFULLY) FOR SOME SORT OF ART RELATED WORK.
THIS MEANT I HAD TO CARRY MY PORTFOLIO WITH ME.
I BUNDLED SEVERAL PLAYBOYS TOGETHER AND PUT SEVERAL OF THESE BUNDLES IN MY PORTFOLIO ALONG WITH WHATEVER ART I WAS GONNA SHOW TO POTENTIAL EMPLOYERS.
PLAYBOY
PLAYBOY

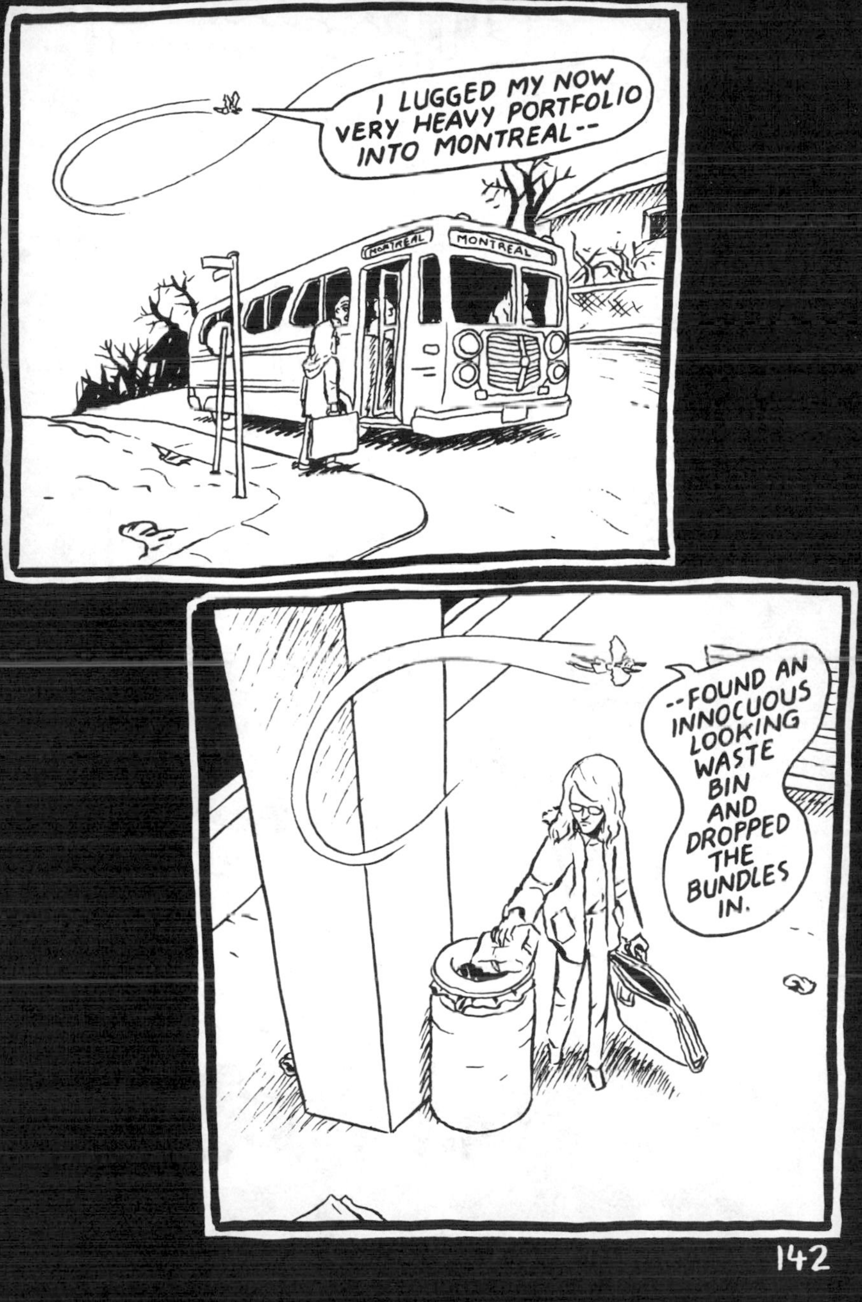
I LUGGED MY NOW VERY HEAVY PORTFOLIO INTO MONTREAL--
MONTREAL
MONTREAL
--FOUND AN INNOCUOUS LOOKING WASTE BIN AND DROPPED THE BUNDLES IN.

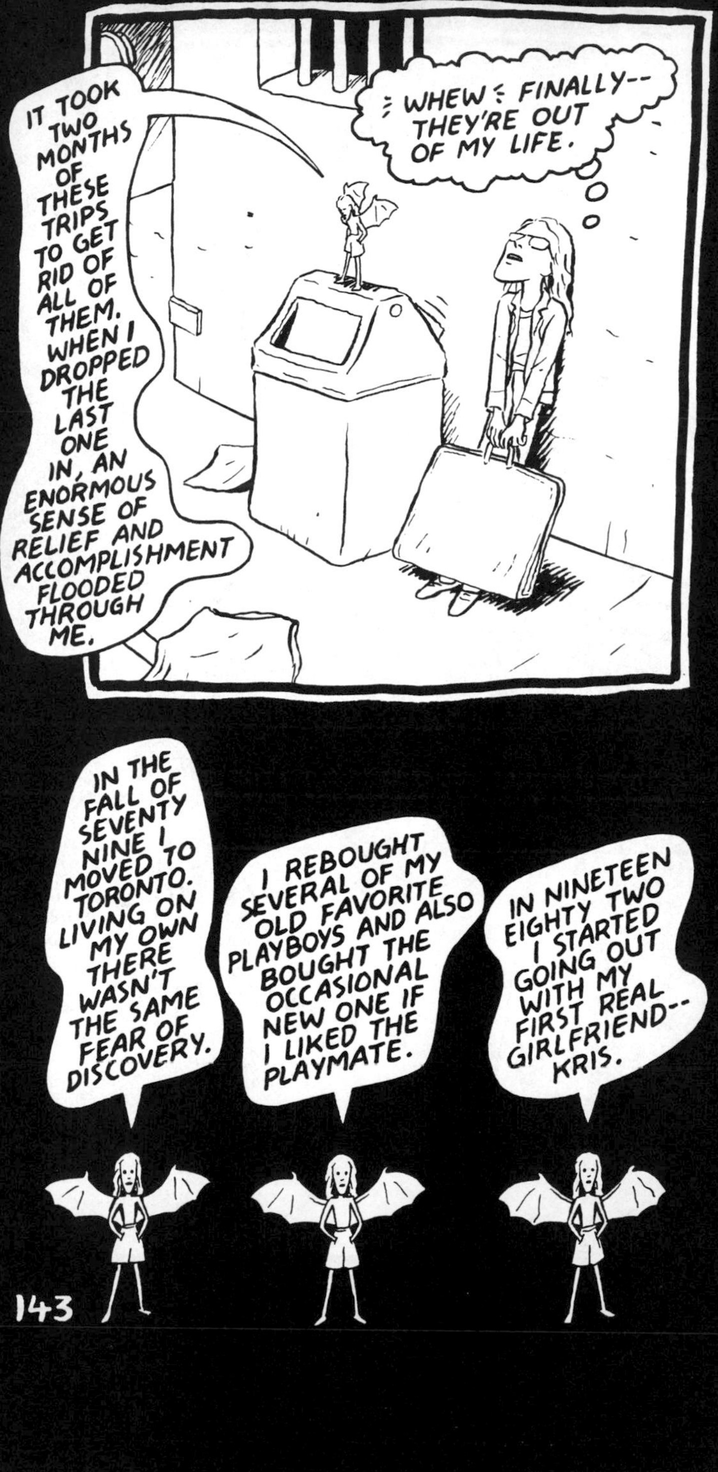
IT TOOK TWO MONTHS OF THESE TRIPS TO GET RID OF ALL OF THEM. WHEN I DROPPED THE LAST ONE IN, AN ENORMOUS SENSE OF RELIEF AND ACCOMPLISHMENT FLOODED THROUGH ME.
WHEW: FINALLY-- THEY'RE OUT OF MY LIFE.
IN THE FALL OF SEVENTY NINE I MOVED TO TORONTO. LIVING ON MY OWN THERE WASN'T THE SAME FEAR OF DISCOVERY.
I REBOUGHT SEVERAL OF MY OLD FAVORITE PLAYBOYS AND ALSO BOUGHT THE OCCASIONAL NEW ONE IF I LIKED THE PLAYMATE.
IN NINETEEN EIGHTY TWO I STARTED GOING OUT WITH MY FIRST REAL GIRLFRIEND-- KRIS.

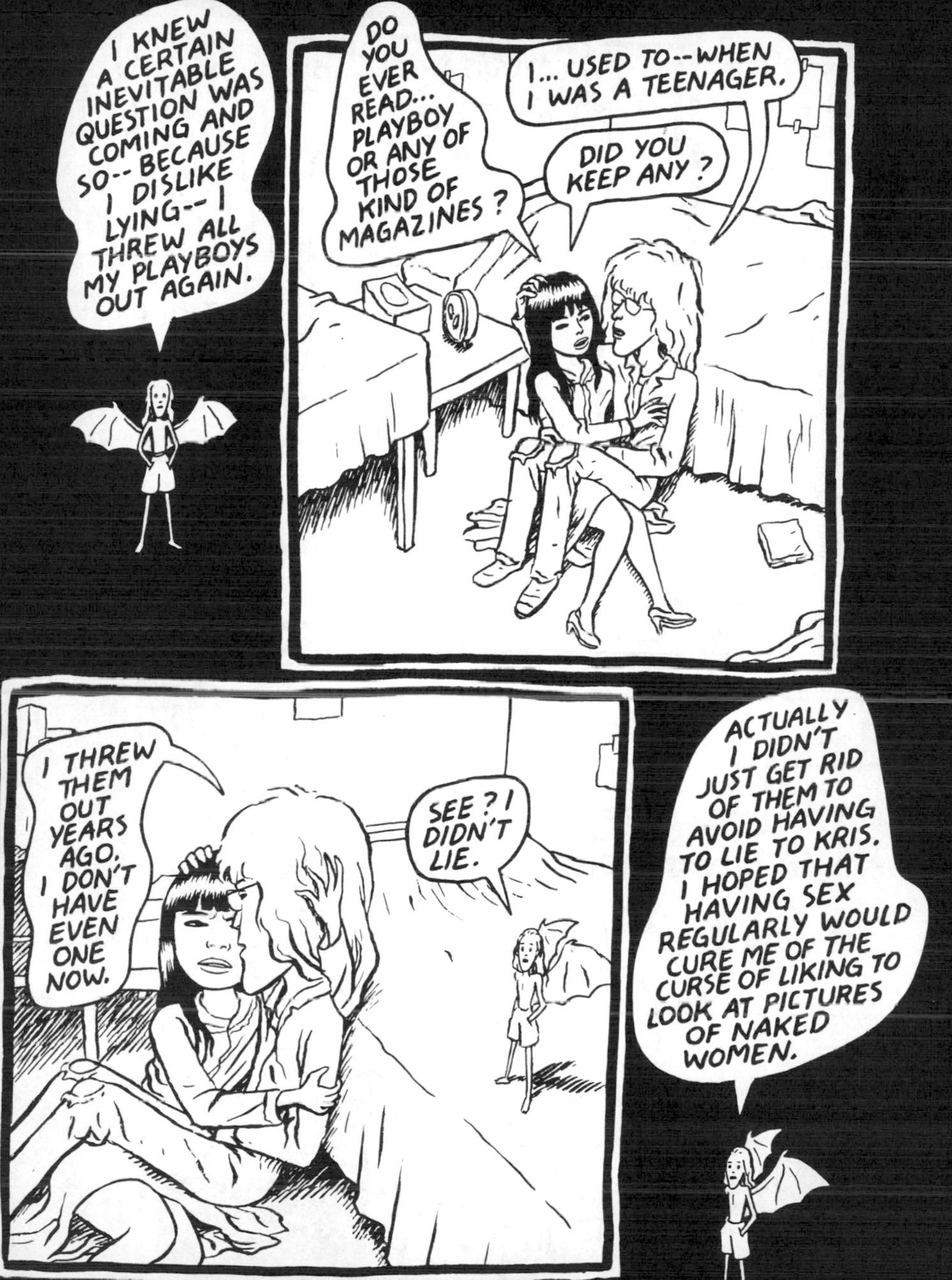
I KNEW A CERTAIN INEVITABLE QUESTION WAS COMING AND SO-- BECAUSE I DISLIKE LYING-- I THREW ALL MY PLAYBOYS OUT AGAIN.
DO YOU EVER READ... PLAYBOY OR ANY OF THOSE KIND OF MAGAZINES ?
I... USED TO--WHEN I WAS A TEENAGER.
DID YOU KEEP ANY ?
I THREW THEM OUT YEARS AGO. I DON'T HAVE EVEN ONE NOW.
SEE ? I DIDN'T LIE.
ACTUALLY I DIDN'T JUST GET RID OF THEM TO AVOID HAVING TO LIE TO KRIS. I HOPED THAT HAVING SEX REGULARLY WOULD CURE ME OF THE CURSE OF LIKING TO LOOK AT PICTURES OF NAKED WOMEN.

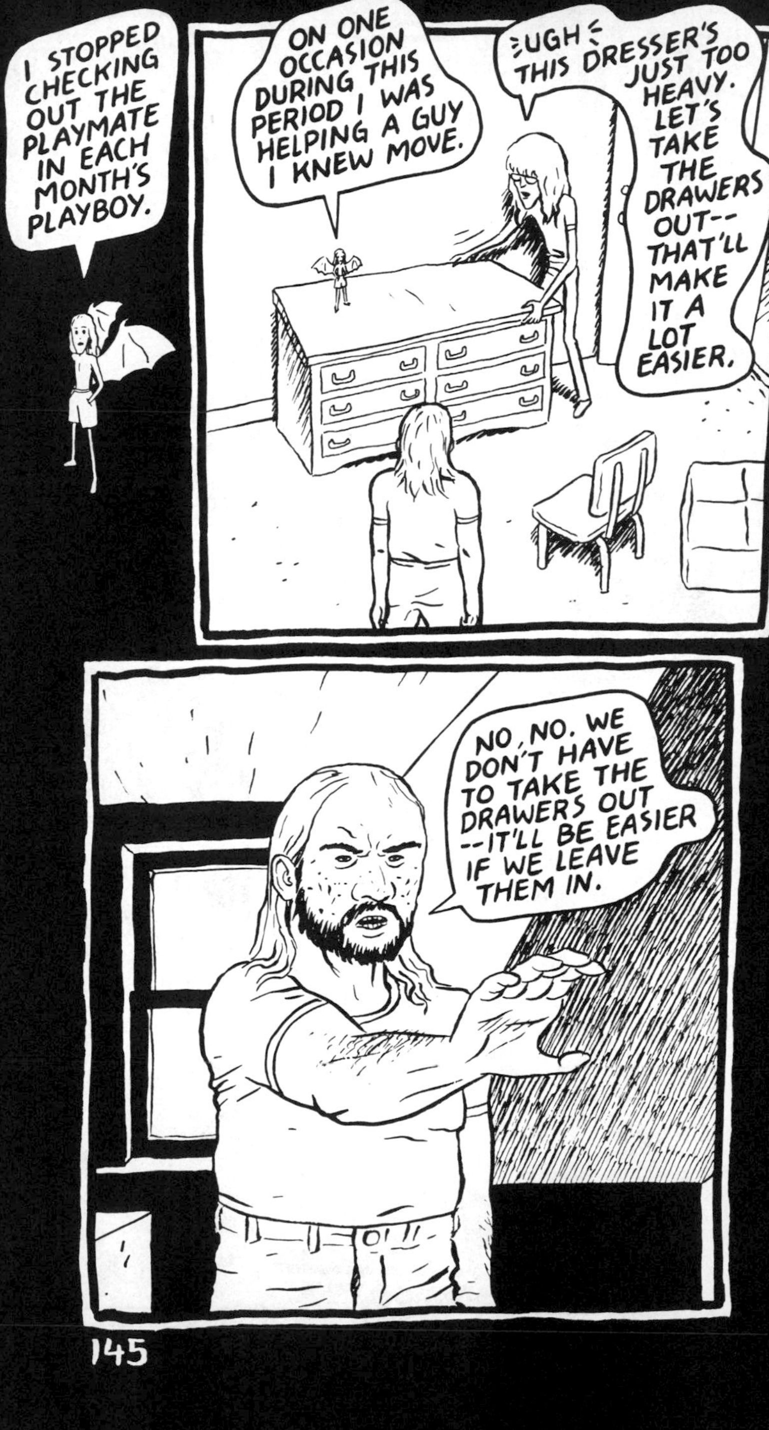
I STOPPED CHECKING OUT THE PLAYMATE IN EACH MONTH'S PLAYBOY.
ON ONE OCCASION DURING THIS PERIOD I WAS HELPING A GUY I KNEW MOVE.
UGH THIS DRESSER'S JUST TOO HEAVY. LET'S TAKE THE DRAWERS OUT-- THAT'LL MAKE IT A LOT EASIER.
NO, NO. WE DON'T HAVE TO TAKE THE DRAWERS OUT --IT'LL BE EASIER IF WE LEAVE THEM IN.

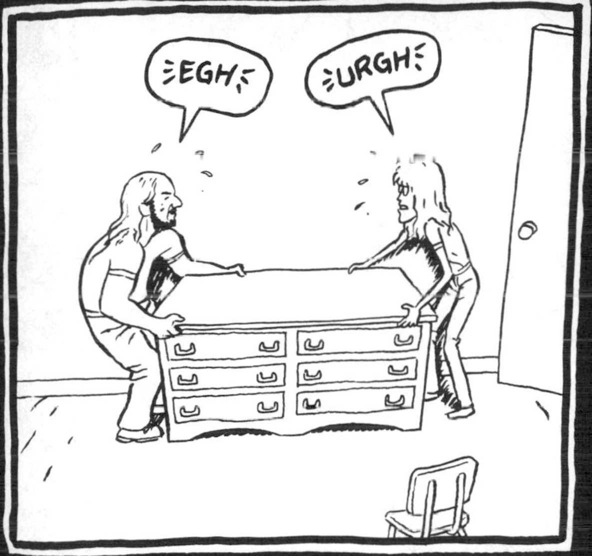
EGH
URGH

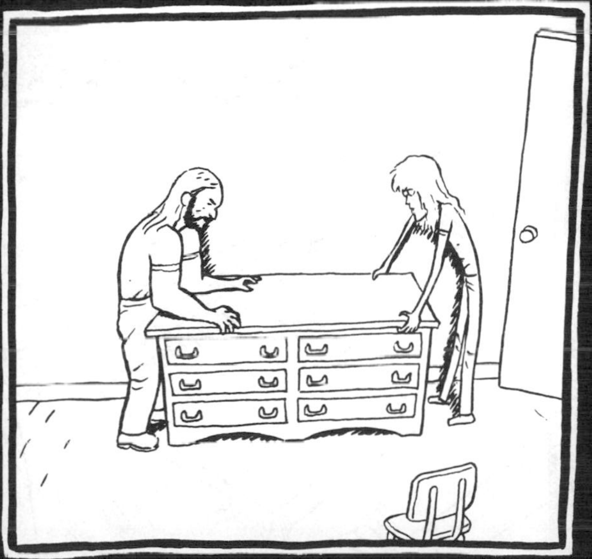

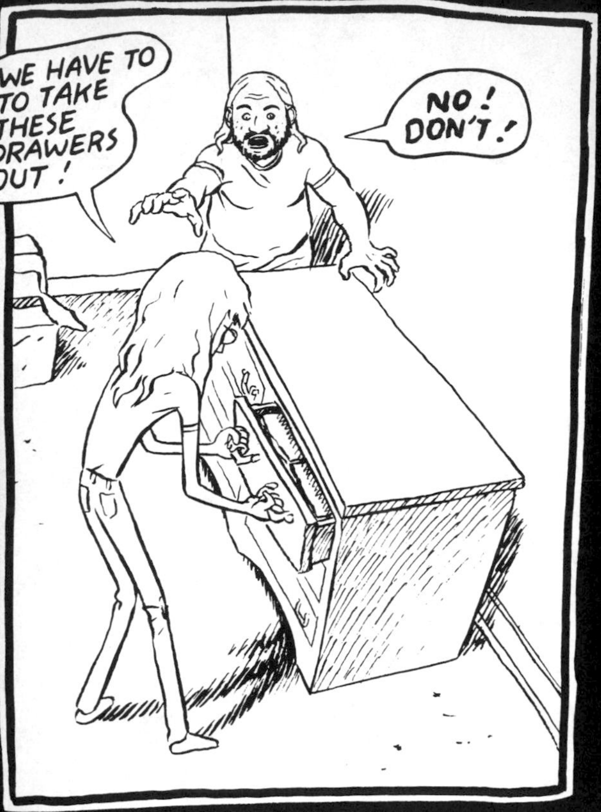
WE HAVE TO TO TAKE THESE DRAWERS OUT!
NO! DON'T!

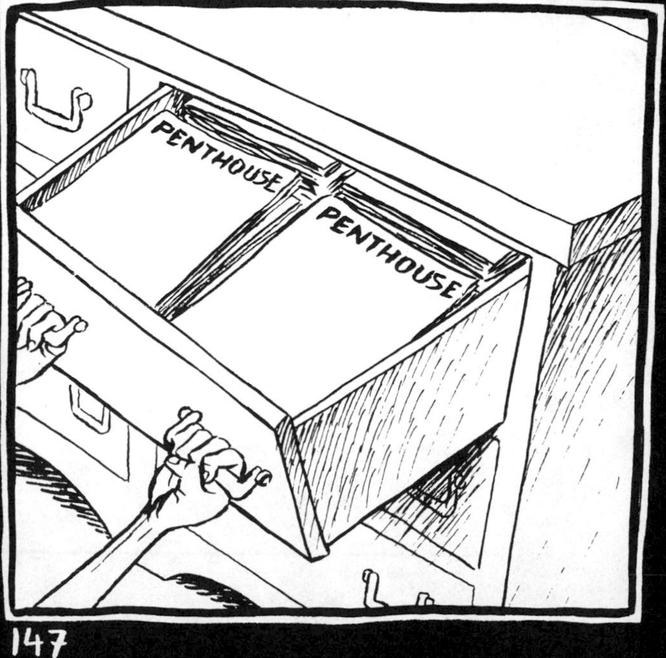
PENTHOUSE
PENTHOUSE

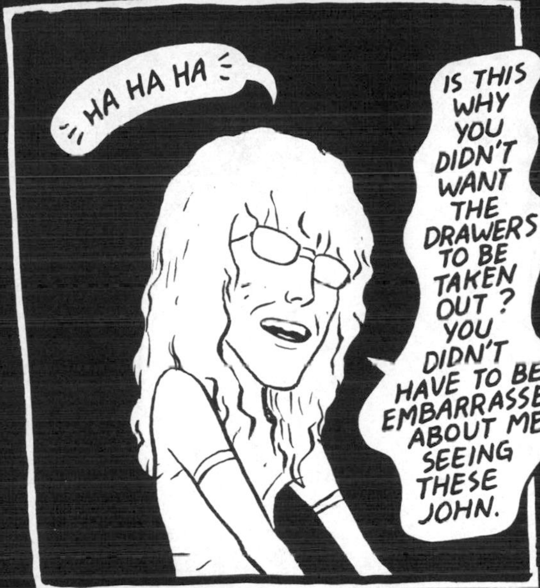
HA HA HA
IS THIS WHY YOU DIDN'T WANT THE DRAWERS TO BE TAKEN OUT? YOU DIDN'T HAVE TO BE EMBARRASSED ABOUT ME SEEING THESE JOHN.

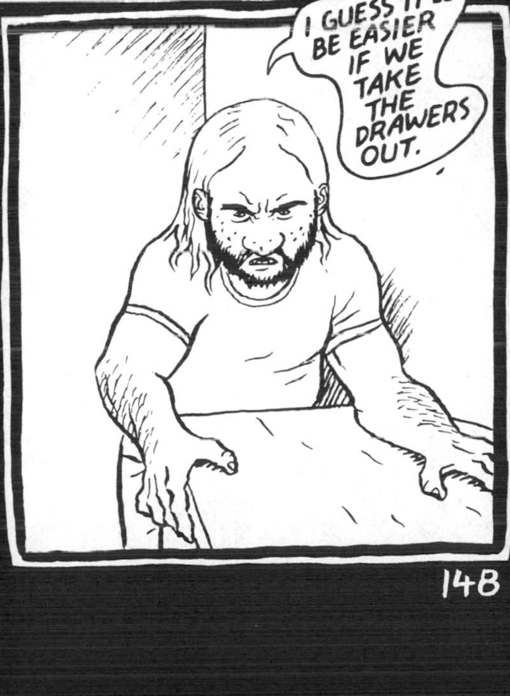
I GUESS IT'LL BE EASIER IF WE TAKE THE DRAWERS OUT.

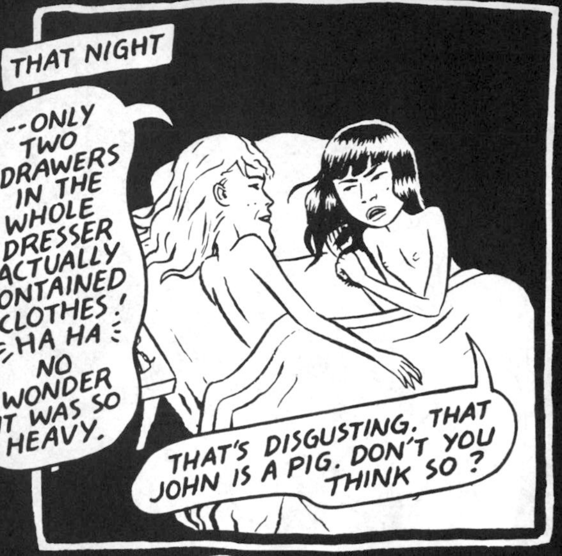
THAT NIGHT
--ONLY TWO DRAWERS IN THE WHOLE DRESSER ACTUALLY CONTAINED CLOTHES! HA HA NO WONDER IT WAS SO HEAVY.
THAT'S DISGUSTING. THAT JOHN IS A PIG. DON'T YOU THINK SO?

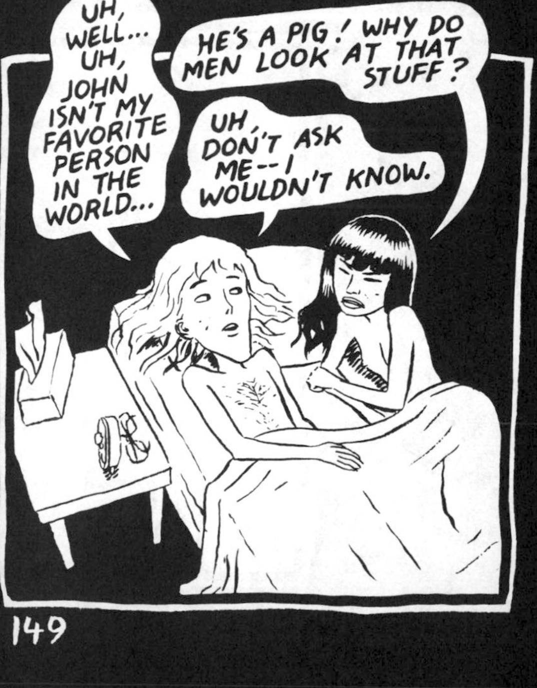
UH, WELL... UH, JOHN ISN'T MY FAVORITE PERSON IN THE WORLD...
HE'S A PIG! WHY DO MEN LOOK AT THAT STUFF?
UH, DON'T ASK ME--I WOULDN'T KNOW.

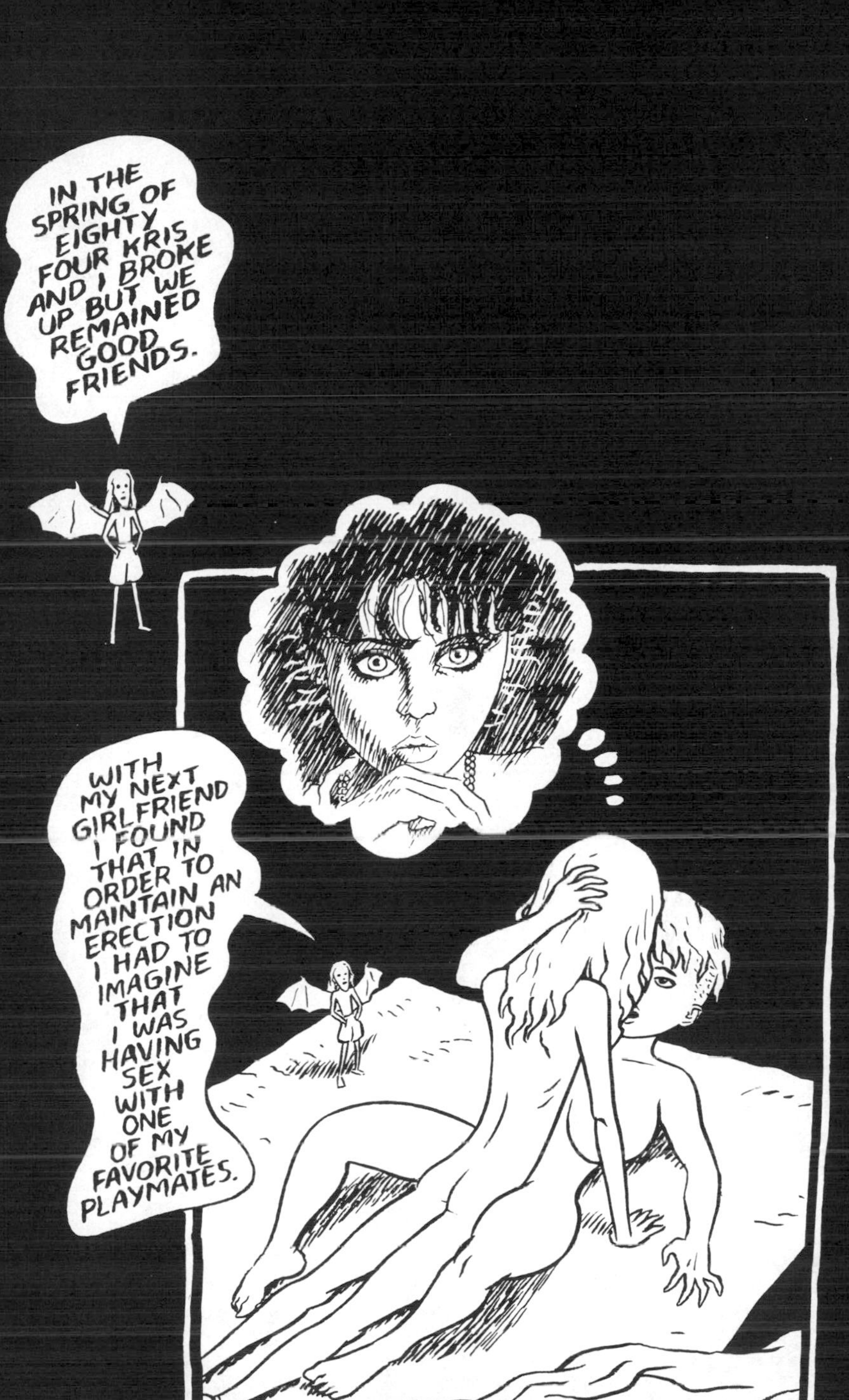
IN THE SPRING OF EIGHTY FOUR KRIS AND I BROKE UP BUT WE REMAINED GOOD FRIENDS.
WITH MY NEXT GIRLFRIEND I FOUND THAT IN ORDER TO MAINTAIN AN ERECTION I HAD TO IMAGINE THAT I WAS HAVING SEX WITH ONE OF MY FAVORITE PLAYMATES.

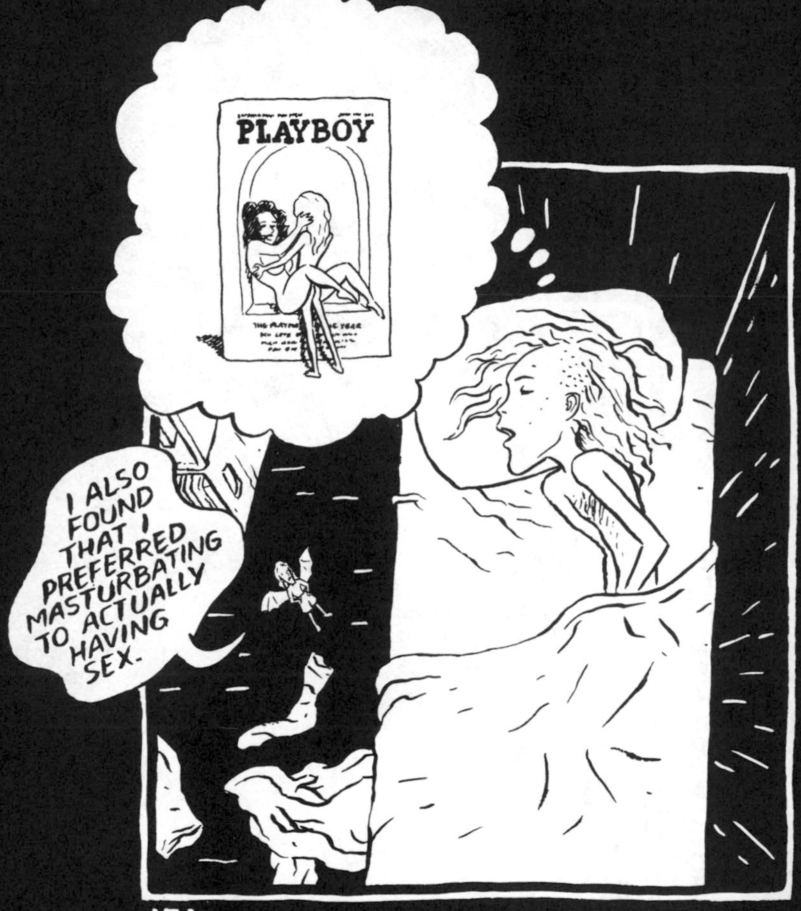
PLAYBOY
I ALSO FOUND THAT I PREFERRED MASTURBATING TO ACTUALLY HAVING SEX.

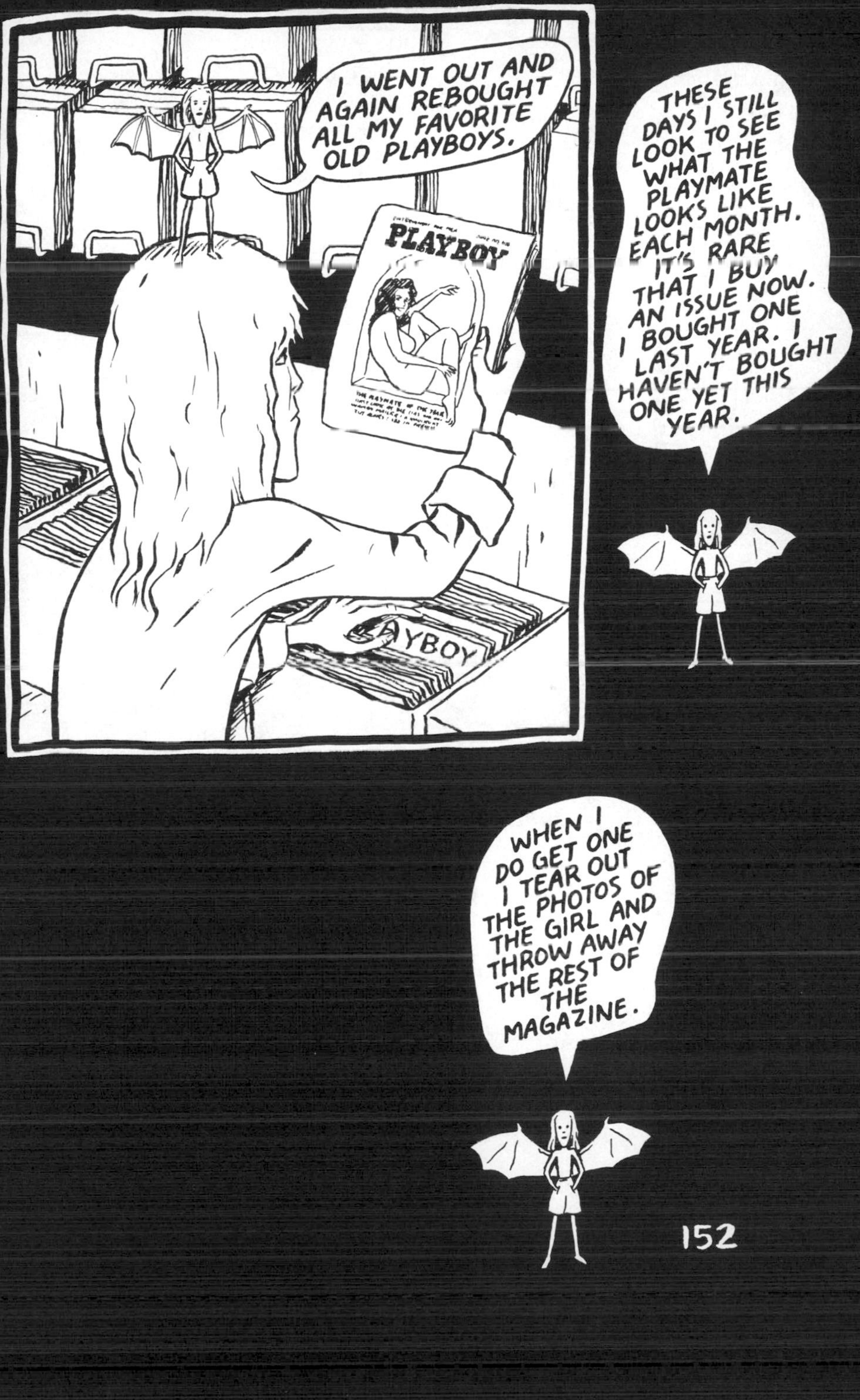
I WENT OUT AND AGAIN REBOUGHT ALL MY FAVORITE OLD PLAYBOYS.
PLAYBOY
THESE DAYS I STILL LOOK TO SEE WHAT THE PLAYMATE LOOKS LIKE EACH MONTH. IT'S RARE THAT I BUY AN ISSUE NOW. I BOUGHT ONE LAST YEAR. I HAVEN'T BOUGHT ONE YET THIS YEAR.
WHEN I DO GET ONE I TEAR OUT THE PHOTOS OF THE GIRL AND THROW AWAY THE REST OF THE MAGAZINE.

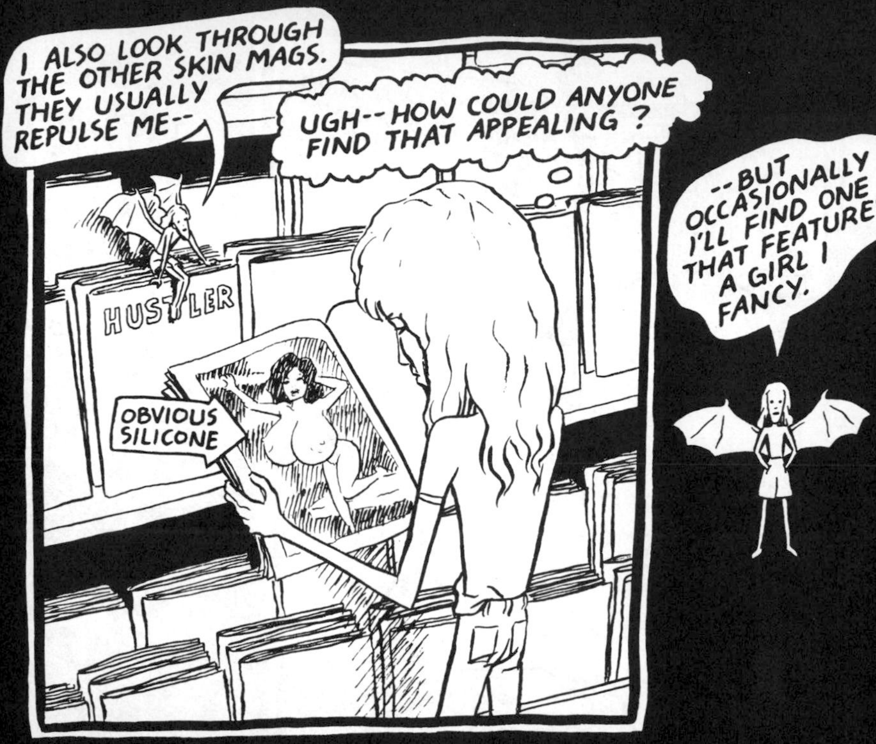
I ALSO LOOK THROUGH THE OTHER SKIN MAGS. THEY USUALLY REPULSE ME--
UGH--HOW COULD ANYONE FIND THAT APPEALING ?
HUSTLER
OBVIOUS SILICONE
--BUT OCCASIONALLY I'LL FIND ONE THAT FEATURES A GIRL I FANCY.

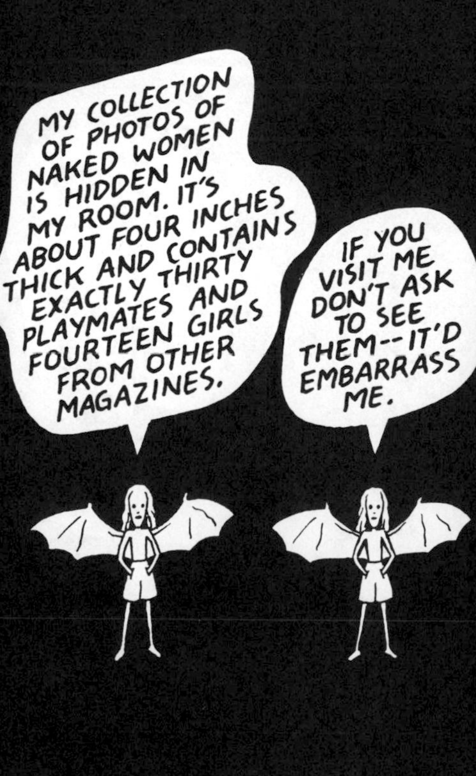
MY COLLECTION OF PHOTOS OF NAKED WOMEN IS HIDDEN IN MY ROOM. IT'S ABOUT FOUR INCHES THICK AND CONTAINS EXACTLY THIRTY PLAYMATES AND FOURTEEN GIRLS FROM OTHER MAGAZINES.
IF YOU VISIT ME DON'T ASK TO SEE THEM--IT'D EMBARRASS ME.

EPILOGUE

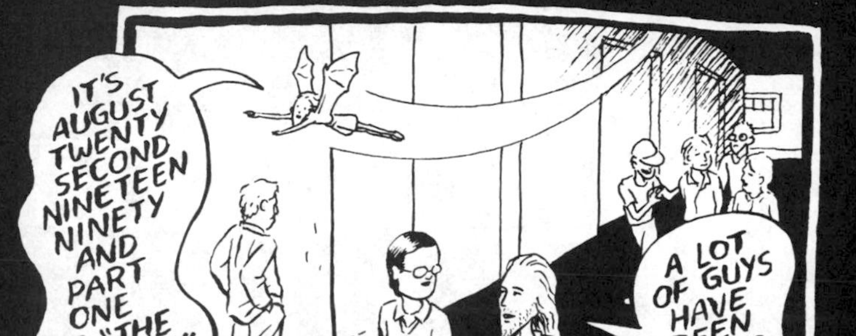
IT'S AUGUST TWENTY SECOND NINETEEN NINETY NINE AND PART ONE OF "THE PLAYBOY" HAS BEEN PUBLISHED.
A LOT OF GUYS HAVE BEEN TELLING ME THEY HAD THAT PARTICULAR ISSUE.
REALLY? I NEVER SAW IT BUT THEN I NEVER BOUGHT PLAYBOY. BUT I CAN REMEMBER THE FIRST PLAYMATE I SAW.

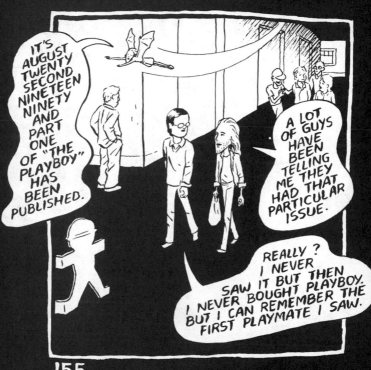

SHE WAS IN A COPY OF PLAYBOY THAT A FRIEND OF MINE HAD. SHE WAS STANDING IN FRONT OF A BOOKCASE AND HAD A BOOK IN ONE HAND AND THERE WAS A LIT FIREPLACE IN THE BACKGROUND.

YEAH RIGHT-- IT WAS... WAIT... MARILYN-- MARILYN COLE. FROM SEVENTY TWO.

156

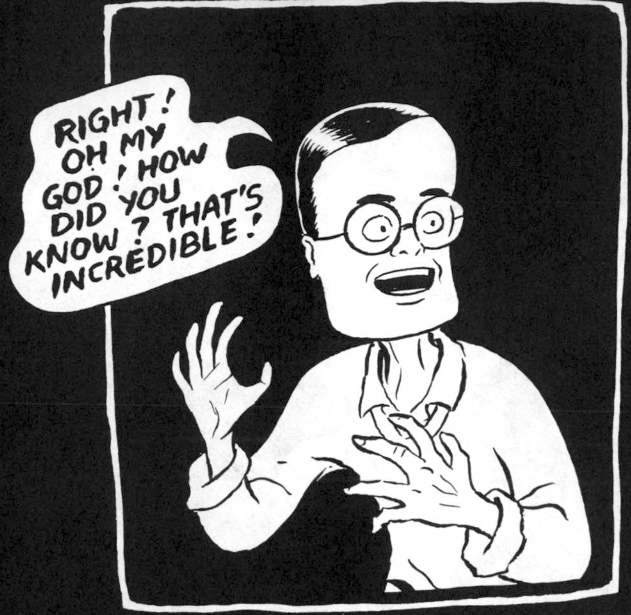
RIGHT! OH MY GOD! HOW DID YOU KNOW? THAT'S INCREDIBLE!

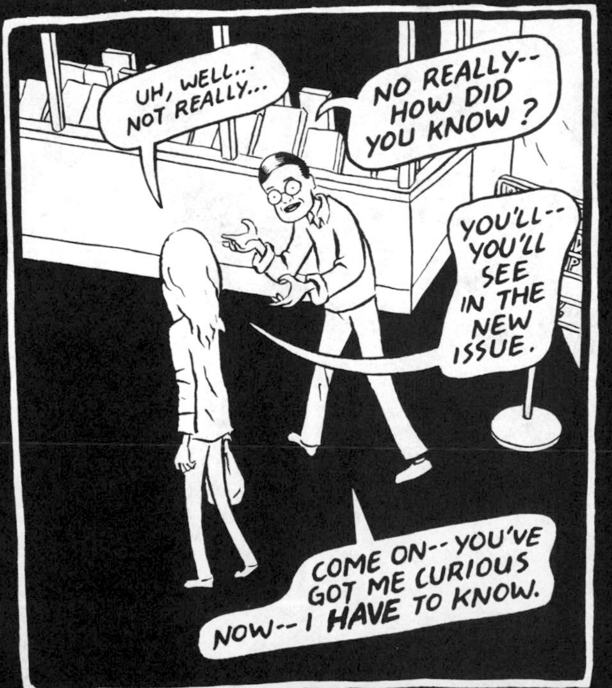
UH, WELL... NOT REALLY...
NO REALLY-- HOW DID YOU KNOW?
YOU'LL-- YOU'LL SEE IN THE NEW ISSUE.
COME ON-- YOU'VE GOT ME CURIOUS NOW-- I HAVE TO KNOW.

WELL, UH PLAYBOY HAS RELEASED SEVERAL BOOK COLLECTIONS THAT REPRINT PICTURES OF PLAYMATES FROM THE PAST--

--AND I HAD A COUPLE OF THOSE BOOKS--

THE JANUARY SEVENTY TWO ISSUE OF PLAYBOY WHICH FEATURES MARILYN COLE CAME OUT BEFORE THE EVENTS DESCRIBED IN PART ONE TOOK PLACE.

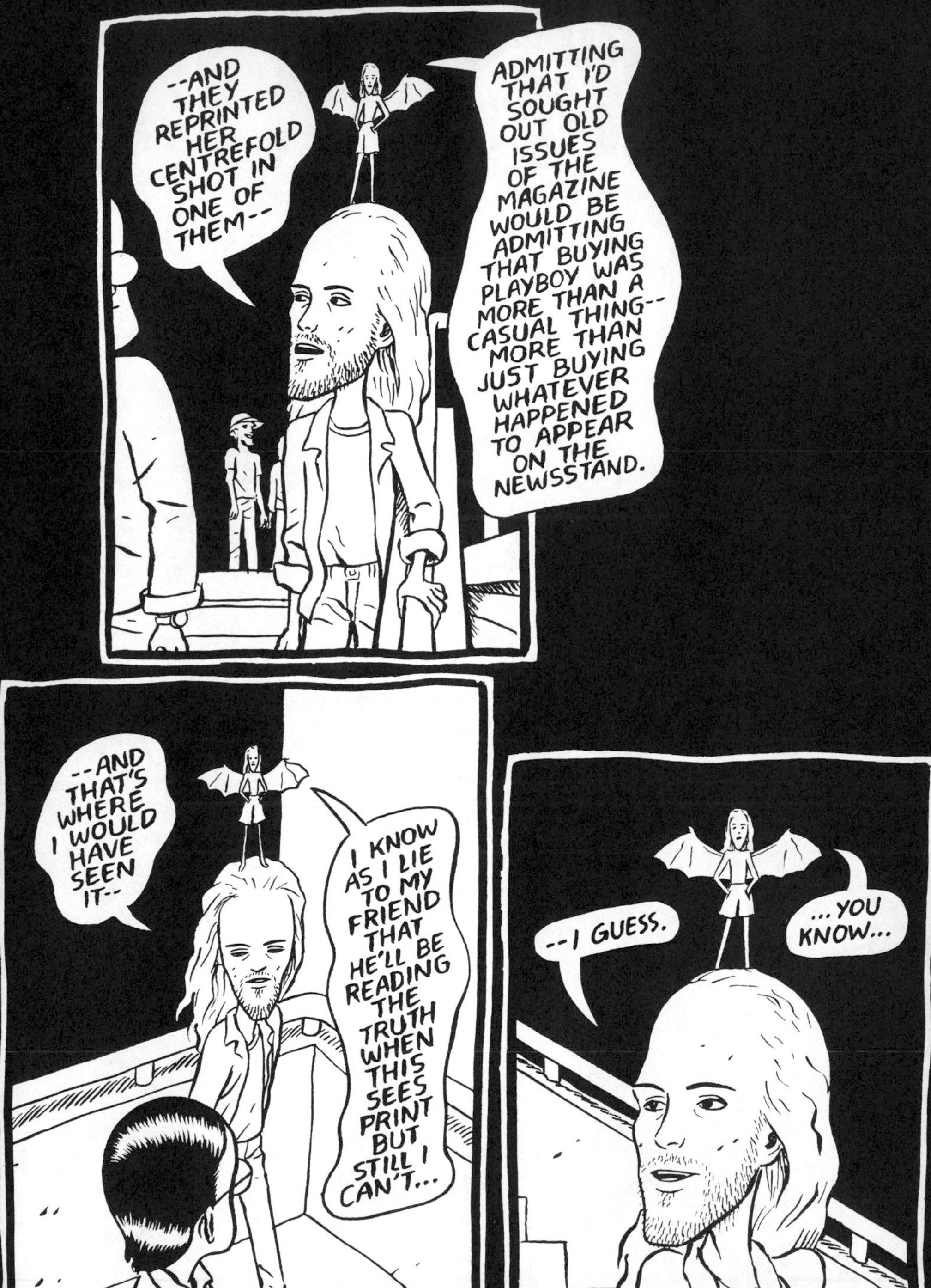
--AND THEY REPRINTED HER CENTREFOLD SHOT IN ONE OF THEM--
ADMITTING THAT I'D SOUGHT OUT OLD ISSUES OF THE MAGAZINE WOULD BE ADMITTING THAT BUYING PLAYBOY WAS MORE THAN A CASUAL THING--MORE THAN JUST BUYING WHATEVER HAPPENED TO APPEAR ON THE NEWSSTAND.
--AND THAT'S WHERE I WOULD HAVE SEEN IT--
I KNOW AS I LIE TO MY FRIEND THAT HE'LL BE READING THE TRUTH WHEN THIS SEES PRINT BUT STILL I CAN'T...
--I GUESS.
...YOU KNOW...

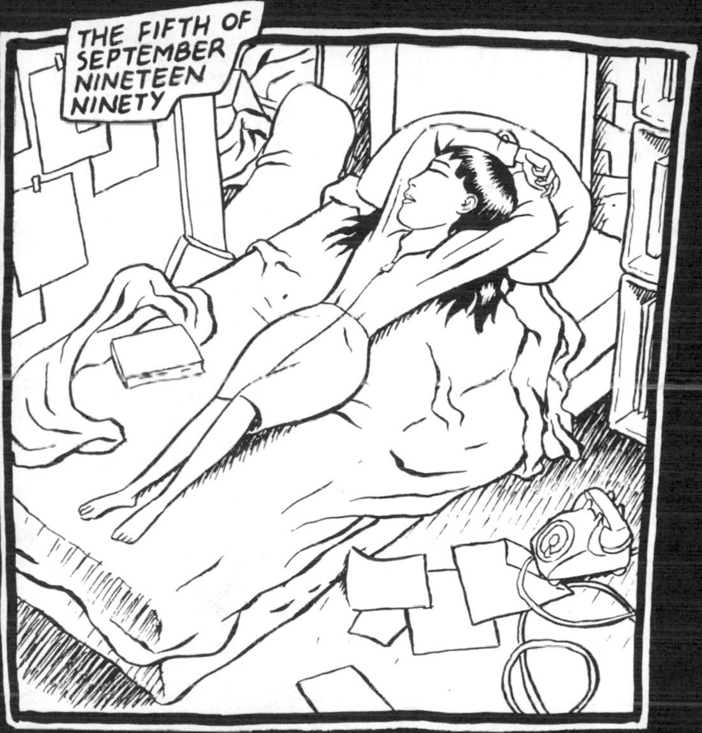
THE FIFTH OF SEPTEMBER NINETEEN NINETY

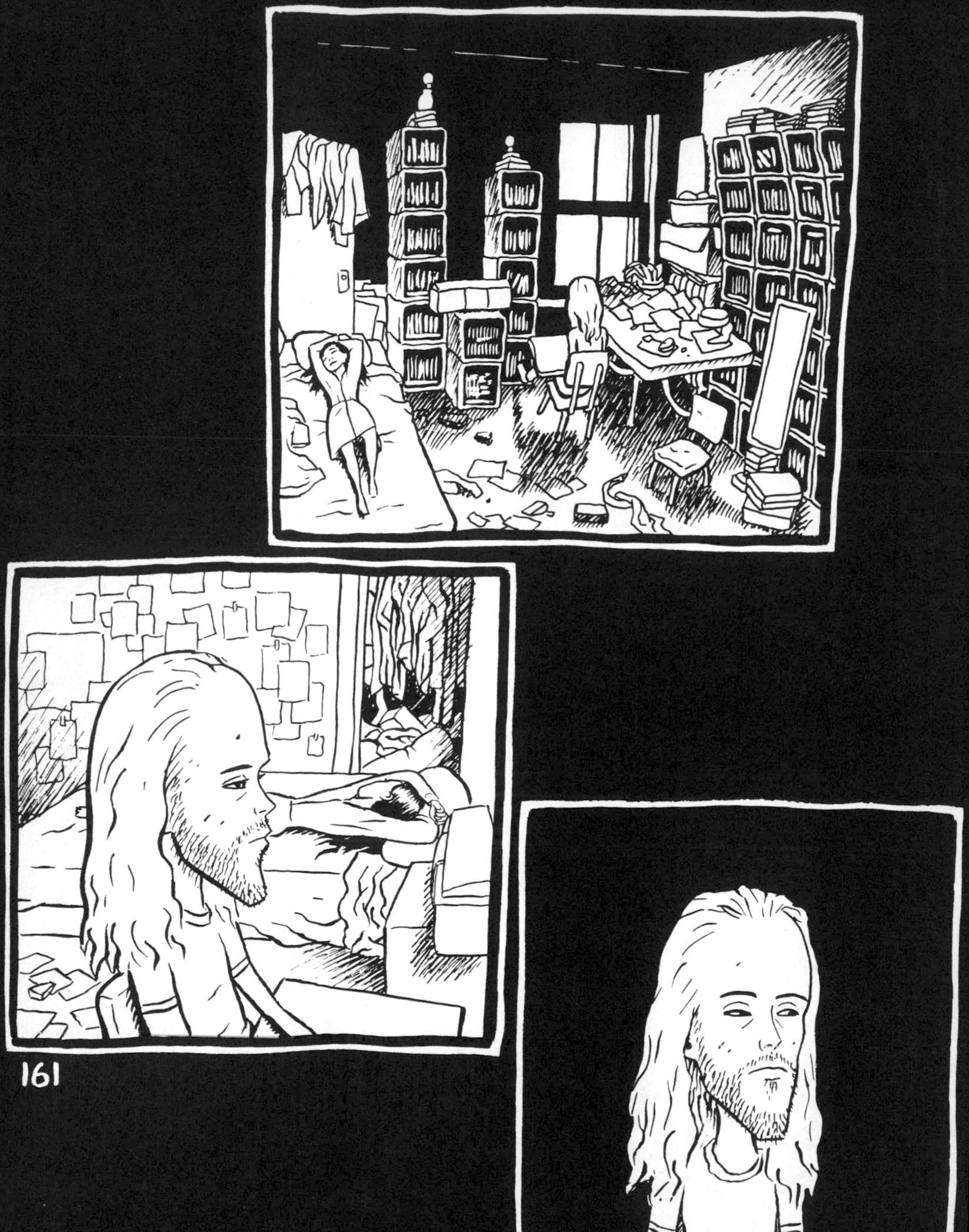

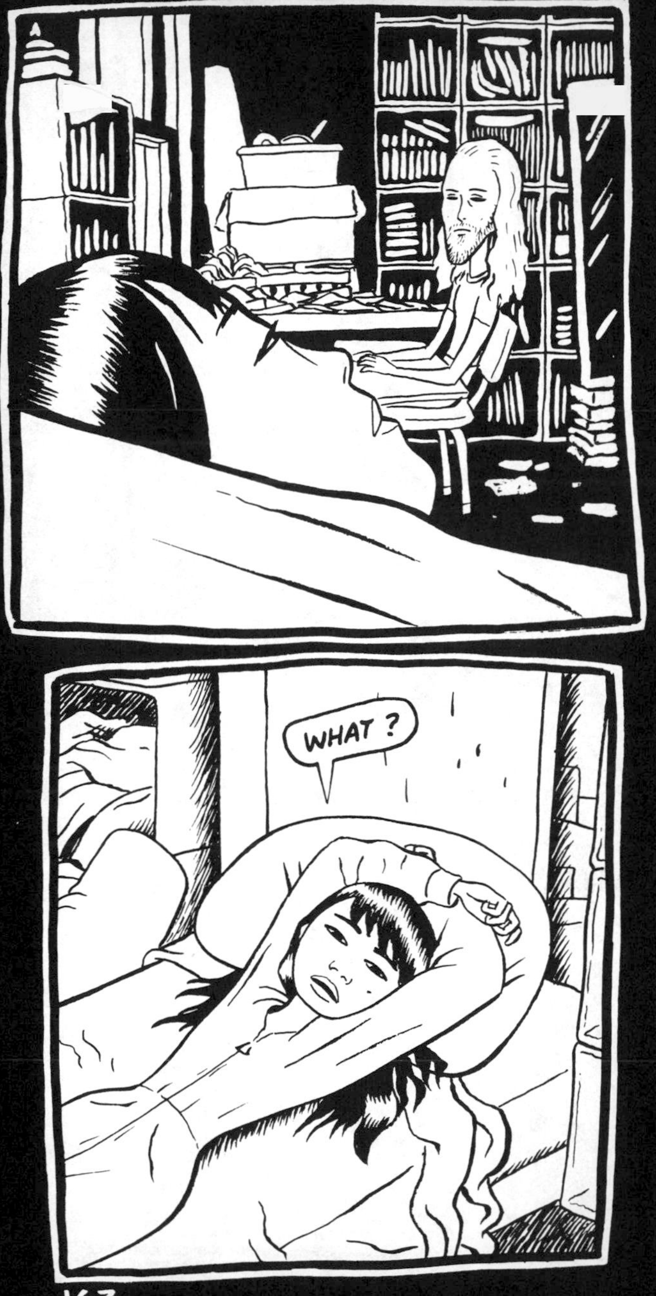
WHAT ?

AHEM

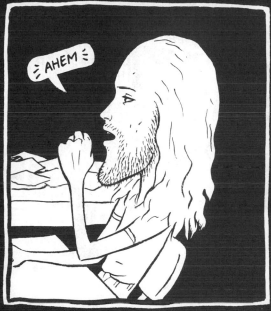

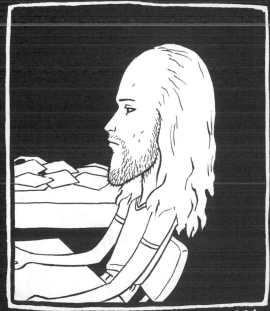

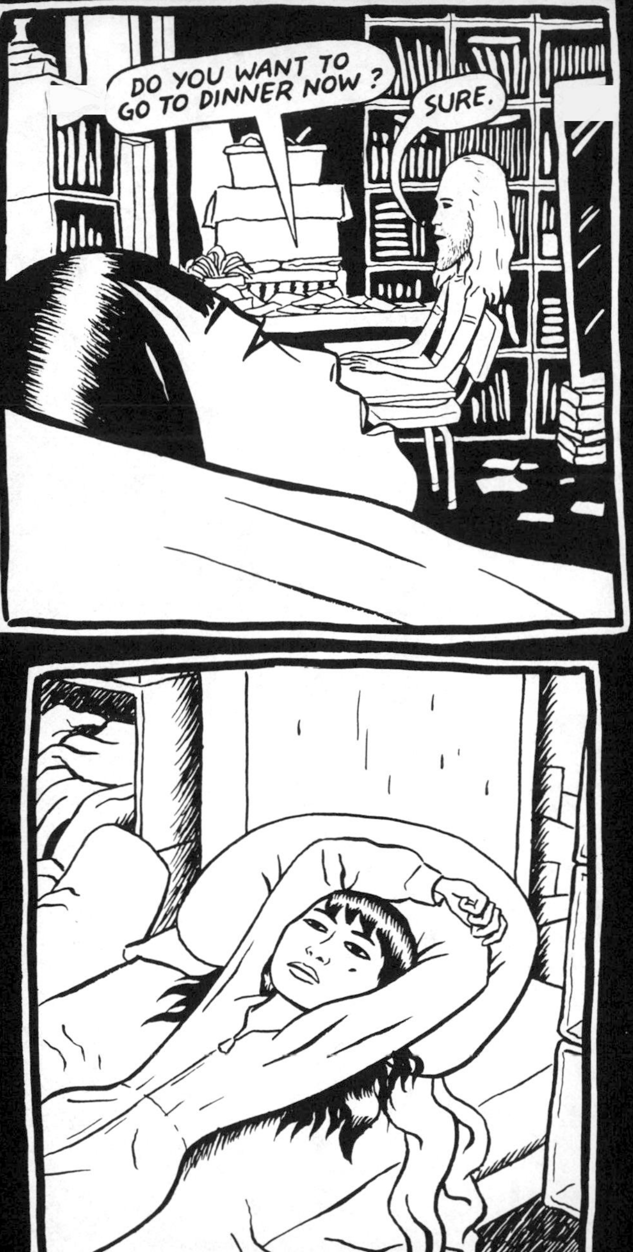
DO YOU WANT TO GO TO DINNER NOW ?
SURE.

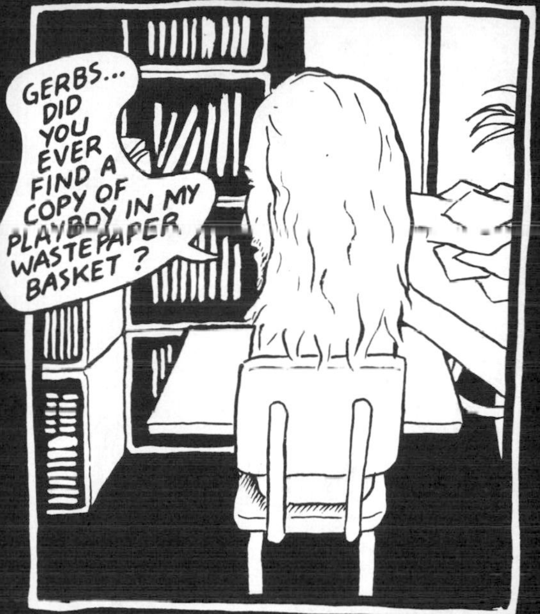
GERBS... DID YOU EVER FIND A COPY OF PLAYBOY IN MY WASTEPAPER BASKET ?

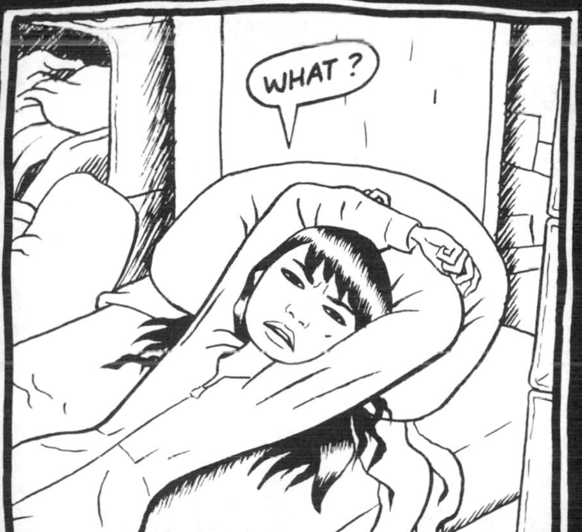
WHAT ?

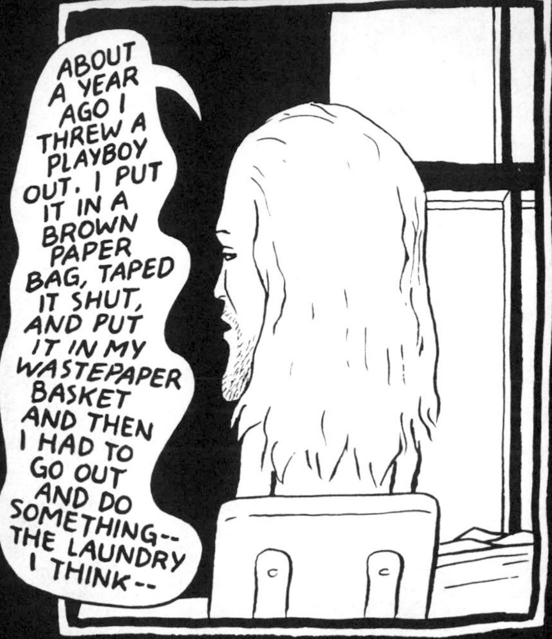
ABOUT A YEAR AGO I THREW A PLAYBOY OUT. I PUT IT IN A BROWN PAPER BAG, TAPED IT SHUT, AND PUT IT IN MY WASTEPAPER BASKET AND THEN I HAD TO GO OUT AND DO SOMETHING-- THE LAUNDRY I THINK--

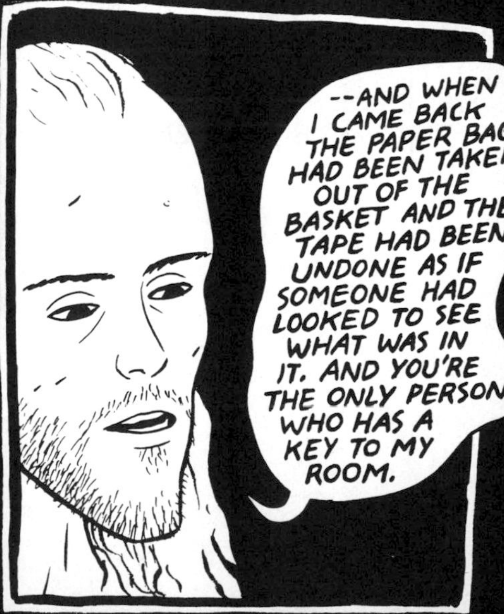
--AND WHEN I CAME BACK THE PAPER BAG HAD BEEN TAKEN OUT OF THE BASKET AND THE TAPE HAD BEEN UNDONE AS IF SOMEONE HAD LOOKED TO SEE WHAT WAS IN IT. AND YOU'RE THE ONLY PERSON WHO HAS A KEY TO MY ROOM.

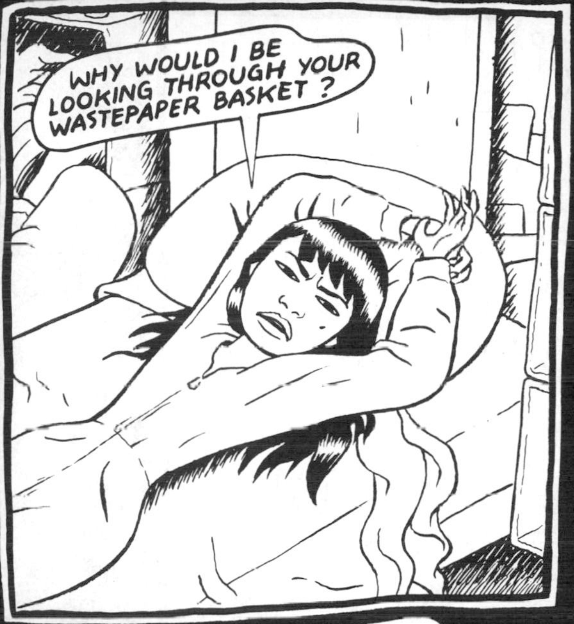
WHY WOULD I BE LOOKING THROUGH YOUR WASTEPAPER BASKET ?

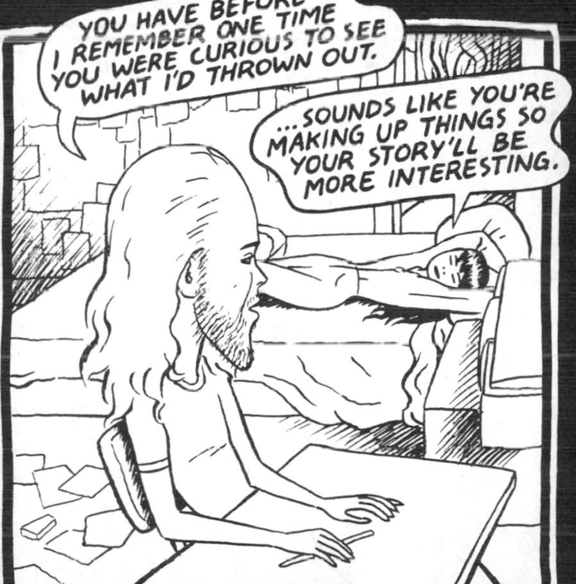
YOU HAVE BEFORE-- I REMEMBER ONE TIME YOU WERE CURIOUS TO SEE WHAT I'D THROWN OUT.
...SOUNDS LIKE YOU'RE MAKING UP THINGS SO YOUR STORY'LL BE MORE INTERESTING.

NO, IT REALLY HAPPENED AND I WAS REALLY WORRIED THAT YOU'D BE, I DON'T KNOW, MAD AT ME OR SOMETHING AND I FELT SICK-- REALLY NAUSEOUS-- I WAS AFRAID-- I DON'T KNOW--
GIGGLE POOR BUNNY.

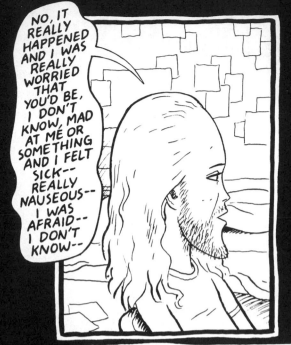

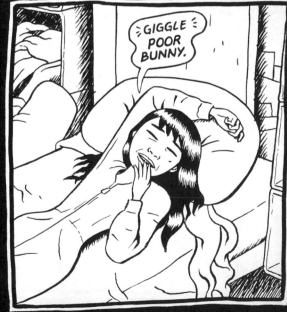

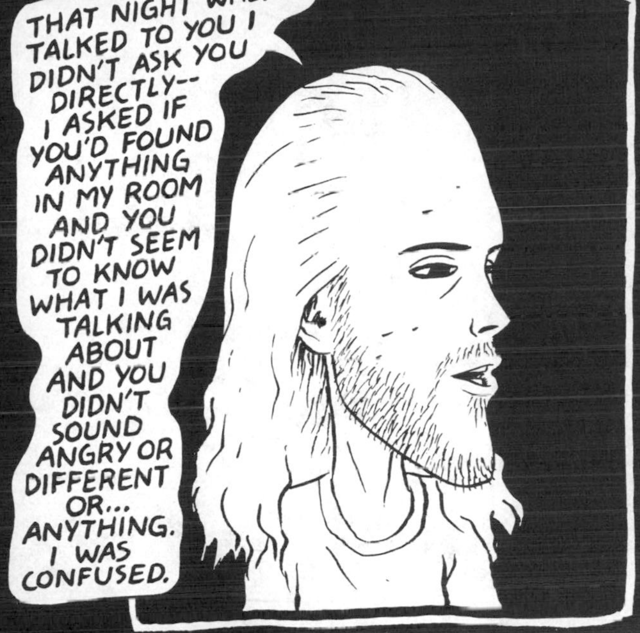
THAT NIGHT WHEN I TALKED TO YOU I DIDN'T ASK YOU DIRECTLY-- I ASKED IF YOU'D FOUND ANYTHING IN MY ROOM AND YOU DIDN'T SEEM TO KNOW WHAT I WAS TALKING ABOUT AND YOU DIDN'T SOUND ANGRY OR DIFFERENT OR... ANYTHING. I WAS CONFUSED.

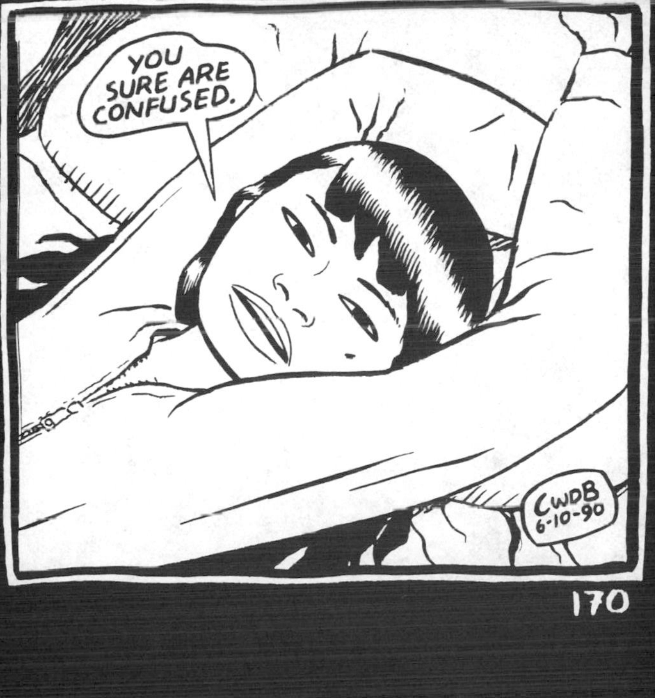
YOU SURE ARE CONFUSED.
CWDB 6-10-90